HISTORICAL RAILWAY MODELLING

(A personal view)

DAVID JENKINSON

PENDRAGON

To all my friends in the hobby, past and present
(with my sincere thanks for allowing me to purloin their knowledge
without shame - and evaluate ideas without conscience!)

HISTORICAL RAILWAY MODELLING

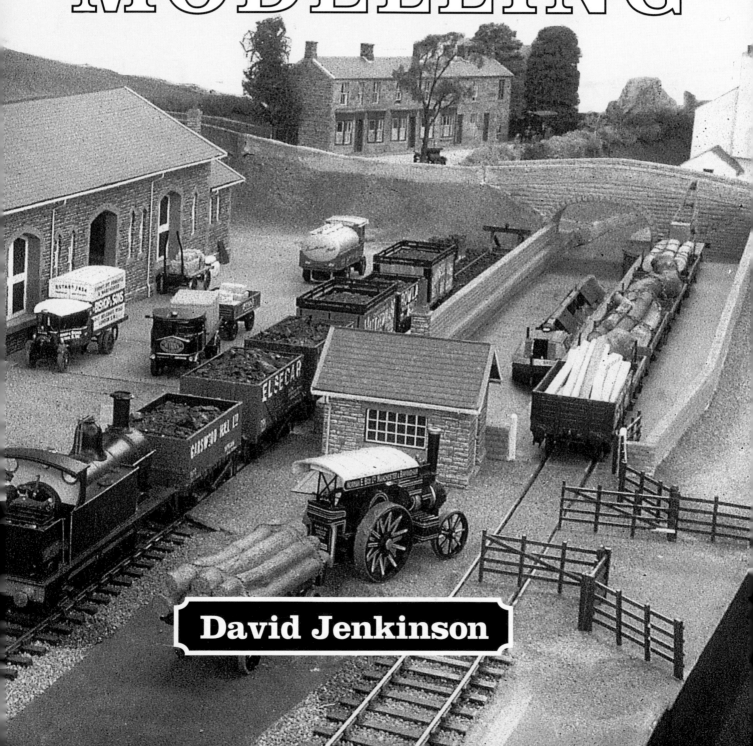

David Jenkinson

Introduction

It was some twenty years ago, whilst photographing the magnificent diorama of Millers Dale in 7mm scale at Matlock, that I first heard the name of David Jenkinson. This is to my shame, for he was already a very well known figure in the world of model railways and railway history. As I watched, a train of Midland Railway crimson lake coaches passed over Monsal Dale viaduct, and I commented to my host, David White, on the superb craftsmanship which had gone into the making of those coaches. "They were built" said David in near-reverential tones, "by David Jenkinson."

Very soon after this, I bought two books on LMS Liveries by the same man, which have become my most reliable source of information on the subject.

My first personal encounter with David was when he, as a publisher, agreed to take on my first book, and although we were poles apart in our approach to modelling, we quickly discovered a personal rapport, summarised by his comment at the time: "Why haven't we met before this?!". The third stage of our relationship came when I stayed with David and his wife, Sheila, in Yorkshire, where a warm friendship developed which has lasted to this day. In all the foregoing lies whatever qualification I may have for writing this introduction, an invitation which I regard as a privilege and a compliment.

So what can I tell you about what you are about to read? What manner of man is David Jenkinson, historian, publisher, broadcaster, teacher and master-modeller? Like all who lead rather than follow, he is a man of strongly held - and expressed - views, but there is no arrogance in him. A friend whom I once introduced to David, later said to me "He strikes me as a man with his head in the clouds and his feet firmly on the ground." Disregarding the purely physical absurdity of the analogy, it was a perceptive appraisal. The 'head in the clouds' describes his width of vision, but his Yorkshire roots suggest an uncompromising personality. But I quickly discovered a deeply compassionate side to David when I rubbed shoulders with my own personal tragedy. Humour too is never far from his enthusiasms, robbing them of any sense of obsessional intransigence. One might well imagine that such a talented man tended to exist on some rarified plane of perfectionism where lesser mortals would find it difficult to approach him. Nothing could be further from the truth, for his enormous zest for life reveals at times an almost ingenuous enjoyment of whatever he is doing. Music too can move him deeply and our evening discussions on railway matters have been known to end up, in the 'wee, sma' hoors', in a mutual admiration of the music of Brahms.

This, then, is the man who is speaking to us through these pages - and that is exactly what he is doing, for I can clearly hear his voice as I read. This is no manual of instruction, nor will you find detailed lists of components or how to assemble them. Nor will you at any time in this book hear David laying down the law or saying "This is how it should be done." In fact, he is highly suspicious of those who adopt this style. What he sets out to do and, in my opinion, succeeds in doing, is to stimulate thought; and this is surely the essence of good teaching. Much of the book is autobiographical, for everything he tells us is drawn from hard-won personal experience. No armchair modeller, David, but a man who, endowed with exceptional gifts, is not afraid to go out and make mistakes; in fact, he parades some of these before us that we might not fall into the same traps.

To the countless readers of other books by David, this introduction will be supererogatory, for you will know what to expect. But for those who are embarking upon the exciting (and demanding) project of a historical model railway, this book will go far in setting you upon the first essential stage - that of thinking it through before making a start. It is a world full of snares, delusions and traps for the unwary, and what David does for us here is to open up avenues of thought which, whilst not guaranteed to give all the answers, will act as a chart to steer us clear of most of the problems. I would go further; I believe this book could well be enjoyed by someone who is not primarily interested in model railways. Not all writers on railway subjects have David's easy and fluent command of our rich English language - more's the pity.

Despite the difference in our respective modelling aims and skills, David and I have at least one tenet in common, and that is that the overriding justification for any model railway is that it satisfies and fulfills the one who built it. This is an unassailable bastion against which no argument or criticism can prevail.

I commend to you both the man and the book.

Jack Ray
Ipswich
July 2001

4

Contents

*   *   *   *   *   *   *   *

NOTE: Unless stated otherwise, all photographs in this book are either by the author or from his private collection where the source is unknown. All other pictures are credited to the best extent possible, but should any mistakes have been made, apologies are tendered in advance and corrections (if any) should be sent via the publisher

© David Jenkinson and the Pendragon Partnership 2001

Published by the Pendragon Partnership, PO Box No.3, Easingwold, York YO61 3YS

Designed by Barry C. Lane, Sutton-in-Craven

Text set in Times Roman and Italic by the author

Printed in England by the Amadeus Press Ltd, Cleckheaton, West Yorkshire

British Cataloguing-in-Publication Data: a catalogue reference for this book is held by the British Library

ISBN No. 1 899816 10 0

Preface

It seldom does any harm for writers to state from the outset from whence they are coming and, perhaps more usefully, to give some indication of where they hope to go, so a few introductory comments seem called for by way of explaining the nature of this book.

During the early 1980s, I was commissioned to write a fairly modest account of my railway modelling which duly emerged as 'Modelling Historic Railways', a title not of my choosing I might add - I doubt I could have made so bold a claim. Whatever, even though not as widely distributed as I would have liked (a typical 'author' reaction, I suppose!), those who did see it were mostly kind and supportive; so that wasn't too bad..... And there I thought things had rested until the opportunity arose for a re-work, which seemed worthwhile, given that the best part of twenty years had elapsed since my first effort, that I had gone on developing ideas and finally, that I had extended my activities into yet another modelling scale.

I was also now able to have a say in the title - and the slight change in main title wording this time is no semantic play on words; it needs explanation. My first effort was criticised mostly for the fact that it was not really what the title implied, 'too much Settle and Carlisle' being a not unheard comment. Nor did the title truly hint at what I really tried to convey. I wanted to advance *ideas* by using, simply for convenience, many examples I knew well from a prototype I had studied in some detail and had also modelled; but the title promised more and this I could not offer, nor can I do so on this occasion. I have therefore sub-titled this effort 'a personal view', for that is what it tries to be; and its resultant autobiographical element cannot really be avoided, nor do I wish so to do.

As a railway modeller-cum-railway historian, I have never modelled the contemporary scene, but since my interests go well beyond the limited scope of my own models, it was always my hope that the ideas I have developed could be used for a far wider range of prototypes than I have chosen to model. I shall, of course, make use of my own efforts by way of examples throughout the book, but I feel obliged to emphasise that the ideas themselves are not dependent on a specific choice of prototype. This aspect did not perhaps come across too well in the first book, so this time I hope to do better. Moreover, since I can now take advantage of much better design parameters, thanks to the happy collaboration between myself and the book designer, my good friend Barry Lane, to whom I owe far more than he will ever understand, I now have more space within which to work compared with last time, and this too should help.

Many ideas previously advanced by me in the early 1980s remain much as they were, and will turn up again, but I have tried to make sure that this more lavish book is not simply an enlarged re-issue of the older story. Quite a lot of its themes will probably be familiar to those who saw the first efforts, of course, but I have added to these and moved onto some new modelling ground as well, hopefully to helpful effect.

Perhaps the most important point to make is that I have no intention of offering a 'how to do it' set of instructions. The techniques of railway modelling are much the same whether or not you tackle the historical scene, and there is a considerable library of excellent books on the subject - not to mention the regular injection of the newest ideas from the many current model magazines. I have benefitted from them all - and also contributed my own 'two bit's worth' from time to time - so here, though I have not ignored practicalities, I have preferred to focus on ideas and (dare I say?) throw in a bit of on-going model philosophy as well.

I have tried to structure the work into a reasonably sequential approach mostly so as to organise my thoughts properly - see contents page. In reality, the areas are usually interlinked, prime emphasis being given to that which looms most important in relation to the development of the model(s) at any specific time. For this reason, though it would have been tempting to offer a chronological account of my own layouts as they have come and gone (12 at the time of writing!), I have preferred to mention them (often more than once) as and when they become relevant in a wider context. I have also used selected examples from other modellers' work when certain points need to be made and my thanks go to their owners for being so generous as to allow me to quote them.

In my earlier book I started by saying that I had gained many ideas from such as John Ahern, Edward Beal and Peter Denny, to whom I feel should now be added the likes of Bob Essery, Ken Payne, Jack Ray, Gavin Wilson and a fair number of others. I remain a little surprised that my own efforts can be added to theirs - and my especial thanks to my very dear friend Jack Ray for his far too flattering introduction.....

It has also struck me forcibly that all the above-named gentlemen place(d) the 'totality' of the modelled scene at the forefront of their activity and I have been content to try and do likewise. The trendy word for this approach is 'holistic' - ie the whole greater than the sum of the parts - and I guess that this 'total' approach is what I too have mostly tried to adopt, usually (like most of my mentors) by attempting to ensure, as best I can, that everything is achieved to a broadly equivalent standard, nothing being wildly out of place by being of markedly different quality to the rest.

So, if this book is of interest and the information in it of value, then much of the credit lies with those who have been my inspiration over a period of, heaven help me, almost fifty years and whose work I have often shamelessly copied - hence the opening dedication.

David Jenkinson
Raskelf, North Yorkshire
October, 2001

PART I

ESTABLISHING A MODELLING STRATEGY

CHAPTER 1

The essential inspiration

"Railway modelling is a pleasure rather than a fad and should be free from the pedantry which dictates.
Yet our aim in this writing is to indicate a consistent course of action....."
Edward Beal: Modelling the Old-Time Railways

WERE IT NOT for accusations of plagiarism, I could well have 'pirated' Edward Beal's book title for my own work, but at least I can start by quoting him, having used his sentences many times, largely because I regard them as probably the most significant words ever uttered on the subject. However, although I have read most of his books, and have quite a few in my library, I cannot say that I have been influenced by all of Beal's ideas - he was a bit too 'freelance' for my liking, as indeed was his highly influential contemporary, the late and great John Ahern. What is more, I had been modelling for over ten years before I even read the book from which the above quotation is taken; but if I have a model philosophy at all, I cannot better Beal's 'consistent course of action' as a way of summing it up.

Beal's exhortation to be 'free from the pedantry which dictates' is also important. Modelmaking is a very personal business and those of us who write about it cannot help but reveal our own preferences. But that is very different from insisting that some ideas are better than others; they are simply different and all have their place. I hope I have never fallen into the trap of telling folk what they *ought* to do; but if my writing on the subject, by drawing on my experience, succeeds in helping a few modellers, especially beginners, from falling into traps and heading up the sort of blind alleys which bedevilled me until Beal's quotation came to the rescue, then I shall be well pleased.

It therefore seems to me that by discussing ideas and principles which experience shows to make sense, others might be saved the time and trouble of finding out the hard way. Little of what I have done and described in print since I started out in the model writing game during the early 1960s is profoundly original, but I have mostly thought it through before starting - and this may well be one key to success.

But 'success' is a shadowy idea. One person's success is often beyond another's grasp or, at the other end of the spectrum, merely a half-way house for those with a greater degree of skill and/or ambition than others may possess. It is, therefore, all very personal and this fact alone makes it hard to offer a blueprint for success, not least in terms of how and where to start. The best I can do in the latter context is to relate some background experiences, a few of which did turn out in time to be inspirational for me, and hope that the reader might thereby recognise something similarly useful in his or her own study of the subject.

The growth of personal interest

I cannot recall a time when I was not interested in railways, nor is it wildly relevant; but it is much harder to answer the question why I am so interested or why I make models. Here, I cannot give a wholly satisfactory answer, nor, in retrospect, do I think it matters over much: maybe, like mountain climbing, I do it simply because 'it is there'. But if pushed, I guess my interest probably started in the late 1930s as a child with a talented father whose skill allowed him to move from crude tinplate on the carpet (it *was* crude, let there be no mistake) to the point where we used handmade Bond's track (or was it Milbro?) in the garden with a scratch built coarse-scale three rail Gauge '0' LMS Jubilee which Dad built in 1939 without benefit of anything save a rather inadequate blueprint, a few not very useful pictures and a lot of patience. I still have it, though it no longer runs on my present 7mm scale layout.

My father was always a 'do-er', so in consequence, my perception of the hobby was always pre-conditioned by the notion 'If you can't buy it, make it - and if you don't know the answers, try to find them out for yourself rather than expect someone else to do it for you.' This has never changed in essence, which may be the reason why some folk see me as a sort of perfectionist - which worries me. I will admit to 'selective fussiness', usually resulting from research which indicates how things ought to be in a perfect world; but I have also learned to live within my limitations in terms of time, skill and inclinations. But I still prefer to make things if I can, rather than buy them, though in recent years, the ever increasing quality of 'ready to run' and kits (in many scales), arguably makes it less necessary than when I started.

But no amount of trade assistance can alter the fact that a strong individual and personal perception of what we want from the hobby is the pre-requisite for everything else. It is not just a matter of wanting (or being able) to make models - many people have this facility in absolute terms - but one then has to move on to the far more complex subject of what sort of models and why, not to mention where to start. I can only answer for myself, of course, so I start by recounting some formative influences which affected my modelmaking, if only to set a background from which I can explain, by analysis, how it came to help me, sometimes by devious means, to extract order from incipient chaos. Some readers may recognise themselves in what follows....

Plate 1: A seminal model. *When I returned to 7mm scale in 1975, I resurrected my father's pre-war LMS Jubilee 4-6-0, gave it a more appropriate tender, converted it from 3-rail coarse to 2-rail fine scale and gave it a repaint. As such, it ran in front of one of my own sets of scratch built carriages during the early days of the first 7mm layout as seen here, c.1978. Unfortunately, my final ministrations had caused the chassis to get slightly out of true, so rather than make further changes, I put the model into honourable retirement with most of the original structure intact. This included the hand made nickel-plated valve gear which, during the mid-1930s, had adorned my bedroom book shelf in a series of re-cycled jam jars containing mysterious coloured (probably highly toxic!) liquids during the lengthy plating process......*

Plate 2: Trains of my childhood - 1. *The first steam trains I recall seeing were those of the old Southern Railway such as that seen here at an unknown location. Orpington (where I lived) was, of course, on the old SE&CR system and many years later, I realised that this sort of fascinating train must have passed my vision on many occasions - a rebuilt Class E1 4-4-0 No.497 at the head of a boat train consisting of narrow width slab-sided SE&CR and/or early SR corridor coaches with matchboard panelling plus, of course, the inevitable 'Pullman Pair' in the middle of the formation for dining purposes. I also later discovered why so many Southern engines (including the E1s) had a sort of 'Midland' look to them (an ex-Derby man was in the drawing office as it so happened), so I guess I was 'programmed' very early in life!*

As a small child, I was taken to meet 'Daddy's train' from the London office and my dear Mum, never realising what she had started, always used to wheel me up to the station well in advance of my father's train - I would have been about three years old at the time, I reckon. We lived in Orpington in those days and all I can really remember - and then only vaguely - is the all-pervading green of the old Southern Railway and the infinite superiority (to my young mind) of the steam-hauled expresses which never deigned to stop, compared with the humdrum electrics which were the only sort of trains on which I ever got to ride.

Curiously enough, although very much a northerner by birth and subsequent residence, I have always had a genuine affection for the Southern Railway ever since those days and have a sneaky feeling that were I ever to abandon my known LMS interests, it would be the Southern to which I might turn, probably the LSWR part of it in the light of my later researches. The moral to all this is never to neglect these early formative influences, for you never know where they might lead - but I digress.

My only travels on 'real' trains (as I had now begun to regard steam-hauled versions) were on the rather infrequent trips north for family reunions in Summer and at Christmas time. Small wonder that with the prospect of indulgent aunts, uncles and grandparents at the far end, coupled with riding on a 'proper' train, I began to regard the railways at King's Cross and St Pancras with infinitely more respect than I ever did their counterparts at Waterloo and Charing Cross - and I had never even heard of Paddington....

I am not sure which route to Leeds (my home city) we used most often - LNER (ex-Great Northern) or LMS (ex-Midland) - but I can clearly recall, with some terror, being hoisted up by

Plates 3/4: Trains of my childhood - 2. *These were the really exciting ones, both these pictures being taken at about the time I first took note of such things; and though the LMS example is heading out of Euston not St Pancras, it is much the same as those in which I rode. The King's Cross shot is, of course the departing 'Silver Jubilee' streamliner behind one of the four silver-grey A4s (unidentified), possibly even the one onto whose footplate I was once hoisted - see text. The LMS view shows an unidentified but named northbound express climbing Camden Bank behind Patriot Class 4-6-0 No.5536* Private W. Wood V.C. *and I chose this picture because I now have a model of the previous LMS engine to have carried the same name - the former LNWR 'Claughton' Class 4-6-0, LMS No.6018.*

a kindly engine driver into the cab of a huge silver-grey monster at King's Cross after a return trip south. It must have been one of the 'Silver' series of Gresley A4s, but what it was doing on Leeds-King's Cross duty c.1937, I do not know.

Whatever, the most vivid memory from that time is of my first positively recalled northbound trip. It was from St Pancras and father had chosen the ex-MR route because, as I remember it: "It is not so crowded and LMS carriages are more comfortable." He was right on both counts; but I did not know this at the time. Meanwhile, the ritual of 'looking at the engine' still had to be observed whatever the route - I was but three or four years old, remember.... My first surprise was that the train was red, never having seen a red train before except for London Transport - and that did not count; but this was as nothing compared with my first view of its red engine, beautifully clean, glinting in the sunshine. I have never forgotten that feeling, though I cannot recall the precise type: probably a 'Jubilee' 4-6-0 or 4-4-0 Compound, I guess. But my young brain instantly concluded that any railway which painted its engines in this fabulous colour simply had to be the most superior system in the land!

Off we went through the London suburbs - including the very exciting sight of seeing an aeroplane taking off from Hendon and flying over our train as we passed - and I now know that I was probably lucky to see a clean red engine on the LMS in the late 1930s and that the company was rather less than perfect (sic!); but I can honestly say that my interest in railways in general and LMS in particular was probably stimulated more by this vivid experience as a small boy than anything which has happened since. And I still had the same thrill when, over half a lifetime later, I was much involved (professionally) with restoring former LMS 4-6-2 *Duchess of Hamilton* to full working order and re-witnessed a clean red engine with steam in her belly and fire in her heart! We are indubitably mad - but who cares?

Unsurprisingly, railway models came onto the scene at much the same time as these vivid childhood experiences, red engines duly emerging in the form of Hornby clockwork Gauge 0 Compound No.1185, followed about a year later by a Bassett Lowke 'Princess' and my father's above-mentioned Jubilee 4-6-0. We ran them all on an elevated track in the garden hauling Hornby Pullmans alongside Leeds Model Co. paper-lithographed carriages and wagons: no scenery or anything like that, but it was fun!

Like so many others of my generation, war intervened, we moved back north, supplies were difficult and things progressed but little for ten years or more, 1946-50 being, in retrospect, very little different from 1939-45 in this respect. But somehow or other the railway interest survived, the track plan of our wartime garden layout, put together on father's rare visits home, being still etched in my mind. We had some tinplate track for indoor activity, but it was the handbuilt nature of the outdoor system which I remember best - and I guess it struck a receptive chord. At all events, when I entered my mid-teens and decided to build my own railway models, it never seriously occurred to me that one could actually buy

Plate 5: The 'shock' of BR - 1. Though not the actual engine I saw in 1948, this official view of ex-LNER Class A3 4-6-2 No. 60059 Tracery on the turntable at King's Cross locomotive depot in February 1949, retaining apple green livery but now with the new branding, still brings back memories of the disbelief with which I and my friends greeted the new order. Cosmetics aside, however, nothing much changed for a few years thereafter and, with benefit of hindsight, we would have been wiser to take more careful note rather then behave like ostriches.....

ready made track - and I never did, until much later and for totally different reasons.

My problem at that time was a combination of lack of money, combined with no firm idea of what I really wanted to do. As an aside, I still find it hard to believe that as a university student in the early 1950s, I actually lived in London on 15/- per week spending money - 75p in modern terms - yet still managed to buy lunches, 'roll my own', take my girlfriend, now my wife, to the cinema and make railway models, the latter interest never having vanished, though it had faded a bit when my friends and I first discovered the delights of female company in the 1940s.....

To be honest, I nearly abandoned it altogether at that time and, apart from young ladies, I can well remember the other reason. It was March 1948 and I was coming home on the bus (as usual) and (again as usual) keeping a wary eye out for the local Leeds-Northallerton train which usually arrived at our local station at about the same time as the bus. On this day, the train got there first and all I could see was the back of a green tender poking out from behind the station building. It was a Class B1 4-6-0 of the LNER and emerged at the same time as our bus set off; but all I now recall is that, emblazoned on the tender were the appalling words 'BRITISH RAILWAYS'. "Oh God," I thought, "they have b....y well gone and done it!" We simply could not believe that 'they' would; but 'they' did!

I was still 'LMS' in persuasion, and had not much liked the sight of the new post war black livery on my beloved and erstwhile beautiful red engines (I could forgive the wartime compromises, being old enough to appreciate why); but even

Plate 6: The 'shock' of BR - 2.
For those of us who were sad that the LMS had finally abandoned its famous crimson lake express livery in 1946, the change of ownership following soon afterwards was no consolation at all and this fine Eric Treacy image shows something of that change. In it, rebuilt Royal Scot 4-6-0 The Boy Scout *is seen at Camden still carrying LMS colours - the new glossy black post war livery with maroon and straw edging was not too bad if kept clean - and albeit 'disfigured' in some eyes by the new BR identity 46169, the new numbers were at least applied in LMS shape sans-serif characters for a few months rather than the later Gill-Sans style which BR took from the LNER.*

on a locomotive of LNER origin this new style of branding was sacrilege in spades and as a result of this experience, I completely lost interest in railways for three years - which was a pity as it turned out, for that period was undoubtedly a most fascinating time had I been more mature in approach.

Interest revived mid-1951 when a very nasty attack of pleurisy rendered me housebound during the cricket season (another love of mine) and all I could do was dream dreams and doodle on a drawing pad. Thoughts reverted to railways - and oh how I wished (even in my mid-teens) for the totally inaccessible (given my state of finances) Hornby Dublo *Duchess of Atholl* in LMS crimson livery, if only to remind me of how things should have been painted!

Interest duly revived, I then discovered *The Railway Magazine* (when it was a proper journal with useful articles about what I still though of as 'real' railways, not this new-fangled BR rubbish!), began to look more seriously at model magazines and, I suppose, first decided that such models as I could assay (I now wanted to model again) would be based on that happy pre-BR period which I recalled so well. That, at least has never changed, though later generations might well substitute the onset of diesels (or maybe the demise of BR itself!) as their defining moments...

Whatever, during the next 10 years or so, lack of money remained the over-riding consideration as far as the model railway hobby was concerned, other matters taking priority, like the establishment of a career, marriage and the arrival of children. But the actual constraints of setting up home at that time against a restricted financial background meant that at least I did have some spare time. I built two '00' layouts at very low cost (neither of them finished), dabbled with kits, not to mention a flirtation with American HO (the latter was all that I could find in the Far East at the time), and tackled some

rudimentary scratch building, but generally did nothing of great note at all. In spite of wide reading (thanks to a good library I could afford this), my activities lacked direction and purpose and an inventory of models in late 1961 revealed three pre-BR British companies, two American ones, a full set of Kitmaster 'Blue' Pullmans, and a train of Kitmaster BR MkI stock (how I wish I still had both the latter....). The only common factor was their 16.5mm track gauge; but all told, it was not the most exhilarating collection from which to try and create a model empire.....

This was the moment when Beal's 'consistent course of action' came to the rescue, so I sold off everything, trading some of the better stuff for a reasonably respectable set of LMS carriages (Exleys) and resolved to have a completely fresh start; it was over 20 years since those halcyon days of Gauge '0' in the garden when it all seemed so simple.

Now I mention these early activities, not because they are of any great significance in themselves, but merely to show just what sort of a 'dog's breakfast' can result from a long period of fundamentally aimless modelling. Indeed, I can well understand why many folk give up altogether and I suppose it was only my deep seated love for all railways (despite my brief mid-teens hiccup) that kept me in the hobby. Looking back, I am convinced that the major lesson learned was the importance of deciding at the earliest possible moment just what is required and pursuing this aim fairly relentlessly, refusing to be diverted into interesting but ultimately unproductive by-ways.

Not that this prolonged early period was totally sterile - far from it, in fact. I acquired, from necessity, quite an amount of scratch building experience, suffered the joys and sorrows of trying to make my first white metal kit hold together and tried to get my first handbuilt track to work. Most important, however, when I finally analysed matters, it helped me decide what I really wanted and, even more vital, what I did *not* want from my models; and I reckon that since that fundamental re-appraisal in the early 1960s, I have not deviated too much in my basic approach, albeit that seven layouts have been and gone during that period, additional to the two on which I am now working......

I would therefore conclude that it is no bad thing for a modeller to go through some sort of 'indecisive period' in which to sort out ideas and techniques; but I would not recommend that it should last for nigh on 20 years! That said, however, it is somewhat unlikely that one's first attempt(s) will last a lifetime, even though some highly talented folk (Peter Denny immediately springs to mind) have demonstrated otherwise. For one thing, we mostly get better at the practicalities as we go along and earlier models do not always 'live happily' with their later brethren, thereby creating part of the inconsistency I am trying to avoid.

Whatever, having thought out all these matters (a long overseas posting helped, given the lack of model shops in Singapore and Malaya at the time), I returned to Britain in 1962, resolved to make a totally fresh start and since then, I have been trying to create models based on what I like to call 'fine scale principles based on a consistent course of action'. If I have achieved any success it is probably by virtue of being a good cribber rather than by offering any profoundly original

Plate 7: Marthwaite MkI, 1964. *This was my first attempt to get the component 'mix' reasonably consistent after my 1962 re-think - see text. The infrastructure, including track and (non-working) signals is wholly scratch built, though the lack of track ballast shows only too clearly. The locomotive too, Stanier 2-6-4T No.2525, is partially scratch built (hand built body on a converted Hornby Dublo chassis with EM Gauge fine scale wheels), but the carriages are from old CCW wooden kits. They did not look too good as built, but later, I became brave enough to apply full 'relief' panelling and paint them properly.*

solutions to the problems of model making as such, so I shall not burden readers with answers to the subject of making intransigent objects adhere to impossible surfaces - there are others far more fitted so to do. But I would like to discuss some of the *ideas* which I believe important if we want to build a model railway. As I see it, 'consistency of approach' is a good deal more than simply ensuring that the models themselves display the same or similar standards of construction. So let me now address this issue in more detail; it pays dividends in the longer run.

These days, we live amongst specialists and I mean no disrespect to these folk when I say that for me, there is no intrinsic interest in modelling a series of company gas lamps, signal finials or whatever other sort of sub-specialisation you may care to postulate. My goal is a model railway in every sense of the word and since we are on this earth for a limited life-span and my pocket is not bottomless, I can neither afford time to devote two years to one engine or, until very much more recent years and even then only occasionally, the cost of others making things for me. However, I do have a great love of railways and to this end, the finished product has to look as nearly right as possible, which, I guess, tends to pre-dispose me towards 'fine scale' standards, hence my move to EM gauge in 1962 and to the finer of the two then available 7mm scale track standards in 1975. But whatever standard I chose had to be capable of application across the board. A super-detailed engine against a hastily knocked-up background is far worse to me than a well assembled kit in a proper setting; and I would rather have a locomotive 2mm wrong in wheelbase if (but only 'if') the price of 100% accuracy is no time to build the layout on which to run it.

My overall aim is to try and reflect in miniature those features of railways which most appeal to me. To this end, I am neither for or against the fully super-detail approach but am trying something which I feel is more important. I like to think of our hobby as something more than the conventional image of grown adults playing with trains - not that I object to being accused of the latter, it is exceedingly enjoyable! But at the same time I see no reason why railway modelling should not aspire to some, at least, of the status accorded to other creative activities - music, art &c.; yet I do sometimes wonder whether some modellers have any feeling at all for the objects they are trying to portray. All I do know is that while there are plenty of books and articles on how to make this or that, there are precious few on why we do it or what we are really trying to achieve. Perhaps it does not matter to many people, but it fascinates me and this consideration will underpin much of what I have to say in this book.

I shall, of course, use my own specific interests by way of example, so there will be a fair amount of LMS and the Settle & Carlisle line in these pages. But I am not trying to make converts to either of them. Rather, I shall try to use them to illustrate general principles which are, perhaps, at risk of being overlooked in our strivings after rivet detail, for when all is said and done, it all starts with the prototype.

Plates 8/9: The first prototype inspiration. These two fine landscape shots, by Bishop Eric Treacy and John Whiteley respectively, show that part of the Settle and Carlisle line which first diverted my attention from the study of geology - see text. It is of course the area around Ribblehead, the 'train-less' view showing the approach to Blea Moor tunnel from the south. The other picture shows a northbound train on the famous viaduct with the fine profile of Pen-y-Ghent on the horizon and I selected it for purely sentimental reasons. It is the famous last official BR steam train on 11th August 1968 headed by now-preserved BR 'Britannia' Class 4-6-2 No.70013 Oliver Cromwell and I deliberately ran the first train through my new 4mm scale Garsdale Road layout on the very same day: I was living in London at the time and could not attend the real thing.

Sorting out the prototype

Concerning the prototype itself, it is impossible to know too much if one is trying to create character and atmosphere in a model. Especially must we pay attention to those aspects which distinguish one piece of railway from another. The 'rolling hardware' is, of course, perhaps the most obvious of the defining elements, but this is only a transient factor: trains alter character with the passage of time and changes in both technology and ownership. But other things are of more permanent nature and although it is impossible to be precise as to exactly what they are in every case, even at the start of the 21st Century, the railway environment still displays tangible evidence in many places of the characteristic elements which were a hallmark of the specific organisation which put it there in the first place.

I shall develop many of what I consider to be the more important of these themes in subsequent chapters, but by way of rounding out this first section, I thought I would simply recount a few anecdotal prototype influences which helped resolve my own thoughts, along with a few prototype pictures which try to point up some of the guiding principles. They have no other purpose save than to explain the sort of initial methodology by which I started my evaluation of the prototype, along with a hope that some readers may thereby be tempted (persuaded?) to give a little initial time to the analysis of the more intangible elements surrounding their own particular favourites, thus clarifying the mind.....

It is, of course, axiomatic that our interest usually starts with the prototype, though there are exceptions. But interests are variable in their intensity, even within a single subject. We may have a general 'interest' in gardening, for example, but on top of that we may then superimpose an over-riding desire to grow prize vegetables, roses or whatever; and I have found that railways are a bit like that. Thus, pursuing the analogy a little further, if railway interest is our 'garden', then model railways may well be the prize plants! But since we cannot cultivate prize specimens of everything, we need to decide on which plants to concentrate. This is often the *real* problem we face and my aim is to help.

In my case, the actual beginning probably had its roots some ten years earlier than my early 1960s re-appraisal, at a time when, having decided to specialise in geography after I entered the sixth form, I was sent on a school field trip in 1951. In retrospect, it is curious that this was the same year as my interest in railways resumed after the traumatic shock of BR (above). The course was located near Malham Tarn in the Yorkshire Dales, the object being to study the classic geology of this famous region. I was not unfamiliar with the territory, having been there more than enough times to fall under the spell of that magical scenery in the 'Three Peaks' area of upper Ribblesdale. The opportunity to find out more was therefore irresistible, so I needed little persuasion to be pitched into an uncomfortable dormitory with a bunch of total strangers - I was the sole participant from our particular school; sixth forms were small in those days.

Inevitably, there came the day when we were looking at the classic limestone pavement at about the 1300ft contour level on the northern flanks of Ingleborough, during which I was distracted by the sound and sight of a very heavy freight train proceeding north with a lot of fuss and palaver on what was obviously a well engineered main line railway; but even at that stage, I perceived a fundamental incongruity: there was hardly a house, let alone a settlement in sight, so what was this massive chunk of Victorian engineering doing in the middle of nowhere? Railways were generally surrounded by industry and people - or so I had presumed - so I asked the teacher in charge of the party the simple question 'Why?'.

Geography, if it is anything at all, is the study of place, trying to answer the three 'W' questions: 'What is it, where is it and why is it there?' Unfortunately, though well briefed on the subtleties of the Carboniferous rock series into which we were burying our geological hammers, our teacher could not answer this 'out of left field' question from a precocious teenager who was supposed to be fossil-hunting! He was not unhelpful, but it was a useful preliminary indication to me that not even the experts know everything and I returned to the limestone pavement none the wiser. But I still remained curious and, I guess, must have made a sort of subconscious resolve to 'find out for myself' - possibly my first tangible realisation that I could not expect to have everything I wanted to know served up on a plate, so to speak. It was a valuable experience for that alone, if for nothing else..

I am, of course, talking about my first fully recalled

Plate 10: Marthwaite Station. Apart from the later addition of track ballast, the terminal end of Marthwaite never changed in essence and was my first attempt to produce genuine Settle-Carlisle type architecture, based on my own field surveys - I later discovered that, had I known where to look, I could have obtained copies of some of the original building drawings from BR, but I still think that my direct study helped. The station building itself was given more accurate windows at a later stage and re-used for Garsdale Road.

encounter with the Settle and Carlisle railway which did, indeed, receive a good deal of my attention in later years, including one of my first and, if I may be bold enough to say so, one of my best full length books*. But it must have gone onto the back-burner of my mind in 1951, for it was not until ten years later (during my long sojourn in the tropics and its consequential re-think) that I began seriously to think about it in the context of modelmaking.

In my first model book (see preface), I felt it needful to devote considerable space to analysing this famous line by way of background, but since then it has become far more familiar. In part, this has arisen from a combination of the mid-1970s threat to its survival, the pioneering response to this threat in the form of the original 'Dalesrail' trains, preserved steam specials following very soon after the 1976 Centenary and, of course, its revival and proper maintenance during the 1990s by way of a better local passenger service than ever before. This has been supplemented by intense and vital local interest and support, much sympathetic restoration of the often quite beautiful stations and, *mirabile dictu*, a renewal of freight workings, ironically by the newly privatised EW&S Railway which, additionally, has had the very good sense to paint its locomotives in a very close approximation to the famous Midland/LMS Red shade!

I shall not, therefore, go into too much additional detail on the specifics of this particular railway on this occasion; they are mostly described in print for those who would know more and also, happily, much still remains to be studied at first hand - which was by no means the most likely scenario when I was writing in the early 1980s. Suffice to say, therefore, that my resolve to make it my main subject of model interest goes back to that time when I was re-thinking the whole business before my return from overseas. By some sort of serendipitous coincidence, this was, simultaneously, the time when I first encountered Edward Beal's philosophy and also found out that the Settle & Carlisle happened to have belonged to that particular company which had so fired my imagination as a very small boy - the LMS. The consequences were probably inevitable - and I have never regretted that choice - but I do sometimes wonder what I might have done had the S&C turned out to have been inherited by the LNER!

I therefore started, after my return to England in 1962, by exploring the Settle & Carlisle in great detail, studying it in depth by the simple expedient of visiting as much of it as I could, taking lots of pictures, measuring as many buildings as were accessible and taking notes on the way. And for 35 years or more, I have been trying to model this fascinating line and the enthusiasm has never really waned. I completed three EM gauge 4mm scale layouts on the theme (1963-74), afterwards developing both of the follow-up 7mm systems (1975-91) to the operational stage before house moves and job requirements forced further changes. This proliferation may seem at odds with my 'consistency' theme; but each and every one of them had its own logic within the circumstances of the time, and whenever I was forced to make a fresh start, I hoped I had

learned a few more lessons. They will all play some part in what follows and when I started my third (and, hopefully, last 7mm system) in 1995, still based on the S&C theme, I could build on the experiences with all of them.

Notwithstanding eight house moves between 1964 and the present time - and several excursions into other railway modelling fields, some of which will also turn up later in this book - I always seem to come back to that primary decision which I made in 1962; and it is the 'I' which is important. A model must, first and foremost, satisfy the wishes of its owner and creator. Whilever it does this without serious reservation, then there is no need to succumb to the often tempting blandishments of others who will try to persuade you to change scale, standards or anything else which may happen currently to be fashionable. One useful quotation states that "If it is not necessary to make changes, then it is necessary *not* to make changes" - and with this sentiment I wholly concur. The only sensible time to make any change is when you, as the person most concerned, feel it to be 100% necessary; and, even then, think carefully!

But that said, I also have many railway interests in no way connected with the Settle and Carlisle and throughout the last thirty or more years have been trying to reconcile these with my main theme, simply because these, too, often lend themselves to modelling. I will go into more detail as they become relevant, but suffice to say at this stage that they involve a lot of disparate prototypes, European and American particularly, together with many irreconcilable clashes in historical period and geography.

Most of these have arisen from my second professional career as a curator at the NRM, followed by a period in railway publishing. Eventually, I finally came to the conclusion that I probably needed *two* layouts to get all I wanted and my semi-retirement in 1995 finally made this possible. Although I concede that this solution may not be available to everyone, I offer it at this early stage as an idea to keep in the back of your mind, just in case....

It is with this background in mind that I have prepared this book. I repeat that it is not a treatise for the model engineer, nor a series of 'how to do it' instructions in the more general art of modelmaking. What I have preferred to do is try and analyse the problems and difficulties involved when trying to model the historical prototype in the hope that others may thereby be helped. And although I am not trying to make converts to my particular choices of prototypes and scales, I would be flattered if I made a few converts to my way of 'thinking through' the many factors involved in pursuing what I like to call the 'total railway' approach.

I am principally interested in the model railway itself as a *totality* and, as far as rolling hardware is concerned, the concept of the *train* rather than any one single element of it almost always takes centre-stage. If this is in the reader's mind too, then my hope is that he or she will find something of interest within these pages.

* *Rails in the Fells*, Peco Publications: 1973/1980

16

Inspirations

".....a clean red engine with steam in her belly and fire in her heart!" - my original inspiration for almost everything - see text. Ever since I was deeply involved with the restoration of Stanier 4-6-2 No.46229 Duchess of Hamilton between 1976 and 1980, I have always regarded her, sentimentally, as 'my' engine - sic! Here she is in all her pride and pomp.

In the second view we see consistency at its best: Peter Denny's Buckingham Central in its final (and current) form, the result of years of constant evolution and showing what can be achieved by a lifetime of dedicated application to a defined objective. (Ron Prattley)

Out in the open air

"Trains of all nations" is my Gauge 1 garden theme and here are two of them: the LMS 'Merseyside Express' and the Pennsylvania Railroad's 'Broadway Limited' running side by side round a truly prototypical radius curve. The LMS train should ideally have a 4-6-0 or 4-6-2 in charge and may well have one in due course, but both trains were contemporary with each other (c.1930-35) and are modelled to a constant 1:32 scale, which really does point up the contrast in size between British and North American hardware - count the carriages.....

But it need not always be serious - the garden line is 'Nowhere Land', so occasional flights of fancy can be permitted. This is another peripheral interest (North American 3ft narrow gauge lines) which I can now indulge in G Scale on my Gauge 1 track. (Jack Ray - 1)

CHAPTER 2

The value of discrimination

"The art of discrimination is not to let the other chap do all the discriminating for you!"
Anonymous

THE SINGLE theme binding this work together is my basic assumption that the reader wishes to model some sort of 'historic' railway scene. I shall, of course, emphasise the British part of the business, but I hope that some of my ideas will travel 'across borders' and be of more universal value.

This chapter will therefore range over principles by way of offering a structural framework which I hope to expand in detail later. I therefore start by reminding readers that since railway history actually began in the mists of antiquity (the Romans had a form of guided transport for wheeled vehicles some 2000 years ago) and ends, literally, yesterday, one has to be selective in choice and fairly rigorous in keeping to the 'straight and narrow' if things are not to become unwieldy. This involves self-discipline and discrimination which I find is best achieved by trying to break the subject down into a few broad but manageable themes.

However, before tackling these notions, it may be worth amplifying what I mean by 'historical model railway', or perhaps more to the point, how I shall approach the subject in this book. It is, like so many aspects of the hobby, a personal choice and different for each one of us, so I think I should start by making it clear that the building of a 100% accurate replica of a real historic scene is not what I have in mind. It can and has been done, often to splendid effect, and I hope that some of my ideas will be helpful to those who are of such inclination; but I also have the feeling that this sort of approach imposes too many tight constraints on most of us and that the 'believable but imaginary scenario based on reality' offers more flexibility of approach. For this reason, I think it is much more likely to be the choice for the majority of readers and this is where I shall lay most emphasis.

That said, however, I have never tried to assert that my approach to the subject is the only way to proceed, nor shall I do so now: therein lies arrogance. But it is useful to know and understand the opinions, prejudices and attitudes of an author if only to assess the printed word in relation to what often may be subtly different needs on the part of the reader. So let me simply state that the main purpose of my historical modelling is to try and combine the 'total' approach, already mentioned earlier, with some form of believable 'historical atmosphere'. It's a tall order and I am still trying.....

However, I long ago discovered that my personal wishes usually interlocked, almost seamlessly, with some far more fundamental considerations, more of which anon; and they led me to the conclusion that our choice of prototype almost always reflects our personal ideas as to what constitutes 'railway atmosphere'. It is therefore not unlikely that the type of model to be made may well fall out naturally from a first appraisal of this somewhat intangible issue - assuming, of course, that we have made one! But for myself, I find it rather difficult to create 'atmosphere' save in context of a complete model railway.

Now this may seem less than original, but it is a useful starting point if only by virtue of stressing the need to lay first emphasis on the broader issues so as to establish the basic framework of ideas before filling in detail. Only after an overall theme is set to the satisfaction of the modeller is it possible to consider the detailed modelling implications - not least 'atmosphere'.

Were it not for an indefinable something called 'railway atmosphere', I venture to suggest that there would be very few railway enthusiasts and even fewer modellers, for there is something about railways, all railways, which holds an irresistible appeal to many people - and a fair number take it further by trying to capture this 'certain something' via the modelling medium. That we don't always succeed does not stop us trying and I doubt if we often stop to analyse the sheer absurdity of it all when viewed in strictly rational terms. But it is possible to sort things out provided we don't try too hard to explain why we do it - that is a much more complex problem which I leave others to tackle....

In the previous chapter, I allowed myself space in which to try and explain something of the circumstances by which my own philosophy developed, based on the detailed study of the prototype, which then led to my chosing my own particular modelling theme(s). Having therefore laid my personal cards on the table, it is now time to move the discussion on to more general principles on which anyone can and, in my view, should build.

The ultimate goal is to resolve (to personal satisfaction) two simple but closely related considerations: the choice and nature of the prototype to be tackled, together with the type of model desired. The two cannot really be separated and in the detailed planning stages of a layout they often become inextricably intertwined. However, if only to try and bring order out of chaos, I will deal with them separately at first, starting with the

Plate 11: A sense of place - 1. *This fine Eric Treacy study at Marsden c.1954, shows a Liverpool bound train behind a non-identifed Jubilee Class 4-6-0 about to enter Standedge Tunnel on the so-called 'direct' LNWR line from Leeds to Manchester. The fact that the late Lord Bishop of Wakefield often stood back from the lineside to capture the essence of the landscape really does allow us to appreciate the sense of place. Clearly it is hilly country, but the four track line also shows that the economic imperative of the route was more important than the difficulty of the terrain. But even had we not known the location, the many dry stone walls in the background will tell us that it is in the north, while closer examination of the non-railway buildings in terms of disposition, shape and type and the somewhat 'blackened' nature of the dry walls themselves, all give a strong hint of the Pennine fringes of the West Riding of Yorkshire, which is indeed where it is.*

character-giving ingredients of a railway are its geographical environment, the identity (and type) of the company which runs (ran) within that environment and the time period in question. Any 'atmosphere' which the modelled end product may display stems from these three and the success of our models may well depend on how accurately we have 'caught' this essential mix. The relative dominance of one or other of the three constituents in this final cocktail can vary widely and in chosing a prototype, the modeller may well be mainly influenced by whichever of them is most important in his or her thinking. I will deal with them in turn, though I cannot stress too strongly that they are interlinked, albeit slightly differently, for every one of us. So in this analysis, I will try to concentrate on universal principles.

Geographical environment and a sense of 'place'

I start with a consideration of location, where we have to remember that the landscape was there first and the railway tailored to it. Into this setting is inserted the railway and the relationships between railway and landscape are meaningful not haphazard. The most obvious clues to this relationship are usually to be found in the amount and nature of the civil engineering, since the landscape itself can only provide a setting into which the railway engineer puts his line.

The engineering response is itself a function of the likely

prototype; they will be linked later.

In the last chapter, I spent some time in analysing the prototype in terms of those direct experiences which finally led to my own models. I also suggested means whereby this sort of appraisal can be applied more universally. But I hope I am not so arrogant as to assume that my own assessment will be of universal appeal and it therefore seemed to me that I needed to distil some fundamentals from this 'personal' mix - so this is where I shall start. I call it discrimination.

Regardless of precisely how we see the real thing, I have come to the inescapable conclusion that the three essential economic importance of the route to be built. Thus a line likely to carry heavy and frequent traffic at high speeds will justify the use of heavy embankments, viaducts, tunnels &c., in order to keep gradients easy and curvature gentle. Usually referred to as 'well-engineered', this was the main characteristic of most British main lines until the end of the Victorian period, the last major example being the London extension of the Great Central Railway. Much the same principles still apply to the new high speed lines of our present day, although modern

traction can make the need for gentle gradients far less critical than it was in early steam days, albeit still desirable if possible.

The need for good alignment in the case of a main line usually took precedence over the oft-assumed, but over-simplified generalisation that railways keep to valleys whereas roads can also go over the hills. There is a grain of truth in this simplification but it was the over-riding economics of any proposed line which really determined things. Here, such lines as the Settle and Carlisle (my choice of prototype) prove the point without doubt, by way of attacking a mountain range head on at very considerable cost and human effort simply because of the economic imperative to get through. Britain and the world in general offer many similar examples - the Canadian Pacific trans-continental route springs immediately to mind, albeit with very different visual impact than the Settle-Carlisle. The point to make here is that rugged territory need not rule out a major main line provided that there is adequate economic justification.

Plate 12: A sense of place - 2. *This further superb landscape study from my old friend Eric Treacy, again gives a fine sense of place - this time in the fell country on the borders of Lakeland. How can we tell? Simply because the hills are high but rather rounded (ie not the Lake District proper) and rather deficient in dry stone walls, thus suggesting either common grazing land (if used for farming at all) or of insufficient value to merit defining by boundaries - note that the lower-lying meadows between the train and the distant hills are more than adequately demarcated by field boundaries. It is in fact Low Gill on the West Coast main line just south of its junction with the secondary main line from Ingleton (marked by the line of cottages) and the train is a northbound empty mineral behind a Class 4F 0-6-0. If the two ex-NER wooden bodied hopper wagons just appearing in view on the extreme right are any guide, then it may well be bound for the North East via Tebay (just a few miles to the north), where it will probably change engines, and thence via Stainmore to former LNER territory.*

Nor must it be forgotten that the human factor can often over-ride geography in the historical context, especially in Britain where the attitude of influential landowners could regularly affect both the course and nature of a main line railway, the by-passing of Stamford by the GNR in favour of Peterborough being a good example. Likewise, the original London and Birmingham line (later part of the LNWR) was forced to deviate east from the easier and logical valley route

Plate 13: Company hallmarks - 1. This finely composed image, again from Eric Treacy, shows LYR and LMS standard motive power in the shape of 0-6-0 No.12230 and 'Patriot' 4-6-0 No.5520 Llandudno respectively. But the signals tell us beyond peradventure that we are actually in the heart of former LNWR territory: Edge Hill c.1937-8.

of the River Gade through Watford (an alignment which *is* taken by the Grand Union Canal), simply because of local landowner opposition to the railway: the expensive Watford tunnels (to re-gain the natural valley route north of that place) were the consequence. Even the Settle and Carlisle has an example: Lazonby tunnel is an unnecessary covered way (rather than a cheaper cutting) to avoid damaging the local vicarage garden - sic!

Perceptive readers will no doubt be able to work out for themselves the possibly interesting modelling implications which this sort of historical knowledge can suggest.....

By contrast with the above, a smaller feeder line was less constrained, being able to follow the natural contours more closely, albeit by compromising in terms of gradient and curvature to keep construction costs down if potential revenue could not justify more expense. But even here, there had to be economic justification for the line in the first place.

Happily for modellers, there are many cases in British history where lines were built without (apparently) too much regard for the over-riding economics. They did not always last

long but they give us more choice. But no matter the precise circumstances, one of the primary decision points a potential historical modeller needs to reach is to determine the type and nature of line to be modelled in order that the background environment may be properly established.

But it is not just the lie of the land which commands our attention. The local architecture (especially older buildings) often makes a region distinctive as, indeed, does the building material used. It is unwise to model a brick viaduct in what is supposed to be granite or limestone country, or to impose a Scottish gamekeeper's cottage in the heart of rural Wiltshire. Maybe the odd freak of this nature does occur in real life but in the modelling context, it usually creates the sort of jarring element which we should take pains to avoid.

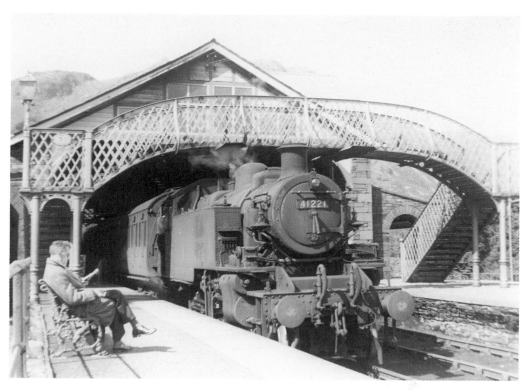

Plate 14: Company hallmarks - 2.
Hilly country again - note the steep slopes just above the station roof. The lattice footbridge has a 'Midland' look but this type could, in fact, be found on the lines of several companies, while the train is clearly of LMS design, though that is not necessarily helpful in the post BR period. But that platform seat has the squirrel and grapes in its supports (see text), so it is quite clearly Furness Railway. The stonework, such as can be seen, is typically 'Lakeland' in terms of treatment and the location is Coniston, c.1960. (B.C.Lane)

So..... study the vernacular architecture; take note of the typical disposition of buildings; analyse the distribution and type of trees; pay attention to the relative proportions of arable, grass and open spaces; consider the basic geological characteristics of the physical landscape.... and so on.

Of course, this is only part of the story, for changes to the human landscape are continuous, many taking place after a railway is built. I shall come back to the time period later, but at this stage it is worth remembering that the 'sameness' of building types, methods and materials is a characteristic of our modern age, only really beginning after the second world war as far as most of Britain is concerned, so whether or not examples of this modern day uniformity are included in a model does rather depend on the time period intended. But we should also remember that even with modern add-ons, most places still contain older buildings and so forth whose form of construction, not to mention building materials themselves, will almost certainly reflect those distinctive regional differences of which modellers should be aware.

Given attention to these matters, the modeller is well on the way to establishing 'where?' in geographical terms. But even if we are able to establish a 'sense of place' for our potential model, the railway itself could be any company operating in such an area. The next step, therefore, is to establish what distinguishes one railway from another.

The railway identity

Fortunately for British modellers, most of the popular 19th Century railways which are likely to attract our interest were big enough to have had distinctive trademarks which have not totally vanished despite almost 80 years of grouping,

nationalisation and post-BR privatisation. Thus, Virgin trains from Euston to Glasgow traverse what is still recognisable as the old LNWR 'Premier' line and its former Caledonian continuation, though I could wish the new name had a bit more of an historic ring to it; the GNER (a rather better name) runs its trains on lines which (if you know how and where to look) are unmistakeably identifiable as having GNR, NER or NBR origins; while 'First Great Western' has even revived the historic name of the old company whose 'house style' is still firmly stamped on much of the present infrastructure. Thus it is that even the most 'modern image' modeller needs to have some appreciation of the historical dimension if things are to make sense.

Regardless of period, therefore, the modeller needs to identify the distinctive features which mark the railway of choice. It may be the signal box design or platform fencing, station furniture or buffer stop design. It may be the signals themselves or even a fondness for a particular disposition of tracks; but it will be something quite distinctive and peculiar to that railway at the time period in question. For example, if my model was based on the Furness Railway area, regardless of whether I favoured FR, LMS, BR or the present day, I might well choose to start by making a dozen or so platform seats where, in the end supports, a squirrel can be seen eating a bunch of grapes. This theme was allegedly suggested by a senior officer of the FR onto whose desk (and its fruit bowl!) a squirrel was a regular visitor if his garden window was open - a nice story whatever its origins - and the seats are still there to this day!

Whatever the points of detail, their identification for a specific company and their replication on the model itself can be essential in creating miniature atmosphere.

23

Plate 15: Company hallmarks - 3. At first glance, this could be taken for somewhere in London on the old Southern Railway third rail electric system, but not so; it is an official view of Liverpool Exchange on the old LYR showing some of the electrified track used by the Liverpool-Southport trains. The revealing company trademarks are the signal box style, the signals themselves and the 'shrouded' nature of the conductor rails (ie set between protective timber longitudinals). The LYR coach in the distance is not, of itself, conclusive evidence of anything.....

This, then, gives us two thirds of the mix - 'where' and 'which railway' - but before proceeding further we may now wish to consider some of the possible difficulties which have already sprung to mind......

First of all, there could be a hopeless incompatibility between geography and railway history. For example, if you like rugged mountain country and your favourite line is the GNR (or its LNER and later successors) then you have a real problem which is best faced from the outset. Something will have to be modified if historical 'believability' is not to be sacrificed and since, for most of us, the choice of railway probably carries rather more weight than the chosen setting, it is likely that the latter may have to go. In the example given above, a compromise might be found where the GNR penetrated some of the steep sided valleys of the old West Riding of Yorkshire, but the chance of operating East Coast main line trains would have to be forgone - and so it goes on.

A second problem relates to the sheer richness of choice available in prototype railway terms. Few of us are totally wedded to one railway to the exclusion of all others and it is frequently impossible to reconcile all our favourites. The most extreme case known to myself was that of a gentleman who wished a joint Midland and Highland system. The LMS era (a possible compromise in terms of rolling hardware) was no use - he wanted the pre-1923 scene - and the layout was never built. I am sure there's a moral there somewhere but despair not, there are solutions at hand!

Another factor might be that of space available, always my own particular headache and to which I shall return later. Even if you can resolve geography with railway, the site available may not permit the development of a model which gives the required effect or atmosphere in the scale in which you prefer to work - so it is back to the thinking stage again. This, in turn, begins to introduce such questions as scale and layout type in the more general sense, at which point the whole matter of choice of prototype and exact type of model to be assayed tend to get inextricably mixed up to the point at which some folk give up altogether! I have been there too (and emerged!), and will try to develop this theme in later chapters, so fear not! Meantime, assuming that we can find a fairly reasonable combination of setting plus company for early planning purposes, let us now move on to the third issue in the aforementioned 'mix', the vexed question of historic time.

Setting the historical period

This is probably the first point at which the locomotives and trains (hitherto pretty well ignored) begin to play any real part in the debate - and then not overmuch! In fact, I would even go so far as to say that the acid test of whether or not a historical model railway has atmosphere is the extent to which it can stand inspection without any trains in view. If it can, then even if trains of the 'wrong' company or historic period happen to put in an appearance, they will merely look like 'foreign visitors'.

However, it is abundantly clear that the design and liveries of the locomotives and rolling stock do much to suggest the historic period represented and, after all, this *is* what we are supposed to be modelling; so it behoves us to try and match trains to period by careful choice of prototype, decorative treatment and so forth. To do this effectively requires accurate pre-knowledge and this, in turn, will almost certainly mean some form of research, a subject which needs special consideration. I have therefore deferred most of its many ramifications until later, and given it a chapter to itself, wherein I try to strip it of some of its perceived (but for the most part non-existent) overtones of fear.....

At this stage, suffice to say that no satisfying historical model can be achieved without some form of basic research, but since this need not cause apprehension, let me get back to the matter of 'period'.

Much period accuracy can be established by little more than the application of common sense, road vehicle design and human costumes being two obvious examples, though I would not always advocate so-called 'period' TV drama as a prime source, especially when it comes to the accuracy of railway

Plate 16: Establishing period - 1. If the source gives us a date, as this one does (Fishponds, Midland Railway, 1885), then we can often use the information gleaned therefrom to help date other images. In this case, the uniform dress is quite helpful, as is the nature of the track ballast (mostly very fine graded and nearly burying the sleepers) but beware the porter with the barrow. Uniform apart, this way of handling milk churns, not to mention the barrow and churn types themselves, was still much in evidence well into BR days.....

hardware..... I have already mentioned the need for appropriate building types (ie watch out for incongruous post-WWII 'development' if you are in the strict pre-BR period), to which might also be added such things as street lamps plus street and station 'furniture' in general, including typefaces and other graphics on station signs, advertising hoardings, &c. You will be surprised how modern some so-called 'old' looking features actually turn out to be when investigated more carefully. Many roads did not get a hard surface until well into the 1930s or later, road marking as such was in its infancy until much the same time and station platforms did not get white edges until the 1939-45 war years, to mention but three common errors to be seen on many models.

Arising from this is the rather more subtle matter of the nature and speed of change and how best to model it. We are apt to see change as a modern phenomenon, but this is not really true. Despite the Internet, computers and many other aspects of the modern electronic age, most of the things which surround us have been here for a longer time than we often think - the military used mobile phones during WWII for example - while motorised transport has more than a century of history behind it as I write and high performance aircraft are almost as long-established.

Plates 17/18: Establishing period - 2. *These two views of Bletchley (LNWR, later LMS and BR LMR), both looking in the northerly direction, show how some things changed and others did not. The earlier view can be recognised as such because of the ash ballast and its deep nature, together with the clearly late Victorian nature of the train in Platform 2. However, the domed clerestory roofs on some of the vans in the distance did not appear until the 1890s and they do not seem brand new, so maybe this view is later than it seems - c.1900, perhaps?*

By contrast, the second view of Platform 1, taken inside the station, is later, though the original roof still remains much as in the earlier *picture. The station signs are a mixture of LNWR and LMS while the track is clearly quite old (possibly still LNWR - the ballast is fine graded and the chairs do not look like those of LMS design), so at first glance a mid-LMS period might well be presumed. But the real clue lies in the dress of the lady passenger which is clearly of mid-20th Century styling. The skirt is rather long and probably contains more material than was used during the economy years of the 1940s. The picture (an official one, though for what reason remains obscure) is actually dated October 1951. What is also interesting is the huge amount of platform clutter, scarcely changed in nature or type for 50 years or more, I guess.*

Contrast this with the really fundamental changes which took place between, say, 1830 (opening of the Liverpool & Manchester, the first fully mechanically powered inter-city railway in the world) and a generation later in the mid 1850s when the whole of Britain was covered for the first time ever with a network of modern transport arteries whose route mileage was at least twice that of the modern motorway network which has taken almost twice as long to build.

We therefore need to remember that it is the shape and style of artefacts which usually changes rather than the basic concept; and herein lies the real problem: style changes are rapid, whether on- or off-rail. Who amongst us has not come across that helpful observer who delights in informing us that our particular choice of engine number represents an example scrapped three days before the so-called period of our model or that two particular carriage liveries could not possibly have been seen side by side in 19xx - or whenever?

There's not a lot we can do about this in the absolute sense (whether it be to counter the nit-picker or reconcile the real historical glitch which lies behind the criticism), which is no doubt why so many of us prefer to represent a rather 'looser' period of time as the basis of our models. It is an imperfect compromise, no doubt, but I venture to suggest that provided the period is not too loose (ie kept to a year or two either side of a preferred date), the achievement of atmosphere will not be put at too much risk.

From all of which it should now be clear that I consider preliminary thinking to be as important as the actual building of models. This is largely because I wasted so much time in my first ten years in the game by building attractive but irrelevant models, that I resolved never to let it happen again. I therefore reckon that the thinking through of a problem can do so much to clear the mind of non-essentials (and thus prevent wasting time on building or acquiring unnecessary or irrelevant items) that time spent on this superficially boring exercise is not ill-spent. Of course, we must realise that

planning is not an end in itself - that way lies permanent 'armchair' modelling(!) - but that said, a similar analysis can also be applied to the question of layout type and models to be attempted, wherein discrimination in all its manifold aspects plays just as much a part as in the topics so far covered. Since this tends to follow logically as the next stage in our thinking, let me now turn to it.

The modelling implications

In building railway models, there are two main areas of activity: the layout itself and the nature of the rolling stock, buildings &c. which will feature on it. They cannot wholly be separated but it helps to try.

During an attempted resolution of the 'Where, which and when' aspects already considered, it is very likely that we shall also have been developing ideas concerning the kind of layout most likely to fulfil our wishes. Setting aside space considerations for the moment, there are few basic types of layout to consider - essentially 'end-to-end' versus 'continous circuit', allied to the matter of authentic operation as opposed to demonstration running of period trains. In one sense, the end-to-end approach goes best with prototypical operation and the continuous circuit lends itself to demonstration running; but the two are by no means mutually exclusive. In an ideal world we might well like to have both options and I have been fortunate that in all my layouts since the mid-1970s, I have been able to combine the two elements. But if the choice is 'either/or', likely to be the case for many of us, then we need carefully to consider our dominant preferences.

It is at this point - and probably not before - that site and space considerations really come into their own for the first time at the practical level. Speaking personally, there is nothing more daunting than to be faced with a blank sheet of paper (save for a site plan outlined thereon) unless you, as the modeller, have already developed some pretty clear ideas as to what should be the nature of the finished product.

IION STATION. NO. 18.

S. E. E. 366

Plates 20/21: Period detail - 1. *The sort of detail which was to be found in and around stations at various times is always helpful. Even if a picture shows a railway which is of no great concern to us, many companies had much in common at specific periods of time and their study can help us get the 'feel' of the times. Here are two pre-First World War images which have much in common though separated by some 200 miles. The first view (the approach to Willesden Junction station) is undated, but the total absence of motor vehicles and the nature of the dress hints at the early Edwardian period, while the elaborate notice board on the station building mentions just about every area served by the LNWR - typical of the time.*

The second (official) view is dated: a near-deserted Bradford Exchange 1912. Again a cobbled road is seen alongside the platforms, this time under the overall roof as befits the major status of the station. Horse-drawn vehicles are equally exclusive while the proliferation of foreground signs and advertisements (on the far wall) is a further common factor between the two images. An interesting point to note is that the railway poster boards, while dominantly those of the owning LYR, include the LNW, North British and Great Central Railways, but not the Great Northern Railway, a tenant of the LYR at this place, whose carriages occupy several platforms in the middle distance and whose posters were on its own side of the station.

Plate 22: Period detail - 2. *This fascinating view of Manchester (probably Queen Street) is characteristic of the 1920s. The road displays a wonderfully eclectic mixture of trams, pedestrians (mostly male) wandering about at random (no marked pedestrian crossings in those days), horse-drawn and motorised vehicles, amongst the latter of which can be seen an open char-a-banc (almost certainly converted from a surplus ex-army vehicle after World War I) emerging from a side street and a quite modern motor car in the foreground. Other details which can be observed are the nature of the dress and the method of loading at least some types of horse-drawn vehicle; and it is worth remarking that, contrary to popular view, the latter type of road vehicle is still dominant in the commercial sense - there is not a motor lorry in sight.*

Plate 23: Period detail - 3. *At first sight, this picture of the entrance to the Mersey Railway platforms at Liverpool Central could be taken as being from the pre-group era, but note that 'LNER' has appeared at the top of one of the poster boards (centre). Virtually every flat vertical surface is adorned by some sort of advertising or publicity material and one can only smile at the Mersey Railway's delusions of grandeur as witnessed by its main display - top left. (B.C.Lane collection)*

29

Now in this respect, it is a moot point whether or not the scale of the model should take preference over the scope of the layout: the accepted wisdom of 'N Gauge in a box room' or 'Gauge 1 for a tennis court' only holds true in the very basic sense. It is sometimes true, of course, that only one scale seems to be appropriate (usually one of the smaller scales chosen when faced with a constricted site) but it is often worthwhile indulging in a bit of lateral thinking by way of considering the options of all the different scales at the planning stage before committing yourself irrevocably (and too

hastily?) to the more expensive next stage and then living to regret it.....

To give a personal example, my first three Settle and Carlisle models were all to 4mm scale EM Gauge, starting with 'Marthwaite' (end-to-end), followed by 'Garsdale Road' (a small basic continuous circuit but fed by quite a large number of running loops to hold the many trains) and finally the 'Little Long Drag' (a 36ft x 16ft blockbuster!). I had always assumed 'the bigger the better' to get the spacious effect I wanted and there is no doubt that the final layout was very spacious and it both looked and performed well; but it never fulfilled my wishes quite as well as the earlier ones had done and at first, I could not think why.

It finally dawned on me in the mid-1970s, a year or two after the layout was operationally up and running (it never was completed scenically), that I had trapped myself into a dangerously myopic '4mm scale way of thinking' and it was only when I considered the possibility of other scales that I resolved the problem. I chose 7mm scale as it happens but, under different circumstances, it might just as easily have been N Gauge.

By then, I had also modelled in the latter scale by way of a somewhat light-hearted excursion into American practice, which made me realise that huge spaces were not the whole answer to modelling problems. Experience with this little venture into what was not much more than proprietary ready to run made me wonder just what I might do in my big shed by going for more simplicity in a *larger* scale. This turned out to be the key which 'unlocked' the problem as far as I was concerned and about which I shall go into more detail in the next chapter. Suffice to say at this stage that many more lessons were learned in the process, not least in terms of layout planning, so all was not wasted.

So much for personal digression, but my hope is that by including it here, I have at least 'fleshed out' some of the problems of sites and space which the dedicated modeller may encounter. The one inescapable conclusion from all these various projects from the 1970s and 1980s is that if one specific criterion is dominant in your thoughts (be it scale, operation or whatever), then something else may need to be given 'back seat' status.

The next stage in the preliminaries is to decide, as best as possible, the question of the overall character of the layout in terms of balance. Are trains to dominate or is landscape to be the main feature? This is a really tricky issue to resolve and best faced at an early stage. Over the years since I wrote my first model book, modelling standards have improved to an amazing extent right across the board in absolute terms as far as accuracy of appearance is concerned, not least in terms of the attention given to the surrounding landscape. This is fine by me, but pursued to excess, it can lead to a landscape-dominated approach which tends to negate those fascinating operational aspects of the historic railway which can really give life to a working model. Since my instincts favour the 'operational railway plus sufficient landscape to offer a suitable setting' rather than a landscape in which there just so happens to be a railway whose operational role is a rather secondary feature, maybe it is as well to say so now......

I suspect that this is because even since I wrote my first modelling book, there has grown up a younger and highly talented generation of new modellers who knew not the historic railway in its prime, save as revealed by the ever-growing number of fine but not always fully interpreted archive photographs. They may, in consequence, be a little unsure of their ground and thus, quite understandably, often take a more 'visual impression' approach, in which I can find no fault as such. But in the hope that a greater understanding of the working of the historical railway may well enhance the enjoyment of the whole hobby, I shall also try to address this issue from time to time as far as modelling is concerned.

We next come, quite naturally, to the matter of whether models are to be made or bought. If scratch building is your metier then the quantity factor may be less relevant than if ready to run equipment is chosen. Here, we need to assess our modelmaking abilities against the excellent components from the trade and it is no good being dishonest in appraising our own talents. There is so much good quality stuff for sale these days that scratch building is no longer as essential as when I started. The fact that I, like many others, still opt for this approach is now far more a matter of choice than sheer necessity and I am quite happy to rely on the trade where its offerings more than match my own skills.

Thus, in conclusion, I hope I have demonstrated that in planning a satisfactory layout, quite a lot of preliminary thinking has to be done. Constraints must be acknowledged, ideas formulated and a fairly ruthless assessment made of the relative importance of the various desirable features which we might well like to incorporate, not to mention an honest appreciation on our part of the extent to which we feel able to carry the project through to completion in terms of both time and skill. All in all, it is a lot to think about and I find it useful to do my thinking with notebook and pencil to hand in order to jot down ideas (however ill-formed) as they emerge.

All my layouts since 1962 (including the rather surreal flights of fancy into the American scene!) have been planned with these ideas in mind and, though never deliberately designed to do so, have all, in their own way, given me valuable experience in a variety of layout concepts, all of which could be put to good use in designing the next one, some of which I hope to share with readers.

They have taught me that there is no perfect solution to what is, in essence, an impossible task - that of condensing the full size railway into the domestic environment. But it is well worth the effort; and the fact that I have, mainly through force of circumstances, put together many model projects in that time (all fully operational though not always scenically complete) suggests that it is not an impossible goal, provided you tackle the subject fairly logically from the outset.

I do not suggest that the reader should copy me in terms of the total number of projects tackled: that was a peculiarity of my own rather peripatetic life style for over thirty years; but since I have found that in every case, logic demands that we start with a degree of initial discrimination in principle, it follows that we must then establish some clearly defined objectives - and that is where I will next focus attention.

HRM

CHAPTER 3

Setting objectives and isolating essentials

"Begin at the beginning and go on till you come to the end: then stop."
Lewis Carroll, 'Alice's Adventures in Wonderland'

WHEN THE King of Hearts addressed the above remark to Alice, I doubt that he had model railways in mind, but his advice is sound, our problem being the common tendency to enter the field somewhere in the middle, then head off happily in several different directions without knowing exactly where any of them may lead. What makes it even more annoying is that although some of these ideas may well offer a useful beginning, none seems to deliver the goods. We then end up disappointed with our efforts or, worse still, doing nothing at all. So.....what is the problem? I am not sure I can answer it completely, but I will try.

When I was a curator at the National Railway Museum, I was privileged both to meet and converse with the late R.A. ('Robin') Riddles, the last proper 'CME' of our railway system in the sense of being the final arbiter in terms of what should be built without benefit of 'design consultants' or other 'hangers on' of the kind so familiar in our modern day. He had been William Stanier's personal assistant on the LMS during the later 1930s and was elderly when I first met him; but his mind was still 100% active and amongst many pearls of wisdom he offered was a particularly relevant comment in any context: "Decision making is easy; it's identifying the problem which causes the headache."

I think this is very true of our hobby, especially when moving on from the issues of principle adressed in the last chapter. I refer to it as 'setting objectives and isolating essentials', from which, hopefully, should stem an approach best suited to our own perception of the hobby; so let me start the next part of the analysis by outlining a fairly familiar sequence of events, well known to me.

Imagine a typical model railway show at which there is a layout which particularly appeals - never mind the reason for the moment, it will be different for all of us. We resolve to do something similar so home we go, inspiration renewed, and get out the drawing board (or whatever) and get down to work. Before long (sooner not later if I am any judge...), we realise that to get a layout remotely like our exemplar, we need to know more about the prototype itself, so research enters the picture: at which point we have no idea where to go. Or perhaps we discover that most of the models on the admired layout were scratch built (and we don't do scratch building, of course!), or that the space we have available is not sufficiently

similar, or that the time required will be more than we can honestly spare, or, or.... So where did we go wrong? Mr or Ms 'X' has done it so why can't we? The answer is devastatingly simple: we have fallen into the familiar trap of trying to model someone else's model.

This is, of course, very flattering to the original modeller whose layout proved this spur to the imagination; but, short of slavishly copying another person - a pretty unimaginative thing to do - what we should really try to gain from other folk is ideas and knowledge. These things can then be worked on and modified to suit our own wishes, skills and experience.

Put at its most basic, the only real way to get going is to appreciate from the outset that we must always create our own model railways and not copy or be over-influenced by other folk. Once this notion has taken hold, not only can we draw many fruitful ideas from other modellers but we can also save ourselves much time and effort by using those of their ideas *which are relevant to us* - and note the emphasis.

Another trap lying in wait for the unwary is that helpful chap (sadly, it is usually a 'he'!) who urges you to 'get something running' as soon as possible. He means well, for it is a very strong-minded modeller who does not want to see the result of much labour up and running. Moreover, it can be a positive disincentive to progress if you can't see some form of mobility fairly soon; but don't rush in too quickly - that was the mistake I made during the 1950s. All I wanted to do was see the trains run and never gave much thought to the overall effect created. Unsurprisingly, no decent effect *was* created - how could it be with GWR, LMS, LNER, BR and Anerican HO all mixed up together? But since any of these choices could have formed the basis of an interesting model in its own right, this experience taught me the need to think through the objectives first: 'Put mind in gear before cash in motion,' if you like..... If this is done first, then there is no reason why the layout cannot be planned in such a way as to have some trains running quite early in the process. There is no mystery about it - just a willingness to think.

I therefore do think it rather helpful if the modeller tries to set objectives and determine priorities at the earliest possible stage - and to show what I mean, I will run through the very comprehensive list of desiderata which I have always had in mind ever since I started modelling the Settle-Carlisle back in

1962. At this first stage, it is no more than a statement of wishes and not set out in any order of importance or priority: that will come later, of course, but first we need to have some ideas to work on:

a) As nearly as possible, correct appearance of track - thus fine scale not coarse. In my 4mm days I chose EM gauge and in 7mm scale went for 32mm 'fine', implicit in both these decisions being the probability that track (or at least pointwork) would have to be hand built.

b) Consistent standards throughout - ie buildings and other infrastructure to be as important as realistic rolling stock and equal care to be devoted to all aspects.

c) Correct station proportions as far as possible - ie no unacceptable foreshortening of station length.

d) Correct balance between scenery and railway and, in my case, if one must dominate, it should be the railway.

e) Main line, scale length trains to be operated.

f) More than adequate hidden storage capacity for the trains, whether by way of concealed running loops or a conventional set of parallel storage sidings - the so called 'fiddle yard'.

g) Maximum curve radius possible and never below 3ft (4mm scale) or 5-6ft (7mm scale), even where hidden from view. All visible curves to be as gentle as possible.

h) Prototypical working to be possible in all aspects - ie essentially 'end to end' in basic operational philosophy regardless of the precise layout plan.

j) Continuous running to be possible for testing and simple demonstration purposes.

k) A branch line for added interest, including the main line junction.

l) All complex trackwork areas to be readily accessible for maintenence.

m) An open stretch of main line without stations.

n) Stations to be visually separated - ie no mythical 'split levels' to explan the proximity of two different locations.

o) The whole concept to present a theme which, even if imaginary, represents a feasible prototype situation.

p) The scheme should allow a gradual build-up with, at least, a modest degree of operation at an early stage.

q) A fairly ruthless approach to the question of 'period chosen' and 'foreign' invaders.

r) (in my specific case) The whole thing to suggest MR and the Settle/Carlisle even when nothing is happening.

Now this is a pretty formidable list - almost a counsel of prefection in fact - but I like to think that with the exception of the very last (purely personal) wish, some or all of the others could be applied to any potential layout scenario as a basis from which to start, provided we add the important concept of 'compromise' from the outset.

I consider the matter of compromise to be so important a factor in the field of model railways that I have given it a separate chapter to analyse in detail, so suffice to say at this stage that it is my firm view that all model railways are a compromise. Regardless of space, scale or anything else for that matter, we must always accept the utter impossibility of

Plate 26: Marthwaite MkI. The first version of Marthwaite was also my initial attempt to meet some of my long list of desirable criteria after my 1962 re-appraisal - see text - and this view concentrates on two of them. Dominant in the foreground is my first attempt at signal construction in a style which would suggest 'Midland Railway' above all else - and I think it probably succeeded, albeit that the signals were non-working at the time. Beyond the signals can be seen my first attempt at producing the sort of flowing look to trackwork which looked as though a real platelayer may have had a hand in things. For the record, the track was built on the late Jim Russell's 'Little Western' principle (an intriguing form of construction, well covered in the model magazines of the 1960s) and ballast was added at a later stage.

modelling every facet of the railway scene. Nobody has done it yet and I doubt they ever will: harsh words, no doubt, but let me explain further.

A likely situation which we may (will?) encounter is that having evolved a suitable set of ideals to be aimed for as far as our own particular personal wishes are concerned, we find that site and other constraints throw up many other factors which make it impossible to design a layout which includes all of them. It is at this point that we need to isolate the essentials and assign some priorities to our first 'wish-list'. It is no easy

Plate 27: Marthwaite MkI again. Another aspect of my wish to create a believable scene - see Plate 26 - was the desire to offer an infrastructure which suggested its (supposed) MR origins. In this second view of the original Marthwaite, this was achieved by making the buildings (in the background) to a genuine Settle & Carlisle style, putting a typicallly Midland 'angled' station nameboard on the platform and adding further (non-working) MR type signals to the scene. The deployment of the Stanier 2-6-4T and LMS standard 'Jinty' 0-6-0 was an early attempt to set a 'period' (c.1936-7) to the scene.

---

task and I would never presume to tell anyone which should be top of the agenda, or the first reject for that matter. But faced with the task of choosing alternatives (unless you have a Dutch Barn at your disposal and almost unlimited depth of pocket), you will soon have to decide which of your many ideas are pre-eminently important - ie 'essential to have' as opposed to 'desirable if possible'.

It has therefore struck me that rather than go on with further theorising, it might be better to consider how my own layouts (for the most part reasonably well recorded in print thus far) have matched up to my own multifold objectives at the time of writing (mid 2001). I gave a brief resumé in the previous chapter but I would now like to expand in greater detail in the hope that this may offer a few general pointers for all.

My first effort, 'Marthwaite', in EM Gauge, was built during 1962-7 when space constraints were at their most critical. It underwent several modifications during that time and at Fig.1, I offer a drawing of the layout in its final and most satisfactory form. From the outset, many of my long term wishes were put

'on ice', largely because at this time the main line option was not a contender. I therefore chose the familiar branch terminus to fiddle-yard solution, but wrote its history based on a real junction location, notionally located at Dent Head, and timed the trains on the layout to connect with known workings on the Settle-Carlisle main line.

The idea for the track layout came from Grassington, the nearest suitable MR terminus to my chosen route. I reversed the prototype plan, mirror image fashion, to suit the site constraints and equipped the layout with a full array of S&C buildings plus a locomotive depot. The problem was that Marthwaite (aka Sedbergh in the real world) represented a larger town than Grassington and with more traffic - yet in reality, Grassington sprawled around whereas Marthwaite had to be confined to c.15ft x 2ft. I leave readers to judge how far it came towards realising the ideal.

In the end, Marthwaite more or less fulfilled about half my above criteria, most of the others being shelved or ignored. I cannot comment wholly objectively as to its overall success, of course, but it seemed to be well enough received. My friends and I had a lot of fun with it and it was with a real sense of regret that I had to close the line in 1967. By now it had grown a sort of 'personality' and become quite well known in the North of England where it was exhibited on several occasions.

But I was not wholly satisfied. My subsconscious 'main line' wishes had allowed it to become far too busy in traffic terms (not to mention the nature of the some of the stock we ran on it for that matter), being physically too constricted for the many trains we operated. In other words I was getting far too close to the believability margin - and it showed.

Custom-built

These views not only contrast scratch and kit-built models, but also allow me to acknowledge quite a few of my friends. The first picture shows my 7mm scale model of the slim boilered Johnson 4-4-0 No.2184 in its full Midland regalia. This model was built by Ken Woodhead (who then decided he did not want it!), so it came to me in exchange for some carriage models and I had Larry Goddard do a 'full

works' paint job on it - in no way could this model be relevant to my main theme! This, in due course, prompted me to make it a suitable train which I added to my 'out of period' display formations and, as such, it will appear later. Meantime, it did some of its running trials on another close friend's layout - that of Ken Payne, who also took this fine view of the engine (including smoke effect) on his turntable.

By contrast, but appropriately in context, the second view shows an equally fine 7mm scale kit-built model of the final version of inside cylindered 'Midland' 4-4-0 philosophy, the LMS standard Class 2P No.635, built and photographed by yet another long standing friend, Dave Austin, with whom I started a model railway club at RAF Seletar (Singapore) as long ago as 1960 - such is the nature of this hobby. The model is posed on Dave's combined indoor/outdoor layout and note that although made from a kit, this one has inside motion which the scratch built 2184 does not have....

Ready to run - large size

Commercial models have improved beyond all recognition since I started this hobby and although still preferring to 'do it myself' in the context of 7mm scale (a philosophy which I also followed with the building of a Gauge 1 LMS train), I took full advantage of the availability of 'ready to run' when I first went into live steam Gauge 1 on retirement from full time work. This was mainly because I felt it was too late and possibly too time-consuming to learn a whole raft of new techniques which hand-built live steam would demand (not to mention the expense of acquiring the additional machine tools which I might need), but also because some of my most favourite non-British prototypes were available in finished form anyway. Not the least of these were several varieties of carriages for the 'Broadway Limited' of the Pennsylvania Railroad, along with the equally well known K4 pacifics which hauled this train.

The engine is by Aster and was my very first Gauge 1 acquisition. It was a somewhat indifferent gas-burner until yet another close friend, former museum colleague Tony Hall-Patch, worked his magic upon it and converted it to spirit burning - and it will now pull a house down and has a wonderful 'voice'. The seven classic heavyweight American 12-wheel carriages in the train are by John Waggott of Dorset and I gain both tactile and therapeutic pleasure by driving this fine train round my garden whenever I feel so inclined and the weather is favourable - note that I run it on the correct right hand track.... (Jack Ray - 2)

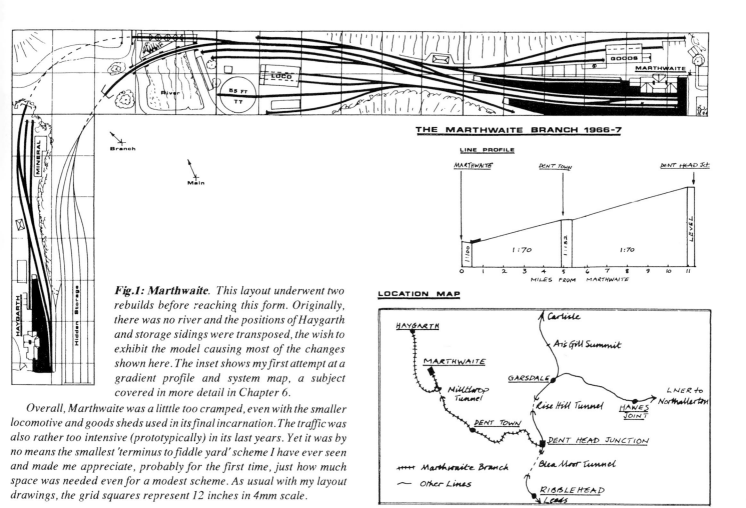

THE MARTHWAITE BRANCH 1966-7

LINE PROFILE

MARTHWAITE   DENT TOWN   DENT HEAD Jct.

1:100   1:70   1:52   1:70   LEVEL

0   1   2   3   4   5   6   7   8   9   10   11
MILES FROM MARTHWAITE

LOCATION MAP

HAYGARTH
MARTHWAITE
Millthrop Tunnel
DENT TOWN
Rise Hill Tunnel
DENT HEAD JUNCTION
Blea Moor Tunnel
RIBBLEHEAD
Leeds

Carlisle
Ais Gill Summit
GARSDALE
LNER to Northallerton
HAWES JOINT

†††† Marthwaite Branch
— Other Lines

Fig.1: Marthwaite. *This layout underwent two rebuilds before reaching this form. Originally, there was no river and the positions of Haygarth and storage sidings were transposed, the wish to exhibit the model causing most of the changes shown here. The inset shows my first attempt at a gradient profile and system map, a subject covered in more detail in Chapter 6.*

Overall, Marthwaite was a litttle too cramped, even with the smaller locomotive and goods sheds used in its final incarnation. The traffic was also rather too intensive (prototypically) in its last years. Yet it was by no means the smallest 'terminus to fiddle yard' scheme I have ever seen and made me appreciate, probably for the first time, just how much space was needed even for a modest scheme. As usual with my layout drawings, the grid squares represent 12 inches in 4mm scale.

Plate 28: Marthwaite Mks II/III. *The original exit from Marthwaite (see Plate 7, Chapter 1) was never wholly convincing to me and the invitation to exhibit the layout at York in 1966 was the only incentive needed to rebuild the approach section. This was when the pack horse bridge over the River Rawthey and the river itself (both of which are features of the prototype landscape near Sedbergh) first appeared in the model scenario: they re-emerged in 7mm scale many years later - see later chapters. In their first incarnation at Marthwaite MkII they went along with some reduction in the size of the engine and goods sheds. The latter is off-stage in this view which shows the MkII version at the river crossing - MkIII only differed by virtue of having a rather more 'rugged' hill to hide the control panel, see Fig.1. The presence of a younger 'yours truly' stems from the fact that it was thought rather eccentric for a serving RAF officer to have a model railway in the main bedroom of his official 'married quarters' and this attracted press attention. Happily, RAF officialdom reckoned it 'jolly good PR' for the service and this was the official result......*

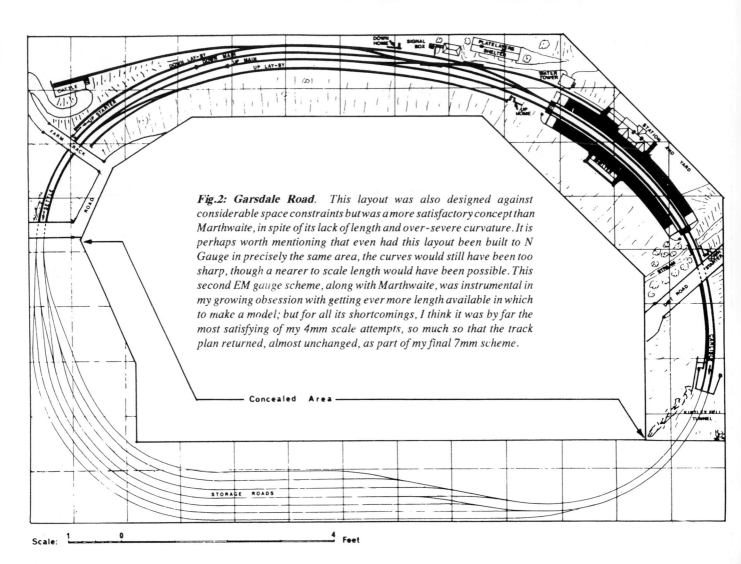

Fig.2: Garsdale Road. This layout was also designed against considerable space constraints but was a more satisfactory concept than Marthwaite, in spite of its lack of length and over-severe curvature. It is perhaps worth mentioning that even had this layout been built to N Gauge in precisely the same area, the curves would still have been too sharp, though a nearer to scale length would have been possible. This second EM gauge scheme, along with Marthwaite, was instrumental in my growing obsession with getting ever more length available in which to make a model; but for all its shortcomings, I think it was by far the most satisfying of my 4mm scale attempts, so much so that the track plan returned, almost unchanged, as part of my final 7mm scheme.

Scale: 1 — 0 — 4 Feet

The second attempt during 1967-72, 'Garsdale Road' in EM Gauge again (Fig.2), was devised to meet some objectives which had been set aside with Marthwaite and again had to cope with considerable space constraints. The site available (13ft x 9ft) just permitted a continuous circuit and enabled a few more criteria to be included, not least my long-wanted slice of the main line. It was getting closer to my ideals than Marthwaite, the standard of construction was better and the concept has had numerous imitators, notably 'Heckmondwike', built to 18.83mm gauge by the Scalefour Society.

Garsdale Road was based on the real life station at Dent, but if one compares it with the reality (Fig.3) and analyses the scale equivalences and overall character, then the layout, though acceptable, was once again beginning to push at the bounds of credibility - hence the fact that although it had a real enough geographical location, I felt obliged to give it a change of name: it was not the real Dent if you see what I mean.... What I needed, or so I thought, was more and more space: real railways occupy a lot of room and it seemed that my layout needed to do likewise.

A change of occupation from the peripatetic RAF way of life in 1972 gave me the chance I thought I needed - a permanent home and the opportunity to build a large shed in

Plate 29: Garsdale Road - 1. Of all the model layouts I have built since 1962, Garsdale Road was my favourite until my final 7mm effort, itself much influenced by that earler 4mm sheme. I am not sure why this is so, but this picture may explain some of it. There is not a train in sight but I fancy it says 'Midland Railway' and that seems to me a more than significant aspect of the story. (Roy Anderson)

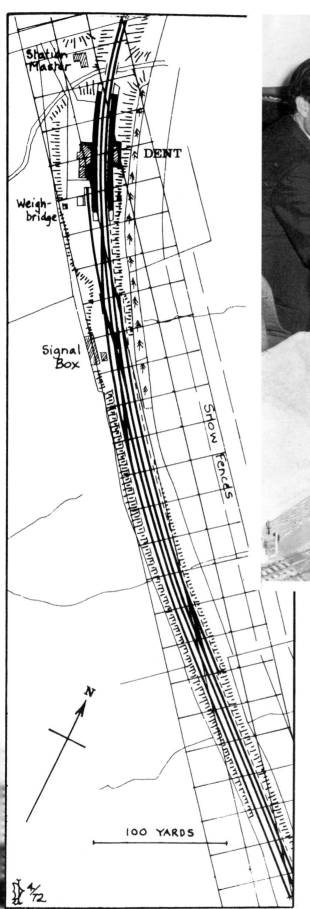

Plate 30: Garsdale Road - 2. This is the only picture ever taken of virtually the whole visible section of this layout (Westminster Central Hall 1970). My unwanted presence (I hate being photographed!) is at least of some value in demonstrating just how small it really was.

Fig.3: Dent Station. This is the real layout on which Garsdale Road was based. I have added 12 inch grid squares (4mm scale), from which it will be seen just how many compromises had to be made with the Garsdale Road plan - far too many for me to have felt happy had I called the model by the prototype name.

which to house the 'Dream' layout. By now, I had amassed quite a collection of models, learned even more about the Settle and Carlisle and thought I knew what was needed; and so began the building of 'The Little Long Drag' - scale length trains, full length stations: in fact, the lot! All my desired criteria were included and for the first time in my modelling life I could actually afford to build it.

Fig.4: The Little Long Drag. *This layout was the third and final EM gauge project in a site which itself was half a mile long in 4mm scale. In spite of its size, the main line was operational in terms of track and control systems by 1974 and the branch had reached the tunnel mouth at Kendal before activity ceased. The terminus at Kendal was never built, partly because I was not totally happy with the track plan (it probably needed carriage sidings as well) but mainly, I guess, because other doubts were by then beginning to cross my mind.*

With the exception of the sharp platform curve at Garsdale Road, retained from the previous layout, there was very little compromise in the visible areas and the trains looked superb when I had completed the main hill masses. Even now, over a quarter of a century later, I am still conscious that this layout represented my ideal concept. But I had made it too big for single handed maintenance and operation, especially against the background of full time employment. However, in terms of the services planned for my later 7mm scale efforts, I always imagine Dent Head Junction to be exactly as drawn here

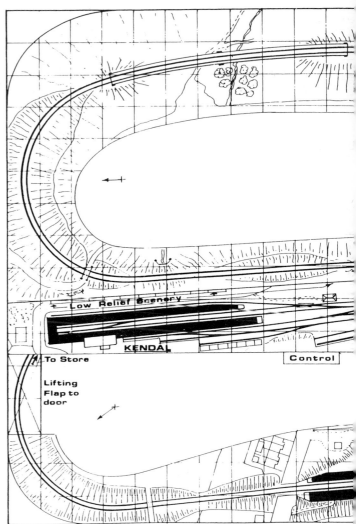

Plate 31: 'Little Long Drag' - early stages. *This view shows the scope of my final 4mm scale effort - plain track already laid (and ballasted in what would be the visible sections), but with pointwork still to add. In the right foreground is a correct to scale length Kirkby Stephen (part finished station building and goods shed to give scale) while in the centre is the huge 10-road, double-ended 'fiddle yard' with its flanking 'through avoiding lines' on the outer edges - the posed 8F gives some idea of its size. In the right distance is the re-located Garsdale Road while far left (upper) are the beginnings of Dent Head Junction. Had it been finished, the branch terminus at Kendal (whose approaches can just be detected above and beyond the far end of the fiddle yard) would have been c.6in above the fiddle yard itself.*

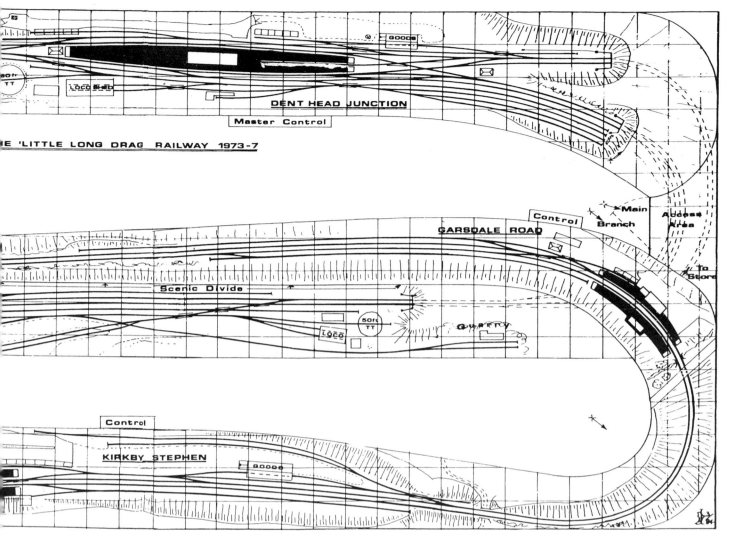

E 'LITTLE LONG DRAG RAILWAY 1973-7

DENT HEAD JUNCTION
Master Control

GARSDALE ROAD
Control
Scenic Divide
LOCO
QUARRY
Main
Branch
Access
Area
To Store

Control
KIRKBY STEPHEN

Plate 32: Dent Head Junction. *Dent Head Junction was based on the real life layout at Hellifield. This view shows the Blea Moor end with most of scenic work well on the way - gaps in the hills left open at this stage to allow for the final scenic touches to be made 'closer to the action', so to speak, prior to closing up the whole area. The main line to Leeds vanished via a model of the north portal of the real Blea Moor tunnel. To its right is a representation of the start of the short tunnel which would have 'vanished' the branch line in model terms but would also have been needed to allow the imaginary branch to Dent, Marthwaite (Sedbergh) and Kendal to make its 180º turn from the main line prior to its 1:70 descent down the adjacent valley. The quantity of carriages in the sidings gives some idea of the size of this layout and, even now, I still feel rather sad that it was never finished. (Ron Prattley)*

Plate 33: Garsdale Road resurrected. Before the 'Little Long Drag' was abandoned, Garsdale Road had at least been given its more spacious new surroundings and this is how it then looked - station buildings still to replace. What is most surprising is that the quite sharp curve through the station platforms seemed somehow less acute in this manifestation than it had been originally. For those interested, the train is in charge of LMS Jubilee No.5562 Alberta. (Ron Prattley)

The general scheme adopted is at Fig.4 and, hidden radii excepted, there was little or no compromise. I even managed to incorporate Garsdale Road into the scheme and gave it the long straight approach from the 'south', a characteristic of the real Dent. I even thought that this time, I might even risk calling it Dent, but sentiment prevailed.... Then, around 1975-6, I realised that although the layout was complete in terms of track and electrics (save for the branch terminus itself), it had only once been operated properly in the two years following completion. Something had gone wrong.

Even now (written quarter of a century after building it), I am still not quite sure why it did not satisfy. Suffice to say that it caused me to think quite furiously. Had I been wrong? Had

my criteria been too comprehensive? Had I become jaded? Was I no longer interested in models? It may well have been a bit of all of these but essentially, it had lost its 'fun' element. I had built a layout which seemed to fulfill all my objectives, yet it lacked the one thing which both Marthwaite and Garsdale Road had offered: the element of pleasure. It had become far more like the Ancient Mariner's albatross round my neck - a veritable 'long drag' in every sense of those words - and I could not actually enjoy the layout because of the huge amount of unfinished work it seemed to represent and which I knew, deep down, I did not really want to do. So I simply ignored it.

When I finally came round to applying myself to the problem, I concluded that both Marthwaite and Garsdale Road had been better, for all their shortcomings, simply because they were manageable single handed. Neither of them fulfilled all my criteria but it did occur to me that maybe a simple continuous circuit with but one passing station of relatively modest proportions and a terminus just a bit more pretentious than Marthwaite might get me most of what I really wanted.

In hindsight, what I think may also have been a partial trigger to this re-assessment had come via an unlikely source.

Plate 34: Seattle and Carliole - 1. *In this American N gauge flight of fancy, the fictional theme was that the S&C, a typical American short line, made connection at Seattle Junction (itself located in wildly improbable and very rugged Appalachian hill country), with the real life Pennsylvania RR, over which the Baltimore and Ohio - equally improbably - had some sort of running powers, and this picture shows the left hand end of the display. In it, a PRR passenger consist headed by a K4 pacific (shades of my later gauge 1 trains!) approaches the junction at the lowest level below the tri-level convolutions of the S&C itself - see Fig.5. If I also mention that the mineral plant in the left distance belonged to the 'Itzawl Mine' company, the general philosophy should be self-evident.... (Ron Prattley)*

Plate 35: Seattle and Carliole - 2. *The junction itself was a sort of transhipment point, much use being made of currently available kits for such things as buildings, water towers and other ephemera, all the locomotives and rolling stock being standard commercially available products of the time, albeit repainted and/or renamed in many cases. This view shows the junction itself with the 'sprig off the branch' to 'Haze Ghyll' via 'Horse Junction' (what else? - !) prominent at a higher level in the background. It was, in all truth, a piece of total and utter conceptual nonsense, but it was hugely entertaining. Moreover, it worked superbly well and caused me to re-think many ideas as far as my more serious notions were concerned. (Ron Prattley)*

At about the time I was embarking on the Little Long Drag, I also built a small N Gauge American system for my two young sons (the only time I ever blamed either of them for my model railway activities) and we produced a typical North American 'Spaghetti Bowl' system which occupied a space of only 9ft 3in x 2ft (Fig.5). This went to a few exhibitions when Garsdale Road had been permanently built in to the larger layout and it was huge fun to operate.

We called it the 'Seattle and Carliole', based it loosely in the Northern Appalachians and most place names were fairly corny puns on the real Settle & Carlisle. A mixture of real and freelance 'railroad' names and liveries were adopted, the whole scheme being very much influenced by (but in no way a copy of) the late John Allen's 'Gorre and Daphetid' system (read the name out loud to get the pun) for those older readers who follow the American scene. Schematically (simple circuit plus branch line), it was not very different from the conclusions I was coming to in the British context (above); and that was not the only way it helped resolve the larger problem.

Fig.5: Seattle and Carliole. *The little N gauge flight of fancy was a lot of fun and acted as very welcome relief to the major 4mm scale efforts in the early 1970s. The track plan, whose grid (exceptionally) represents 12 inch squares in N scale, shows just how much operational interest can be packed into a small space at this scale and was to prove instrumental in my re-appraisal of scales in general (see text).*

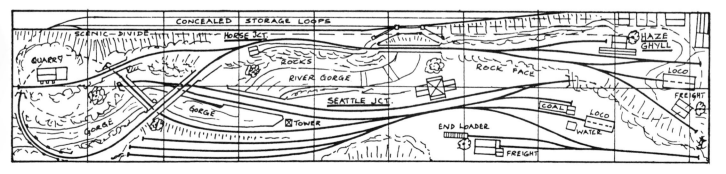

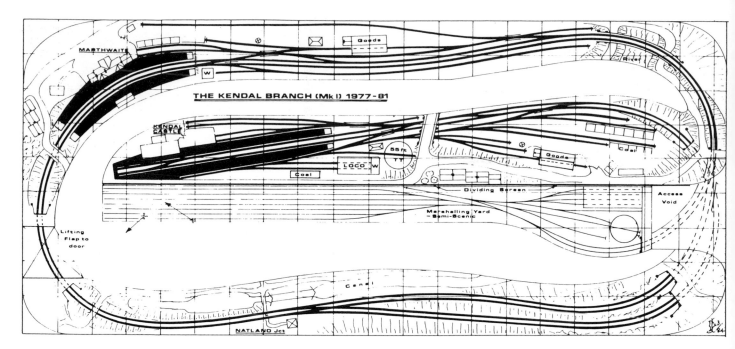

THE KENDAL BRANCH (Mk I) 1977-81

A simple circuit plus terminus in 4mm scale seemed a very modest ambition in my 36ft x 16ft shed until I began to re-appraise the scale factor. Here, the little N Gauge flight of fancy proved the key. We had gone to the smaller size to fit an operationally interesting layout into my son's bedroom and it had worked, so why not go the other way in the shed and move up a size? And once I cleared 4mm scale thinking from my head, I could then look at the very positive virtues of a larger scale - better running, more accurate appearance and so on - the 'Seattle and Carliole' in reverse, so to speak.

Another thing which then occurred to me was the fact that a common factor existed between Marthwaite, Garsdale Road and the N Gauge system: all of them had, above all, given much operating satisfaction. Having by now tackled many different sorts of layouts, I finally realised that what mattered most to me was this aspect of the hobby. Whatever else I did, I wanted to re-create the *operational* aspects of the historic steam railway above all, using models which looked as accurate as I could manage (against the inevitable cost and time constraints, of course) in a setting which did not lose operational interest after about ten minutes!

My 7mm scale ventures have therefore gone back to themes something akin to the Marthwaite/Garsdale Road degree of complexity but with the advantages of the greater solidity, reliability and running quality of the larger scale. I had always acknowledged this fact but could never reconcile it with my thus far obsessive desire for space, space and yet more space.

Fig.6 shows the first scheme to be tackled in the big shed which had hitherto housed the 4mm scale empire. Even this was roughly equivalent to 20ft x 9ft in 4mm scale so was not exactly small. It worked beautifully for a few years but when it was about half complete, outside considerations gave rise to a house move. This was somewhat frustrating (I had not moved

Fig.6: Kendal MkI - 1977-81. This plan represents the first 7mm scale attempt and when compared with Fig.4, gives a very clear indication of the difference in scope between 4mm and 7mm scales in the same area. However, to maintain consistency with most of my track plans, I have marked it with the more usual 12in squares for 4mm scale. In the latter scale it would just about fit inside a long(ish) single garage, though there may have to be some slight adjustment of the width of the operating wells between the modelled areas.

This layout was very reliable and I was somewhat irritated, to say the least, when it had to be abandoned. The only real 'down' side was the concealed double junction (somewhat difficult to access) and the lack of adequate provision for my out of period 'display' trains. I particularly liked the storage siding scheme where I made no attempt to hide things but merely screened the area from Kendal - one of my friends referred to it as the 'fully frontal' approach (sic!) and had it reached completion, I would have made the area mildly scenic and added a locomotive depot (as drawn) to house any spare engines and give something else for visitors to look at between trains. The through station was incorporated in the NRM's permanent display in 1983 where it still remains in regular daily use (written in 2001).

house for 10 years - an amazing period compared with my RAF days), but I could at least take consolation from the fact that it coincided with the time when the NRM (where I then worked) had decided to embark on a model railway display and I was asked to co-ordinate activity.

A working 7mm scale layout was to be the centrepiece (the museum had a fine collection of 7mm models simply crying out to be seen) and to speed things up, I offered to hand over the completed through station on my soon to be dismantled layout. It was recovered intact and by 1983 had been re-installed at York where it remains to this day. Since I left the museum, there have been many additions and improvements, but it is satisfying to see that the trackwork which I handbuilt in 1978 has stood up to over 20 years of far more intense operation than I had ever envisaged when I put it there....

Plate 36: Kendal I. The first 7mm effort had hardly got under way and was not comprehensively photographed before domestic matters were to intervene. Plate 1 (Chapter 1) shows aspects of its early development and this view, taken in 1980, shows the only near-finished part of the scheme as far as I took it: Royal Scot 4-6-0 No.6159 The Royal Air Force heading for Kendal while a trip freight working behind a Midland 0-4-0T approaches the junction - Fig.6. (Ron Prattley)

Meantime, the new house offered me the weirdest site I have ever tried to utilise - a complex of inter-connected basement cellars plus a low level garden patio which I could access via a 'hole in the wall' from the basement. It took me two years to come up with a scheme and there were very many rejects on the way. I even thought of going back to 4mm scale at one point, but the attractions of 7mm scale in terms of reliabilty finally won through and at Fig.7 I show the final version which did get built.

Schematically, given the overriding operational priority I had finally determined (above), I found that I could not improve on the first 7mm concept, nor did I want to. But I have to confess that the through station as drawn had to be simplified part way through construction largely because I had

pushed the track geometry a bit too far and was getting many unpredictable derailments which I could not fully cure. This was a hitherto unknown factor in my modelling life and made me rather annoyed - especially when I came to realise that it was all my fault anyway for trying to be too clever by half.....

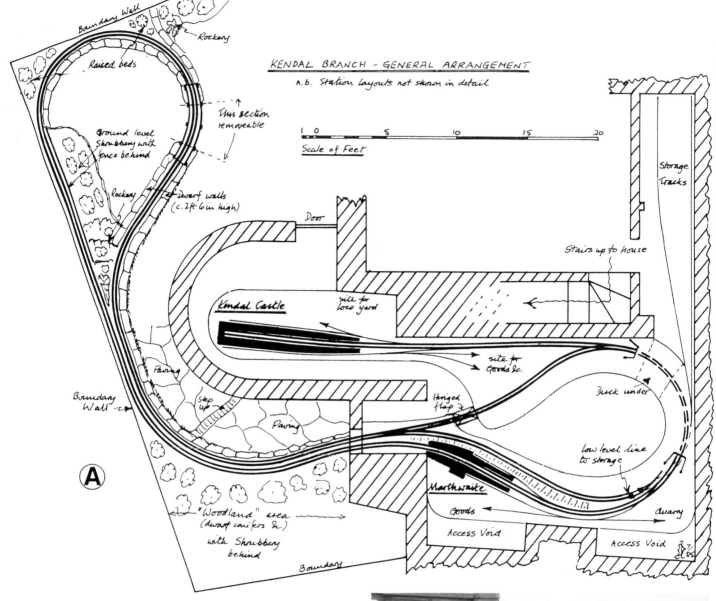

KENDAL BRANCH - GENERAL ARRANGEMENT
n.b. Station layouts not shown in detail

Scale of Feet
1 0   5   10   15   20

Boundary Wall

Rockery

Raised beds

This section removeable

Ground level Shrubbery with fence behind

Rockery

Dwarf walls (c. 2ft 6in high)

Door

Storage Tracks

Stairs up to house

site for loco yard

Kendal Castle

site for Goods &c.

Paving

Step up

Paving

Boundary Wall

Duck under

Hinged flap

Low level line to storage

Marthwaite

Goods

Quarry

Access Void

Access Void

"Woodland" area (dwarf conifers &c) with Shrubbery behind

Boundary

Ⓐ

Whatever, this scheme had one great benefit which the first 7mm layout had not offered. Copying my good friend Ken Payne's original 7mm idea, I had achieved the essential continuous circuit by going out into the garden via a return loop and this gave me a huge length of uncluttered main line in the garden on which I could simply enjoy watching the trains go by. The fact that it overlooked the famous Nidd Gorge and viaduct in Knaresborough whereon I could also witness the real railway (including passing steam specials from time to time) made this side of the layout so pleasurable that work inside the cellar tended to slow down more than somewhat. It may also have had something to do with my real irritation at having to rebuild Marthwaite as well, but it was definitely a new experience and a bit of a mystery too, given all I have said so far about operating fidelity.

Part of this new problem was compounded by a move to self-employment in 1988 which, during the last three years of the period in question, took up virtually all my spare time and

Plate 37: Kendal II. *A view through the 'hole in the wall', showing two freight trains about to enter the cellar from the four-track garden section. The prominent cable down the centre of the tracks (of outdoor waterproof mains standard) carried the electrical feeds to the garden section and was eventually buried in the ballast. (B.C.Lane)*

gave little enough time for modelling anyway. But since the main circuit and storage sidings were complete, I could still run the trains very often - and I did. This layout lasted eight years (1983-91) and was never completed inside the basement.

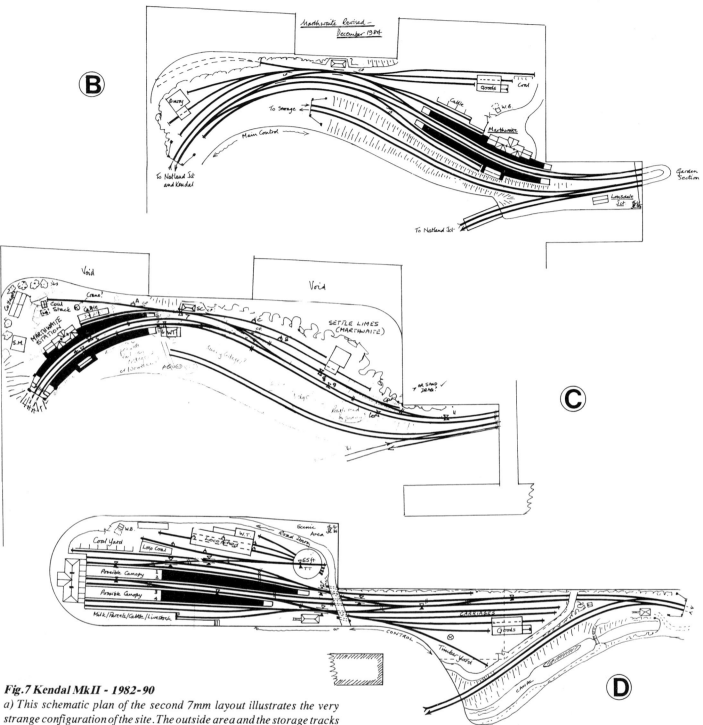

Fig.7 Kendal MkII - 1982-90

a) This schematic plan of the second 7mm layout illustrates the very strange configuration of the site. The outside area and the storage tracks were completely finished, as was the continuous main circuit in a sort of 'bent dog-bone' arrangement.

b) This was the original track arrangement at Marthwaite on the second layout and was virtually finished before I realised why I was getting the unacceptable but wildly intermittent derailments mentioned in the text. I had stretched the track geometry beyond that which was totally wise by putting rather too much complex pointwork onto the sharp curves at the quarry end of the layout.

c) This revised and simplified version of Marthwaite managed to eliminate all the tricky pointwork and stopped all the derailments as well.... It was looking quite promising (albeit operationally simpler than I would have preferred) when yet another house move intervened.

d) I had many attempts at designing the terminus in its round-ended room, this being one of about six or seven attempts to get it right on this site alone; and it would probably have appeared in something like this form had I not had to spend so much time in rebuilding the through station before I could start work on it and we were obliged to move yet again. I still quite like this plan, in spite of its funny shape, and even thought in terms of making it portable for exhibition work, with a plug on fiddle yard to the right of the goods shed and a showcase in the angle between the turntable and approach tracks.

Plate 38: Kendal II. This wide-angle view shows the main indoor part of the second 7mm layout looking across the site towards a part-finished Marthwaite. As can be seen, most of the scenic substructure was set in place before I met with track problems - see text. The girder bridge (left foreground) was actually a small lifting flap to gain access to the terminus site behind the camera.

Plate 39: Kendal II. The most nearly completed section of Kendal II was Natland Junction which, in this particular scheme, would have been a fully scenic part of the layout. The general idea for the scene was loosely based on the juxtaposition of railway and canal at the Marsden end of Standedge tunnel on the LNWR line between Huddersfield and Manchester and I think it would have looked rather attractive had it been finished. The train is the overnight sleeping car working behind ex-Midland Class 3 Belpaire 4-4-0 No.773. (Ron Prattley)

Plate 40: Kendal II. The space inside the return loop on the outdoor section of the line was a popular train watching site on Kendal II, but viewed from the outside of the loop, the sharp curvature was cruelly obvious. 'Watching the trains go by' became quite a time-consuming and popular distraction at that time and as far as I recall, these two trains were being 'tested' (you understand) for some two hours while refreshments on the table were gently consumed...... (Ron Prattley)

The next stimulus was yet another house move, this time prompted by my four children leaving home to set up their own lives (ie we no longer needed quite such a large house) and my wife retiring from full time teaching - and she now wanted a far bigger garden than we had ever thus far owned. Given that the second 7mm layout was still a bit unresolved, this prospect was not as irritating as the abandonment of the

first Gauge 0 effort had been, especially when we found a house in the country which not only had a big garden, but also possessed a huge garden shed of about the same size as the one I had left behind in 1981.....

So back to the drawing board again, fortunately conducted against the background that since 1976, I had already gone a long way towards building up the stock of 7mm models I felt I would need for the project. The only problem was whether or not the desired concept could be realised in the new shed which, at 32ft x 18ft was shorter and wider than the first one.

It did not take long to realise that the original 7mm scheme (Fig.6) could not be re-created in the new shed: the shorter length was against me and memories of pushing track geometry beyond reasonable limits in the basement setting had taught me a valuable lesson. There was also the very recent and new aspect of the hobby to factor into the planning - the sheer joy of sitting in the garden and and watching the trains go by in a spacious main line setting. Should I therefore think in terms of another combined indoor plus outdoor system?

A quick appraisal of the relevant ground levels soon made me realise that a combined system was not a viable proposition - but what about building *two* new layouts, one to fulfil the already established 7mm criteria, the other to take care of the main line fixation? They would continue to be 'historical', of course, but should they both be LMS?

The relevant point here is that during my museum life, I had developed a much wider interest in and appreciation of the non-British aspects of railway history and it seemed to me that I could perhaps use an outdoor layout on which to display a wholly eclectic mixture of famous historic trains. Given that I do not believe that an outdoor setting can be wholly realistic in terms of scenic fidelity to prototype, even though it has a lot of

Plates 41/2: Gauge 1 in the garden. *This railway came together very quickly in the summer of 1994, mainly so that the garden itself would not be disturbed for too long. The first view shows the scheme just after tracklaying was complete and ballasting started. All baseboards were built from tanalised timber sections, designed as a kit of parts - ie pre-cut to shape before being assembled in one 'hit' in about three days. Track, of prefabricated commercial origin, took a further two weeks to lay and trains first ran within a month of starting! The second picture shows a close-up of part of the same area some two or three years later when flanking brick walls had been made and the 'V' back-filled to give a raised 'alpine' bed. Other methods of cloaking the wooden substructure include miniature lonicera hedges and a long, purely cosmetic viaduct, some of which are seen, fully matured, elsewhere in this book.*

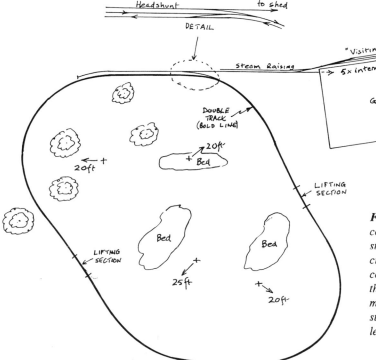

Fig.8: Gauge 1 in the garden. *By contrast with the many and varied convolutions of my basement site, the design of a garden circuit for live steam work was a painless exercise. I could get 20ft radius minimum curves, long sidings capable of holding at least ten coach trains and a continuous circuit of some 230ft (1.4 scale miles at 1:32 scale) on which they could run. It is essentially a display stage for a variety of trains and makes no pretentions to prototype working, save that the outlet from the storage sidings via a long lay-by alongside the main line is via a trailing lead, involving double reversal to get at the inner circuit.*

other compensating virtues, I was thinking more in terms of a 'display stage' on which could, of course, be paraded anything which took my fancy, including the odd American example, thus allowing me to reinstate some earlier favourite ideas.

Furthermore, I had also by now spent time watching and participating in the live steam Gauge 1 activities of some of my former museum colleagues and found that the tactile joy of actually 'driving' a miniature steam engine rather than twiddle a control knob had its own attractions, albeit very different from those I had hitherto known in this hobby - so why not adopt Gauge 1 live steam for this putative new outdoor venture? After all, I was approaching retirement age with the prospect of some sort of gratuity money to spend..... So thus it was that in 1994, following a brush with ill-health which caused my retirement from full time work a tad earlier than planned, I embarked on my new 'two layout' venture.

By then, I had had a year or two in my new premises in which to make the necessary plans and Figures 8 and 9 show them. In order that the garden should not be disrupted for too long, the Gauge 1 system was built in its entirety during 1994-5. Length apart, it is essentially very simple in concept and it took me only a few weeks to lay all the track (ready made this time, not handbuilt) once the baseboards were in place, the latter with outside help since my health no longer permits me to tackle heavy work single handed.

Its chief plus value was that I could have my 'Trains of all Nations' (most of which I 'bought in' rather than made for myself) stomping round the garden at an early stage - and this was great fun, especially during that wonderfully fine summer of 1995. But as with the earlier indoor/outdoor 7mm system, it was very much a fair weather activity with all that this implies. What is more, I soon found out that tail-chasing as a sole form of activity (even with the added challenge of getting live steam to perform properly) can soon get restricting to an 'operational' sort of person such as myself, albeit highly therapeutic if taken in moderation. So once the garden was tidy again, it was not long before I wanted to get back to the 'all-weather' albeit more complex 7mm system, which I also managed to start in 1995, free from the need to accommodate the sort of massive main line trains which I could now run in the garden.

I computed that this final 7mm effort would be my 12th layout since I started out in the mid-1950s. I therefore decided that there would *not* be a No.13.....

Curiously, events since the mid-1970s have caused me to adopt larger scales in order to keep up the momentum, but had

---

Fig.9 Kendal MkIII

a) This plan was conceived in 1994 and construction began in 1995 using this drawing as the basis. The track is arguably too complex in the hidden areas, this being a function of both my operating wishes (which I explain in more detail in Chapter 6) and my need to provide more storage areas for the out of period display trains. In practice, it has been found that there are no totally inaccessible areas should the need arise, while at a very early stage it became apparent that the layout did not need much more than a simple turntable at the storage sidings - ie one dead-end locomotive standing road at most.

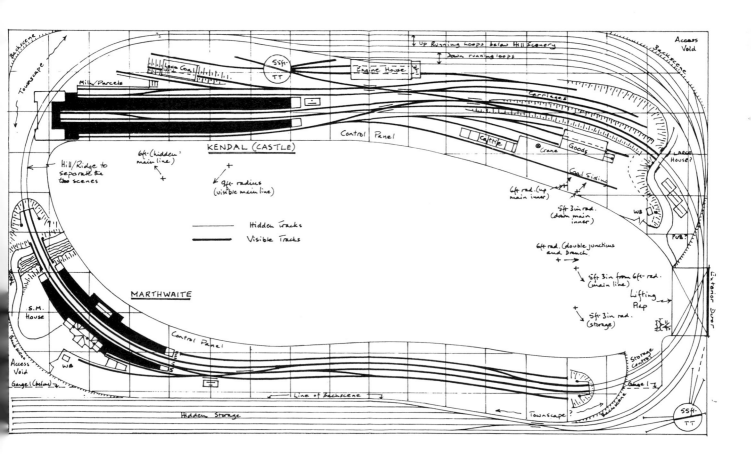

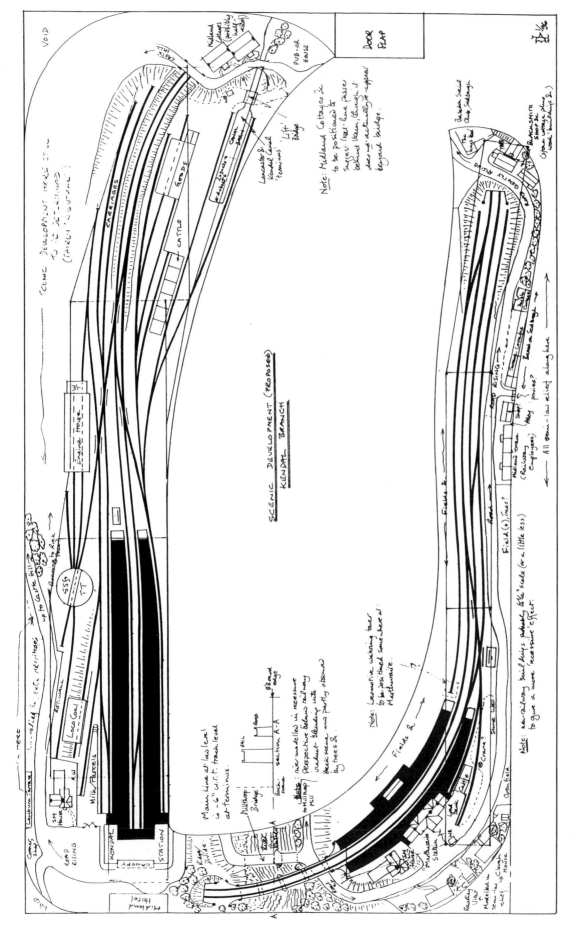

Fig.9 Kendal Mk III

b) This slightly later drawing concentrates only on the visible parts of the layout but was prepared after it was decided to add an extra siding at Kendal goods yard. The rectilinear lines (replacing my usual grid) show the extent of the solid top baseboards at Kendal and Marthwaite, the rest of the visible area being open top construction. As building proceeded, further slight changes were made to the locomotive yard at Kendal and after two years or so of operating, it was felt desirable to slightly improve the facilities at Marthwaite. Both these latter changes will be found on the finally revised track plan offered at Fig.20 in Chapter 6.

52

Trains in the Garden - 1

Despite the many frustrations with the indoor parts of Kendal II, the garden section was an unqualified success and undoubtedly the major factor behind my decision to do the same sort of thing in Gauge 1 live steam. These pictures of the 7mm line show a general view across the four track part (trains posed for effect), looking towards the famous railway viaduct at Knaresborough, and the Barrow line local about to traverse the return loop. The stone walls were all built by myself, an interesting aspect of garden railway modelling (sic!) and an idea which was to be repeated in brick on the Gauge 1 line. (Ron Prattley - 1)

Trains in the Garden - 2

'Trains of many Nations' is my design theme in the garden. The choices were largely based on some of the overseas prototypes which I had either studied or seen and make no attempt to be in period with each other. The general view shows a typical ten-coach Wagons-Lits train as might have been operated in France c.1950, headed by a live steam working four-cylinder compound model (by Aster) of the famous 4-6-4 No. 232U1 (as preserved at the French railway museum in Mulhouse), which I had seen and admired. The close-up view shows the unique Bavarian 4-4-4 No.3201 (as preserved at Nuremburg and also seen and admired) heading the 'Rheingold' of the 1930s. The engine is another Aster model, converted from gas to spirit burning by former museum mentor John van Riemsdijk, who also designed 232U1 for Aster. In truth, 3201 never pulled this set, being withdrawn before the carriages were built. But since some of them are also preserved, I felt that a bit of 'modeller's licence' could be called into play..... (Jack Ray - 2)

Plate 43: Kendal III. *Construction of Kendal III began in mid-1995 and the basics of this much more complex layout also came together quickly, all baseboards track and power circuits being in position within 18 months of the start. At this point, the layout was very comprehensively tested before starting work on the scenery. This picture was taken during that first running session early in 1997 and shows the bulk of the track layout at Kendal plus the main line running loops behind and below that station. They are all now fully hidden and this viewpoint is no longer available to the photographer. (B.C.Lane)*

my site possibilities gone the other way, I hope I would have had the courage to reduce the scale. Indeed it has more than once occured to me in recent years that my original 13ft x 9ft site for Garsdale Road might well have looked better had I adopted precisely the same plan in 3mm or 2mm scales - but I never even considered it at the time.

Nevertheless, in the light of my experience over the best part of 40 years, I think I should now add three more vital points to my original list, quite apart from my digression into choice of scale during the last few pages:

a) Keep things as simple as possible consistent with your fundamentally essential wishes.

b) Keep it manageable single handed - unless you have a guaranteed clutch of semi-permanent helpers.

c) Make sure it will be fun - arguably the most important factor of all.

My current (1995 onwards) 7mm scale system is a sixth attempt to produce a layout inspired by the Settle-Carlisle - *that* has, at least, remained consistent - and it is undoubtedly the most satisfying. It is not as simple as Marthwaite or Garsdale Road; it is not as spacious as the Little Long Drag and it was not as simple to build as the first two 7mm attempts. But I think it combines, better than all its predecessors, those essential elements which most appeal to me.

Perhaps the most encouraging sign, even before a foot of track was laid, was that the concept had begun to develop a personality; and that had not happened since Garsdale Road was on the drawing board. Mind you, while I was building the Gauge 1 outdoor system, I sat on a quite different 7mm track plan (essentially a junction scheme) for a year or two before deciding to go back to the 'circuit plus terminus' theme.

Thus it was that well over 30 years after deciding to base my modelling on the Settle and Carlisle, I finally arrived at a scheme which I am sure will outlast all its predecessors. With hindsight, I should not, perhaps, have taken so long but I have discussed it here, warts and all, in the hope that reading of my experiences may help others to shorten the thinking process.

But don't worry too much if you don't get it right first time.

Despite all I have said, there is great pleasure in 'starting anew' provided we learn from our experiences: I have thoroughly enjoyed building all my layouts save, perhaps, for the final stages of the Little Long Drag.... Moreover, the only person known to me who has continued to develop his original scheme without starting completely afresh is Peter Denny with 'Buckingham'. It was many years before I met Peter and saw the layout which had most served to inspire my own efforts. He is, without doubt, a quite exceptional person and one of the very few modellers whose advice can, unreservedly, be followed by us all.

In conclusion, though I may have strayed a little from the main theme of this chapter from time to time on some of the previous pages, I have quite deliberately concentrated on what I consider to be the essential preliminary thinking processes as I see them. And while I do not recommend that anyone should take quite as long as I did to arrive at a satisfactory conclusion, I do hope that I have managed to convey the feeling that a degree of self-discipline has to be imposed upon an instinctive liking for railways if we are to succeed in attaining a believable historical model. And lest this latter comment should seem to be at odds with a leisure time activity, it may be worth reminding ourselves that the railway itself is a highly disciplined form of transport in which order and rationality have mostly been pre-eminent in the development of the system from the earliest days.

It thus seems to me that if our models are to succeed, they should try to reflect the order and discipline which the real railway exhibits. 'Anything goes' is not really the railway way of doing things, nor should it be evident in our models. Funnily enough, however, I have also found from experience that far from putting us into a straightjacket, it is this very discipline of the railway mode of transport which offers one of the most satisfying challenges to the modeller. Yet it is still possible to bend quite a lot of the rules in model form without destroying the credibility of the end product - and it is this aspect of the subject which I shall try to appraise in the next chapter.

HRM

CHAPTER 4

The vital matter of compromise

"Regulations are made for the obedience of fools and the guidance of wise men
Old military saying (Anon.)

THE MODEL railway hobby is littered with the remnants of half finished, inconclusive models which must represent, *in toto*, a prodigious amount of time, money and effort; and if one tries to analyse this situation, it seems to me that why they do not satisfy is bound up, somewhere, with a failure to come to terms with the question of compromise.

The Oxford English Dictionary defines 'compromise', *inter alia*, as: "...(finding of) intermediate way between conflicting opinions etc, *by modification of each* [author's italics]." In model terms this means that we have to decide how much 'modification' we can permit ourselves in order to find an acceptable 'intermediate way'. The problem is that the modifications apply, simultaneously, to more than one aspect of the subject and at times defy separation; but we must try, and that is the subject of this chapter.

Before devising any layout scheme, the modeller must realise that all model railways are a compromise in some form or other. Something will have to be sacrificed if anything is to be achieved and each modeller has to decide, at a personal level, what this has to be. It is hardly the most world-shaking observation but bears repeating, for I never cease to be surprised by the number of modellers who, to judge by their statements (and sometimes their published offerings), seem to think that no compromise is needed - I think they are living in 'cloud cuckoo' land! I will therefore put my head on the block and suggest the main areas where I think that compromise will be needed and try to deal with them in turn:

a) Space and scale
b) Modelling standards
c) 'Historical believability'
d) The period factor
e) The operational factor

Space and Scale

I put these two factors at the head of my list because they are the key to everything; and I tackle them under one heading because they are closely related and need to be connected quite early in the planning phase. Of the two, however, the space available is probably the first of all considerations in any railway model - we are all constrained by site space, whatever

the depth of our pockets or however skilful we may be as modellers. Therefore, above all (and presuming a preferred scale), the model must be appropriate to the size of site available. Only when we have decided what can and cannot be accommodated in the space on offer can we start to consider the many other relevant factors.

But this does not necessarily mean 'smaller site - smaller scale.' Our choice may evolve from other considerations and I will return to it later. Meantime, having entered that caveat, let me start by looking at those aspects of site space which are, to a very large extent, independent of scale.

The question of layout size resolves itself into two main areas - curve radii and linear dimensions; and I put them in that order because curve radii determines everything else. The real railways rarely go below a six chain radius curve (396ft) and even this radius is most often found in sidings. This is equivalent to 5ft 2½in (4mm scale) and 9ft 2½in (7mm scale), to quote but two common choices. But railways generally prefer more generous dimensions and on main lines, even a 10 chain curve (8ft 8in - 4mm; 15ft 4in - 7mm) is considered with reluctance. In consequence, unless your site is at least 11ft square in 4mm scale or 19ft square in 7mm scale, you cannot use scale radii at even the minimum value if you want a continuous circuit..... Yet between these two areas are likely to be found the bulk of site possibilities available to most of us - spare rooms, garages, lofts &c. - and many acceptable layouts have been constructed within these dimensions without serious loss of realism. So we can reasonably conclude that curve radii can be compromised; the question is 'How far?'

Clearly, the final arbiter will be the minimum radius which our models will traverse and this can, depending on standards (see next section), be quite severe. But the point at which severe curvature may cause unsatisfactory appearance can also be relevant and is often determined by the way in which the layout is viewed when complete. If from within the curve, then a sharper curve radius will usually prove more visually acceptable than if seen from the outside of the curve. This is caused by the attitude taken up by vehicles on a curve and at Fig.10, I offer a diagram to explain the point.

Of course, if a continuous circuit is not wanted, then the need for sharp curve radii may be less and although I do not

wish to be dogmatic, the following general principles seem to me to be generally sound:

    a) Use the largest curve radius you can manage to fit in.

    b) Never work to the smallest practicable radius simply because the vehicles will negotiate it.

    c) Where possible, try to confine sharp radii to hidden areas (Fig.11A)

    d) It is better to have two minimum curves connected by a gently curving near-straight section with transition curves rather than sharp geometrical curves connected by a long straight, though there will almost always be a slight width penalty (Fig.11B)

    e) (As a corollary to (d)) Do not be afraid of putting turnouts on curves, always provided that they never impinge on the areas of minimum curvature.

Putting this into actual dimensions, I have never worked to less than 2ft 9in - 3ft radius (4mm scale EM gauge) or 5ft - 5ft 6in radius (7mm fine scale) and have always managed to get something better than these values where tracks are visible. But even with the tighter constraints, I managed to build a continuous EM gauge layout in 13ft x 9ft and my present 7mm system employs 5ft radius in one or two hidden places simply to allow the concept to work at all (Fig.9, Chapter 3). But I fell foul of my own injunction at (e) - and paid the penalty - when I built my second 7mm layout (Fig.7, Chapter 3) and located turnouts too far into the sharpest curves.

The linear dimension is a far tougher proposition. Here we are dealing with the area wherein is likely to be found the bulk of the visible interest on the model and where we meet up with the really fundamental characteristic of the railway itself - its predominantly 'long and thin' nature. Somehow or other we must try to capture this element and I am inclined to think that

Plate 44: A good example to follow. *I have mentioned the Rev. Peter Denny several times in these pages already and will do so again, for he is probably the most influential of all the modellers I have met in terms of my own approach to the hobby. Moreover, he is a past master of creating believable scenes against considerable site and space constraints, not least in his tackling of curvature problems, a point well shown in this view of the principal Marylebone express leaving the terminus at Buckingham behind the biggest engine on his line. That curve is not much more than 3ft radius at best, but can only be seen from the inside of the bend, while the insertion of many other attractive and distracting features into the scene tends to 'fool' the eye. During the early 1990s I was able to commission a series of pictures of his famous layout for a magazine I was then producing and editing (Modellers' Backtrack) and this is one of them. I had never seen the layout before and, despite Peter's typically self-denigrating comments about his own modelling, I was constantly astonished at the clever subtleties which he had used so as to get round the many space and site problems. There is a lesson in this for all of us, of that I am sure. (Ron Prattley)*

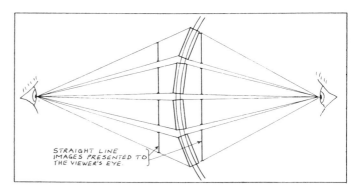

Fig.10: This drawing attempts to show why it is better to view sharp curves from the inside. The relative proportions of vehicles and gaps between them is clearly much better.

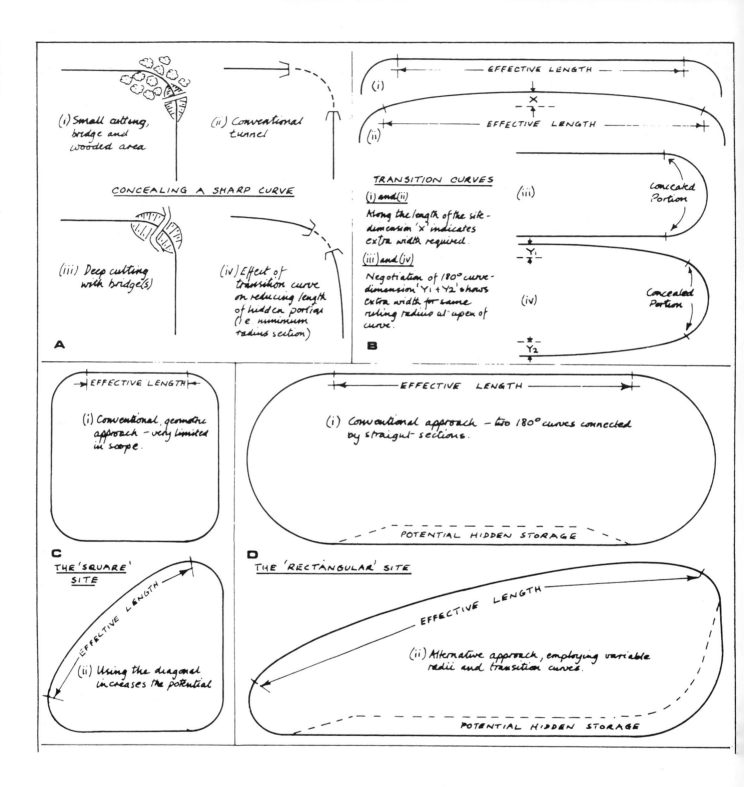

Fig.11: *These diagrams attempt to offer a few ways by which extra visible length can be coaxed out of limited spaces. In all cases, the use of transition curves serves not only to assist in this process, but also improves the appearance in more general terms.*

---

for a given area, a longer narrower site is better than a square-ish shape, even if we have to sacrifice the 'continuous' option, presuming we want it, of course.

Needless to say, we may often have no choice in terms of site - and I am no stranger to that one after so many house moves over the years - but it is worth trying to do something even in an awkward location. I have therefore offered at Fig.11(C,D) two more ways in which extra usable length can be coaxed from awkward shapes. They tend to sacrifice the straight line element altogether where the tracks are visible, but I happen to believe that this is more railwaylike than purely geometrical formations can ever be.

Plate 45: Further distractions. *When I built Garsdale Road, I too was faced with all-too-visible sharp curves at both ends of the layout and felt I should do something about it. I employed bridges with scenic 'cameos' to divert attention from things I did not wish folk to notice too much and this was the 'south' end of the display - anyone who has travelled the Yorkshire Dales will recognise the frustration caused by peripatetic flocks of sheep ahead of one's motor car. I might perhaps also mention that the two 4Fs (both from that very well known Wills white metal 4mm scale kit of the time, of which I also had three further examples) were given different tenders, liveries and weathering treatment so as to hint at period - late 1930s in the case of this layout.*

Plates 46/47: The viewing level. *When faced with looking at a layout from the outside of a bend, the over-sharp radii we are often forced to use can be unhelpful. This was a major problem with Garsdale Road, always viewed from inside the circuit by the operators (where the tight curves did not show too badly) but usually seen from the outside by most spectators (where the curves were only too obvious). The interesting point is that if we lower the viewpoint, this problem can be reduced as this pair of pictures, taken from almost the same position (save for the height of the camera), show only too clearly. The problem is that while the near eye-level view gives a more natural perspective, thus arguing in favour of the high level baseboards which some folk advocate, it is far simpler to build a layout at the more customary 3ft or so above the ground. My solution, as I get older, is to adopt the practical level for building the thing and offer visitors a chair from which to observe the layout if they prefer the eye-level view.....*

For the record, the 2-6-4T and carriages are the same as on the original Marthwaite (Plate 7, Chapter 1), but the carriages now have full raised panelling, properly lined-out; while the engine has been renumbered 2503, later research having shown this to be correct in terms of the bunker configuration of this model (straight-sided and only applicable to some of the class). The Class 5 4-6-0 (from a kit) represents one of only four named examples, No.5156 Ayrshire Yeomanry *and was chosen simply because it happened to be the very last example I saw in regular BR service on the Settle-Carlisle line.*

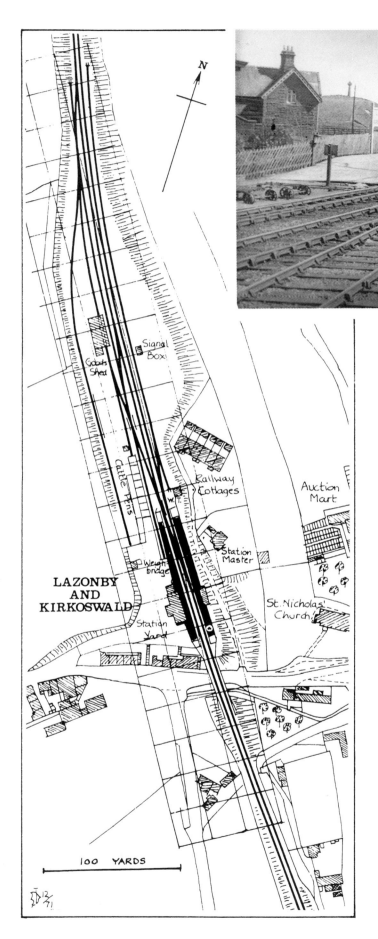

LAZONBY AND KIRKOSWALD

100 YARDS

Plate 48: Lazonby, 1938. This view, looking south, shows that although the tunnel in the distance forms a useful visual 'exit' for a possible model, it is still a long way off and the approach is dead straight.... Note too the amount of length taken up by the simple but characteristic trailing crossover plus single slip in the foreground - too much compression here on a model would tend to spoil the effect.

At the end of the day, we eventually arrive at a linear dimension beyond which it is impossible to go, and it is only when this critical value is established that we can decide just what sort of feature can be modelled. Note that I say 'feature' and not 'station'. Most of us try to model a station as a first essential, but perhaps we should first ask ourselves whether we want a station at all: better, perhaps, a nice piece of countryside with, maybe, a small lineside quarry (or some such), all of which looks believable, rather than try and cram a station in where no room exists. Real stations take up rather more space than you might think and to show what I mean in terms of layout implications, I will analyse just one example in some detail - Fig.12.

Lazonby is a typical Settle-Carlisle through station of medium size and the first thing to note is that the overall length is at least four times that of the passenger platforms. I have gridded the drawing to indicate the conventional 12in squares

Fig.12: Lazonby Station: Settle and Carlisle Line. Lazonby, Kirkby Stephen and Armathwaite (where near-identical track layouts were to be found), have always represented my favourite Settle-Carlisle stations, especially in those days when all had a full array of 'supporting features'. For one thing, the whole concept was typically and recognisably Midland in approach and, architectural differences excepted, could be found all over the MR system; but secondly, the track layout itself is very interesting in terms of its operating potential. Had I ever been forced to model but one typical 'S&C inspired' scene (and presuming I had the length available) then it would be based on one of these. This drawing shows the real layout, gridded with 12 inch squares (4mm scale), which shows that even a 20ft x 3ft site would not get you much beyond the boundary fence.

Plate 49: Armathwaite, 1962. The layout at Armathwaite was almost identical to that at Lazonby and this picture shows the station from the opposite orientation to that of Plate 48. The very gentle curvature through both stations adds to their charm but can be difficult to model. Note too, how little the essentially Midland nature of the station remained intact well into BR days.

Plates 50/51: Kirkby Stephen, 1912 and 1935. This, the third of my favourite S&C stations, displays much the same track layout as Lazonby and Armathwaite, though the gentle curvature goes the opposite way and the station building is of a slightly larger type. To get some idea of how much linear space in 4mm scale is needed to get a near-accurate representation of this layout, see Plate 31, Chapter 3

at 4mm scale and we can see at a glance that the overall length scales to over 20ft in this scale; yet the platforms will only accommodate four or five normal size bogie carriages. How much shorter can we make this layout without destroying the essential nature of the prototype?

If we halve its length, then to keep things in proportion, the platforms will only hold two or three coaches. But we cannot halve the building size or the distance between tracks to keep the balance, so we end up with a station building two thirds the platform length, along with over-short sidings and other undesirable features - a patently absurd state of affairs which would present a visual horror. And the track itself also poses a problem. You cannot, for example, halve the length of a crossover or turnout, simply to save length, or else the whole thing looks more like a tramway than a railway - not that I have anything against trams by the way; I love them.....

Plate 52: A 'no compromise' layout? The scene here does not give much indication that we are looking at a model, and 7mm scale at that. It belongs to a friend of mine, Neil Corner, who, in 1980, had asked me to design a scheme to fit into an empty outbuilding c.80ft x 40ft as I recall. I give more details in Chapter 9 and, to be honest, I did not really think that it would happen, but it did - Neil is a determined sort of chap! Few of us are fortunate enough to have this sort of space available, but what can be mentioned at this point is that if the essential idea had been fulfilled to total perfection, the converging main lines (MR and LNWR respectively) would have displayed nearly straight alignments - even the available 80ft length was too short......

Fig.13: Essence of Lazonby. In this drawing, I have tried to show how Lazonby might be scaled down for model purposes without losing too much character. The drawing is annotated to indicate the areas of compromise and speaking personally, this is about as far as I would be prepared to go and still call it by its proper name. If the essential layout was to be further compressed in width or given more acute curvature, then I would adopt either a change of name if it was based on a real line (as with Garsdale Road) or the 'might have been' approach on an imaginary line - eg the first 7mm scheme at Fig.6 (previous chapter)

This is a prime case where, if you want this sort of facility above all else and only have 10-12 feet or so of length available, you would (anticipating somewhat - see later) seriously consider a change of scale. But if you have a strong desire for a larger scale, then you can 'squeeze' it a bit if you are careful; and at Fig.13, I have tried to produce the essence of Lazonby in as short a length as I feel could be tolerated in the 4mm scale context.

I have slightly shortened the pointwork to c.1:6 crossing angle (in prototype terms more suited to sidings by the way), rather than the 1:8 value of the real main line, and increased the curvature of the approach tracks too. But neither of these should go too far, or else the gently flowing nature of the prototype would be lost. But were this plan to be combined with minimum radius approaches beyond 'station limits', the length would still be too great for many people. Furthermore, it is at least debateable whether or not one should now call it 'Lazonby' at all. It was precisely for this reason, when I made my 4mm model based on Dent, that I called it Garsdale Road - I felt it had gone a little too far from reality although the result was fairly acceptable, visually.

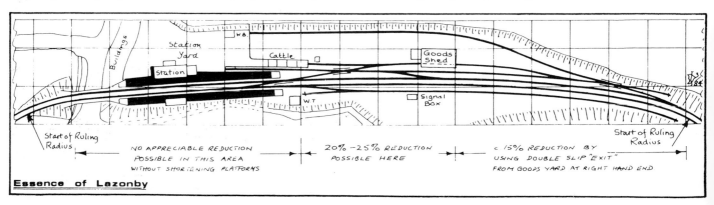

Essence of Lazonby

Start of Ruling Radius

NO APPRECIABLE REDUCTION POSSIBLE IN THIS AREA WITHOUT SHORTENING PLATFORMS

20% - 25% REDUCTION POSSIBLE HERE

c 15% REDUCTION BY USING DOUBLE SLIP "EXIT" FROM GOODS YARD AT RIGHT HAND END

Start of Ruling Radius

Fictional stations are not much better, for the normal rules of track geometry, building size &c still apply. But since they don't really exist, we need no longer worry quite so much about certain aspects. This was the thinking behind the through station on my first 7mm layout (Chapter 3 Fig.6), where I did manage to get a Lazonby style layout, including its approach tracks, in not much more than the 4mm scale equivalent of 20ft, largely by putting fairly large radius 90° curves at each end. Viewed from the inside of the curve, they were not too bad (see Fig.10), but when it was moved to the NRM, where it would be viewed from the opposite side, we straightened the approach lines at each end (ie beyond the pointwork) which gave a vastly improved effect.

Paradoxically, a terminal station handling the same or more traffic than a place like Lazonby, need not necessarily take up as much length, if only because the approach tracks are confined to one end. But we may not want a terminal, or it could be that the chosen prototype, like the Settle & Carlisle, had no terminals anyway.

Reverting then to the fundamental problem of length: in my judgement it is a difficult task indeed to compromise the length of a real station for model purposes and still retain its essential nature. As a crude rule of thumb I would say: 'No more than 25% reduction and still be very careful!' As a consequence, I believe it better to have the length available in which to fit a scale length reproduction before tackling a model of a real location. It can be and has been done and, indeed, I once did it myself - well more or less...

This was the incomplete model of Kirkby Stephen on the final 4mm system (Fig.4, Chapter 3) and even with 3ft radius hidden approaches (and a non-existent cutting at the south end to hide one of them) it still needed a 36 ft length to get it all in. To be fair, it did look right; but so much so as to convince me that it would not have done so in 25ft of length.

Whatever, it is now time to introduce matters of scale, so far mentioned only *en passant*. I said at the start of this section that site and scale were linked, but we can only do this when we understand the various site constraints I have outlined. The point here is that choice of scale is not simply a matter of chosing what can best be fitted into a given site; the really interesting fact is that we need not even adopt the scale which convention often decrees is the best choice in relation to that space - eg more space = larger scale &c., &c.

It is an easy trap into which to fall and given that, like most of us, I did not have too much space available in the early days, I too was thus 'programmed' for over 20 years, hence my adoption of 4mm scale. But, having finally let my reach exceed my grasp in the 4mm field, as I have explained already, I finally came to the conclusion that the premise itself was fundamentally flawed; for when we get down to the 'nitty gritty', there are many other things to consider. Indeed, those of more mature years may well recall the late Professor Joad (BBC Radio 'Brains Trust') who regularly prefaced his often witty comments by the vital caveat: "It all depends upon what you mean by...."

Plates 53/54: Minimum space - 1. Apart from the little 'N' scale layout, the only other time I have ever tackled a truly restricted site was the case of Haygarth on Marthwaite MkII/III in 4mm scale - all of 6ft 6in length from tunnel to station building. The higher level view shows how it was designed to 'cloak' the fiddle yard, while the more frontal image could only really be seen properly when it was on exhibition. The station building was based on the quaint and non-standard prototype at Culgaith on the Settle-Carlisle itself, the simple goods shed came from Woodchester on the Midland's Nailsworth branch (Gloucestershire), near to which I was stationed at the time, and I set the tracks on a sort of diagonal to try and increase the apparent visual length.

I now feel that almost any scale can work regardless of available space, provided that we can first identify our real wishes before decisions are made - and since it works at a multiplicity of levels, let me use my own situation by way of making the point.

I eventually chose to try to create a 7mm system with quite complex operational potential in what (7mm wise) is by no means a vast area: a large garden shed, equivalent in size and shape to a single garage in 4mm scale and a small spare bedroom in 2mm terms. But now let's look at it from the other direction. This site, like one of its predecessors, could equally well have housed a vast 4mm scale empire or an arguably mind-blowing 2mm set up; yet at the other end of the scale it could also accept the Gauge 1 equivalent of a 12ft 6in x 7ft 3in 4mm scale system - which proportions, many folk in 4mm scale would find quite luxurious.

Now you cannot, of course, extend this particular line of discussion into every possible site situation, especially at the smaller end of the space scale; but I reckon that there are very few potential sites which do not offer us a choice of at least two, if not more modelling scales. At the end of the day, it may well be determined by precisely what sort of layout you want and I shall come back to that later.

But whatever scale you finally choose, the fundamental space parameters will not be very different from those already

Plates 55/56: Minimum space - 2. Minimum space requires some sort of compromise with standards and when I first saw Peter Denny's small terminus (Leighton Buzzard - Linslade), I was interested to note how he had managed to pack so much operational interest into a space not much longer or wider than was available to me with Haygarth. The first view shows the entry from 'off stage' where wickedly sharp curves had to be adopted - and viewed from the outside too. This cannot avoid the sort of compromises with track geometry which the real railways did not much like, though I once found a near-equivalent to that foreground turnout at Colne (MR/LYR) by way of a 1:4 crossing angle so as to gain access to at least two places in the goods yard. I measured them out of interest but although I have long lost the pictures I took, they convinced me of the truth of the 'prototype for everything' statement.

But once into the main part of the scene (second picture), Peter lessens the compromises, straightens the whole thing out and returns to his favourite flowing reverse curves, an idea to be recommended at all times, no matter how much space you may or may not have available; and he also uses the diagonal much as I had done at Haygarth, though I don't know which of us did it first.... I shall go into this in more detail in Chapter 9 but meantime, note how Peter has also made use of smaller engines and shorter carriages (albeit all authentic) to help increase the apparent length of the modelled scene. (Ron Prattley - 2)

outlined, save in one particular respect; and that forms the subject of my second area of compromise.

Modelling standards

Let me start this section by stating as a self-evident truism that the purer the modelling standards you desire, the more likely it is that you are going to have to match the prototype in almost all respects, especially when it comes to matters of space and scale such as discussed above.

However, it is equally self-evident that we all differ in our fundamental needs and wishes. For example, although most of my above analysis of size and scale is predicated on the assumption that the standard gauge British system (which could well include its secondary lines and/or branches) is likely to be the choice of most modellers, there will be exceptions. Likewise, I have based my comments on the not unlikely assumption that reasonably fine scale models will normally be desired, albeit ignoring the often fatuous debate about what, precisely, constitutes fine scale and accepting too that many will choose otherwise and/or come up with their own particular variation......

In general, this particular debate usually, though not always, tends to home in on the fundamentals of track and wheel geometry rather than the accuracy of the 'upperworks' which are most usually cosmetic - live steam locomotives excepted. It is therefore perfectly possible to envisage an exquisitely made superstructure running on rather coarsely dimensioned wheels and track (indeed I have seen many) or, albeit rather less likely, to see a basic body shell fitted with superbly proportioned wheels matched to equally accurate and well made track. In an ideal world, we would maybe like the best of both options; but we don't live in an ideal world and in any case, this ultimate perfection is unattainable for most of us - I am even tempted to say 'all' rather than 'most'...

Just about the only thing which can be said without doubt in terms of wheel and track standards - and the only thing that really matters - is that they should be fully matched to each other and that the track should be well laid. Do this to the best of your ability and I guarantee that a vast number of perceived operational and mechanical problems will vanish overnight, regardless of the standards you adopt, and certainly without the need for many of the elaborate and often 'quack doctor' solutions which are often recommended, especially (usually?) by those without working layouts. In this latter respect, I often recall that well known saying: "Theoretically, the bumble bee cannot fly; but nobody told the bumble bee!"

The main point to remember is that although standards are different, they all compromise to some extent, even in their 'purest' form - eg electric motors in most steam outline locomotives in the sub-Gauge 1 scales. There are exceptions, of course, but in planning terms we mostly need to bear in mind that standards are merely part of the totality which most of us strive to achieve, so we have to decide how and where we wish (or may need) to compromise. Now I have no wish to enter into the dimensional minutiae and other aspects of the various standards which we may adopt, nor do I wish to take sides, but I do think we need to consider the implications which arise therefrom, not the least concerning how much we can get into a given space, assuming the scale is decided - and here the selection of appropriate standards can help us.

If you are not too concerned about certain aspects of the subject - or maybe you wish to model an industrial scene - then maybe curve radii can be tightened up to get more into a limited space. Likewise, if it is main line running at all costs

Plate 57: Pushing at the limits. I am instinctively a 'main line' sort of person and trying to get this right has caused me quite a few problems over the years which I have, I hope, finally put to rest with my final 'two layout' philosophy. This problem first came to the forefront at Garsdale Road which, although really too small overall, did need a goodly quota of main line trains to be wholly convincing. This view of my 4mm scale kit-built No.6159 The Royal Air Force on a 'Saturday Special' shows something of what I mean.

Starting with the track, it is fully chaired and ballasted bullhead (appropriate to the late 1930s) but that release turnout from the lay-by to the main line (straddling the barrow crossing) is not quite gentle enough to my way of thinking. It worked well enough in EM Gauge, which is why, given my restricted space, I kept to that standard rather than adopt the new and logically better 18.83mm gauge parameters of Protofour. But it was a compromise, as was the fact that the train itself (eight coaches in all with the hidden bits) encompassed a near 90⁰ angle on the curve itself - never mind the direction of view. The curve, gentle enough by 4mm standards and not below minimum scale value, was actually of a radius which would demand a continuous check rail in reality (and a speed restriction) had it been on the main line, but I felt this would not look right in context. I think I just about got away with it, but I was always uneasy and readers must decide for themselves where they stand.

and you don't mind a little widening of the six foot and/or a few tighter curves, then by adopting something less than the ultra fine wheel and track standards which usually look superb, you might just do it - 00 Gauge rather than EM or P4 in 4mm scale for example.

The permutations and possibilities are endless, but they always come back to that essential personal wish which I have so often emphasised. Even so, speaking from my own experience, I would always counsel caution whenever you are tempted to push standards beyond their acceptable limits - better perhaps to change scale and/or standards and/or thematic ideas in these circumstances. Only the individual can decide; there is no 'quick fix' universal solution.

However, since I have had a go at quite a number of options over the years, it might be useful to conclude this section by once again using my own final choices to sum up my views as far as standards are concerned.

The Gauge 1 live steam was easy to decide. There was no problem with curve radii - I had plenty of space and could adopt a minimum radius of 20ft, ie just under 10 chains full size. Nor was there any imperative to model a real scene or full prototype operations for that matter. It is, in all truth, simply an outdoor parade ground for some favourite historic trains. All that mattered was that the trains should look as nearly like the real thing as possible (including length) and, given the wish to compare British with French, German with American &c., &c., they had to be at a constant scale with each other: 1:32 in my case.

I therefore chose the standard Gauge 1 track and wheel standards - much the same, proportionally, as EM gauge or 7mm fine as far as wheels and track are concerned. There is a finer option, as with the smaller scales, but since I was 'buying in' quite a lot, including track, I went for the readily available, virtually universally adopted and well proven standard which is especially relevant to outdoor use. The only snag (shades of British 2mm and 4mm scales and all their associated gauge problems) was that most British outline models are to 10mm scale (1:30.5). Why this should be so when 1:32 is such a lovely, wholly imperial and 100% accurate linear ratio in terms of track gauge is quite beyond me. But there are some 1:32 scale British outline locomotive models available and I could and did scratch build my British train - LMS, of course....

So in this instance, I assigned a specific priority to the 'train' and live steam, almost to the exclusion of everything else. But in the context of my new indoor layout, I intended to tackle the whole picture as best I could. So why did I make the choice I did and what compromises were needed?

Plates 58/59: Where ample space can help. *I have found it a curious fact that although the customary track/wheel Gauge 1 standards are normally marginally less accurate than those used in 4mm scale EM and P4, or 7mm scale 'fine' for that matter (ie 32mm gauge rather than 33mm for Scaleseven), that the spatial parameters offered by the (usually outdoor) nature of what is often called the 'Premier' gauge, tend to negate many other of the more arcane aspects of the hobby (which we so like to debate) in terms of some aspects of the finished impression created. I am not sure why this should be so, for it is easier, I think, to build a totally holistic model railway (see my preface) in the smaller scales. However, the 'big stuff' has a lot going for it, certainly sufficient*

to persuade me make the change in terms of some of my long-held wishes, so I offer these pictures in support.

I have a feeling that it is a combination of correct 'scale to gauge' ratio (when modelling at 1:32 scale) and the large radii which are often available. The first image, totally devoid of trains, shows the effect of the latter. This is a 20-25ft radius curve through my garden, fully transitioned and superelevated and with the 'six foot' set 100% correctly. The half-log and fully matured lonicera 'cloaking' of the timber sub-structure is part of the garden scenario and designed to look harmonious when no trains are running. The second picture shows my scratch-built ten-coach LMS 'Merseyside Express' in charge of live steam ex-LNWR 'Jumbo' 2-4-0 No.5050 Merrie Carlisle *and Midland compound 4-4-0 No.1000, traversing the 100% 'cosmetic' 24-arch viaduct through the orchard. Even with this amount of space, I have preferred to adopt a gentle reverse curve between two major arcs of the circuit (Fig.8, Chapter 3) rather than go for the simpler dead straight alternative.*

It is, of course, yet another form of compromise, though I doubt if too many folk will be counting rivets or measuring track and flangeway clearances in this particular context.... Neither do I suggest that this, or any other approach for that matter, is a total solution to the many ideas we may wish to replicate in miniature. I merely offer it as one of many possibilities to consider before we start, depending on our own view of 'Railway History', how we would like to reproduce it in model form and, of course, our own individual circumstances.

Plate 60: A personal compromise. In Kendal MkIII, having rid myself of all ideas of making the 'impossible to achieve' all-embracing layout which included everything I most liked, I felt it better to home in on the possible by concentrating on a narrower set of criteria, given that I could now get my hitherto obsessive main line 'fix' by way of Gauge 1 in the garden. So, in terms of the permananent indoor layout, I resolved to try and concentrate on the sort of period and other detail which might offer clues to that which most attracted me and in this view, camera posed in a position not available to the naked eye, I think I may be getting quite close. It shows ex-MR '990 Class' 4-4-0 No.809 (formerly MR No.999 and representing a design much associated with the Settle-Carlisle - the LMS renumbered it in the 1920s) entering Marthwaite 'en route' to Dent Head with a three coach local passenger train of scratch-built 'square light' clerestories. The engine was built from a kit, while the other 'Midland' elements in the scene (platform fencing, water crane, nameboard and station architecture) are a combination of commercially available parts and my own scratch building.

As far as scale is concerned, I stayed with 7mm because experience had already shown me that in terms of reliability, Gauge 'O' was far easier to make 'work' properly than the smaller scales as far as I was concerned. It had nothing to do with fine/coarse scale or whatever current shibboleths were fashionable; it was simply a matter of size - ie 'rolling mass' and the fact that you can't scale down real dust and dirt! I am, above all, an operational modeller, so trains must run without fault (or as nearly so as possible) and here, the sheer reliability of 7mm scale (in any of its sub-specialities) was the deciding factor, supervening the more spacious effect of 4mm scale in the same area. But the trains must still run with real purpose for real reasons with locomotives and stock making sense in terms of what they are trying to represent; and it all had to

happen within the setting of a believable historic scene which did not jar the visual senses.

The next decision was whether or not it should be built to 32mm gauge fine scale (as before) or whether I should move to the more recent S7 standards - ie 33mm gauge and tighter clearances at pointwork. The latter would necessitate much re-wheeling, of course, and the better logic of S7 in terms of the prototype (as with the 4mm scale Protofour equivalent) was unarguable; but the decision was taken out of my hands when I looked at the sort of track plan I needed, this being the over-riding operational priority. I would have to use tighter curvature than was ideal in some hidden locations and when showing my ideas to my friend Bob Essery who models to S7 standards, his first comment was 'It will not work in S7.' In other words, I was faced with the truth of my above comments regarding the benefits of easing the standards. To use S7 would mean, at best, a 6ft minimum radius (and even then, some of the stock would not like it very much!); but the whole scheme would work in 32mm fine scale, where I had already proved that 5ft radius curves could be used.

As it happened, all the tight curves could be hidden, so almost everything in view could follow prototype practice. Indeed, by careful tracklaying, we managed to close up the track clearances from the recommended dimensions by a small amount in most 'front of house' locations (with huge visual benefit) and still get sound running. This slightly technical modelling point, bound up with an appreciation of what is going on between wheels and track, is not really germane to the main thrust of this discussion, but I mention it mainly for the benefit of those modellers who may wish to do a bit of experimenting to see what can be achieved. I am pleased enough when some visitors ask if the layout is S7!

Historical 'believability'

It is probably a *non sequitur* that if we model a real station to true scale length and with high accuracy then it ought to be historically believable. Of all the examples I know, Geoff Williams' 'Aylesbury' was the first real proof of that and, in more recent years, layouts such as 'Bodmin' in Scalefour. But as I have outlined above, this presupposes close attention to the length factor for ultimate success.

At the same time, I firmly believe that it is possible to use the 'based upon an idea' theme as opposed to the modelling of a real place and still create a totally convincing picture. The doyen of this approach was, and still is, Peter Denny with 'Buckingham'. He has had numerous imitators since, including myself, but we don't always succeed in creating an end product quite as well as he has done or we would like to do. Here, I think the main reason is a lack of sufficient attention to the 'ground rules' governing this alternative approach.

The key word is 'believable', and it almost defies real definition. In a sense, for a model based upon an idea to be believable, the observer has to suspend belief in the true prototype reality and substitute for it the quasi-fictional reality of the miniature scene - and this is what Peter does so well. I guess it was the best part of 40 years after I had first encountered his work in the magazines before I was able to visit and watch Buckingham in operation, but it was well worth the wait. He adopted what I soon discovered was a typically self-denigrating appraisal of his workmanship, frequently drawing my attention to areas where the model standard in absolute terms was not quite as 'Hi-Fi' as a later generation had achieved - and he was right: there is much impressionism in Peter's work as he will be the first to admit. But I had not noticed these infelicities - it was far more vital to make sure that the milk train was running to time!

I was glad of this experience, for it convinced me that this too was what I wanted from my models and from time to time I have managed to get close. And although it is not easy to make this sort of convincing switch to a miniature reality, there are a few basic principles we can follow, the first and foremost of which must be a convincing story line.

My very good friend of almost 40 years standing, Arthur Whitehead - talented modeller and a master layout operator who has been closely involved with many of my projects, including the latest one - was (and is) very fond of starting a debate on proposed layout schemes with the words: 'Just supposing....'; and herein lies the key. If we are to make a model of a line or station which did not really exist at all (and that is what it boils down to) then it must have some sort of economic and geographical feasibility. Fortunately, the history of Britain's railways is festooned with abandoned 'might have been' proposals and a bit of research into these can often generate ideas for models.

This is only the second time in this book that the word 'research' has been seriously mentioned - deliberately so. Research is so fundamental to good historical modelling that I have felt it desirable to devote a whole chapter to the subject.

But I do not think it worthwhile for the modeller to get too deeply involved in the fascinating world of research until he or she is very clear just what it is that needs to be researched in relation to the specifics of the modelling ideas in mind. It can, all to easily, become an end in itself, so I have deferred its consideration until the next chapter.

Be that as it may, we are still at the interface with research and if we are going to adopt one of the many 'might have beens' as the basis for a model - or even invent our own bit of history for that matter - then it must be a story which carries conviction. I said at the end of the last chapter that the railway was a stuctured organisation and it can be stated categorically that no group of entrepeneurs would have built a real railway had there not been promise of sufficient traffic to justify the cost of construction. The fact that many of the unfulfilled proposals never became reality was probably as much due to the lack of real traffic potential as anything else, so the modeller must beware of adopting what I like to call a 'geographically nonsensical' approach.

It can get even more complicated when we bring in the historical period, because what might have been sensible in the 1850s, could have become a geographical nonsense by the late 1870s - or vice versa. That is why many railways arrived late and died early. This need not stop us modelling them if we so desire, provided we are aware of the real life situation; and, of course, quite a number of the marginal proposals did get built so why should not the modeller add to the list? After all, the Settle & Carlisle itself was probably the biggest geographical aberration in our railway history, save perhaps for the London extension of the Great Central; but they were both built and I find it strangely interesting that Peter Denny should have chosen one of these two for his imaginary world while I have picked the other.....

The period factor

Somebody once said that 'History begins yesterday' and in railway terms it could not be more true. To those of us whose stable world of railways had begun to collapse with their nationalisation in 1948 (see Chapter 1), only to be given the *coup-de-grace* by the elimination of steam 20 years later, it is quite reassuring to realise that the 'Deltics' (which killed off the East Coast 4-6-2s and themselves suffered a similar fate less than 20 years later with the arrival of HSTs) are now just as much an historical anachronism as LMS 'Duchesses', GWR 'Kings' and, from an earlier generation, LNWR 'Georges' and Caledonian 'Dunalastairs'. But I cannot resist commenting that the steam locomotives usually enjoyed a longer active life before they had seen out their time: *'Plus ca change, plus ç'est la même chose'* as the French put it.

What I am trying to say is that unless the modeller is prepared to be so dedicated to authenticity as to place his model at, say, 16th June 1944, it is almost impossible to select any historic period without encountering problems. God willing, we enjoy this earthly life for the appointed 'three score and ten' (hopefully more), during most of which time we are consciously reacting to the scene around us. If, like me, your railway interest has been maintained for most of your life, it is usually impossible to pick one period for a model which has all the desired elements within it. Even though one may succeed in resolving the size, scale, standards and, if imaginary, the 'believability' factors already discussed, I venture to suggest that the time factor will always trip you up.....

Now I am very fond of the LMS Railway (and its many constituents), but I can't run a North Western train on my favourite Settle-Carlisle (much less a Highland one), nor, even if I painted them all in LMS colours, could I operate an ex-Furness Railway Sharp Stewart 4-4-0 (scrapped in the later 1920s) alongside my favourite Stanier 4-6-0 *British Legion* or a red-painted ex-HR Loch' Class 4-4-0, all of which latter engines were black by the mid-1930s. Yet all three types are amongst my favourites and I have models of two of them, so what can be done?

The first thing to realise is that there was not and never will be a time when things do not change. Sometimes change goes quickly, at other times (rarely long-lasting) there can be a modicum of stability. In railway modelling terms it would therefore be unreasonable to expect to find a period when nothing was likely to change - and even if we did, chances are that it would be the wrong period as far as our railway preferences are concerned. The solution to this dilemma, like so many others, is simply to ignore it. This is not to say that we cannot reach a compromise, but simply to suggest that we do not get too 'uptight' about the period factor.

Not surprisingly, I have tried to factor this into my thinking too and have come to the conclusion that there are three reasonably satisfying solutions which we might do worse than to consider:

a) The 'purist' approach - a fixed year (or, perhaps more realistically, a season of the year) when little or nothing of any significance actually changed.

b) The 'semi-purist' approach - essentially much as (a) but allowing for a little bit of time stretching to permit a few out of period items to appear on the scene, under controlled conditions, of course, and with a bit of due thought as to the overall consequences.

c) The model museum approach - in this option, period accuracy is sacrificed to the wish to model typical items from a variety of historical times.

Which of these three is chosen is very much a matter of personal inclination; but nevertheless, let us see where they all, in turn, can lead, once again offering some of my own experiences by way of example.

In terms of decision making, the purist approach is the simple one. A time is chosen which most fits the desires of the modeller and all non-appropriate out of period notions are ruthlessly suppressed. It sounds remarkably simple and I have tried it for myself. My EM Gauge layouts were, at first, quite

firmly based on the 1937 situation where I could have pre-group, early LMS and Stanier items all intermixed, as long as I painted everything in LMS colours appropriate to the year - *en passant*, this was one of the spurs to my researching (and publishing) LMS locomotive liveries in detail, having got one of my engines wrong in 1965 and having then had to suffer the consequential flak!

There seemed to be no problem until I suddenly fancied a Johnson 4-2-2 and a Deeley 990 Class 4-4-0 (both types scrapped c.1928) and a non-streamlined 'Duchess' 4-6-2 (1938 and later). Frankly, I funked it and, in a sort of wishy-washy way, temporised at the LMS c.1928-38. But, gentle reader, you cannot reproduce the LMS accurately over such a long period - think about it for a moment and you won't need me to tell you why. And this is where my modelling stood when I abandoned 4mm scale in 1975. In other words, purism is for purists!

The opposite end of the spectrum, the 'model museum' approach, is also pretty simple. Here, suspension of belief in time is paramount and you simply make models of things which appeal and run them in a pleasantly neutral (or should it be neutered?) setting. Why not? It is no great secret that I was employed at the National Railway Museum in the 1973-88 period and, unsurprisingly, became involved with the museum's model display, somewhat reluctantly I may add - it was my hobby after all and I did not much fancy it being seen as part of my, quite different, official job. Whatever, I allowed myself to be persuaded and donated part of my first 7mm effort to the NRM to save a bit of time.

In the presentation we were faced with space problems somewhat analagous to the domestic situation, but not quite so severe, additionally complicated by the sheer range of available models - basically pre-group to BR. We therefore chose the 'model museum' option, not because we *were* a museum but because it seemed the only possible way of displaying the concept of 'British trains down the ages', the dominant wish. It seems to have worked, provided that the observer is prepared to reconcile the broadly 1930s/1940s nature of the scenery and lineside effects with the c.1900-1970 characteristics of the trains which pass through. It did not particularly satisfy me, and I have to say so to myself if to no one else; but it has nothing to do with the fact that my erstwhile solidly Settle-Carlisle through station lost all its regional identity, track layout apart, taking on distinctly GWR overtones instead.....

Interestingly, however, I later concluded that my lack of enthusiasm for this sort of theme needed to be modified by way of an added personal caveat: it was only unsuitable for me if it was the *sole* option available. When I finally decided to have two layouts, I soon realised that my 'Trains of all Nations' Gauge 1 theme (Chapter 3), being not a thousand miles away from the concept which I had helped instal at York over ten years earlier, had its own virtues.

Meantime, however, after I had moved to 7mm scale for my main interest after 1975, I soon found myself coming down strongly in favour of the semi-purist solution. In this case, we

Coping with curvature - 1

Curvature (and lots of it....) is endemic in most model railways and the best we can do is to accept the problem and try to cope with it as best we can. On my current 7mm layout (for reasons explained elsewhere), I tried to resolve the issue by putting all the essential but over-sharp curves out of sight, thus allowing the visible parts of the layout to be given more generous radii. Even so, that through Marthwaite station platforms (about 10ft radius) was getting to the critical minimum prototype value (6-7 'scale' chains), but since it is normally viewed from the inside, it is less obvious (see Fig.10). Purely for curiosity, I wanted to see what it might look like from outside the curve at scale 'eye' level -

see Plates 46/47 for the rationale - so I put the camera where I could not go myself and took these two pictures, more or less 'blind'.

One of them shows Claughton No.6018 Private W. Wood VC on the sharpest part of the curve with the down 'Lakelander' train (the tail of which is still emerging from the distant tunnel), while the second picture shows 4-4-0 No.809 on a down local at the start of the transition to the more gentle curvature which starts at the platform end opposite the signal box - see cover picture for a third view in this series, further into the transition section. I was agreeably surprised with all of them.

Coping with Curvature - 2

In the great outdoors, we can usually get much nearer to correct scale values for our curve radii, but even then they are normally a bit less than the prototype would use. Here I show examples of my two garden schemes. The first picture shows the 90° four-track curve from cellar to garden on Kendal MkII. Memory tells me that it was about 12-14ft radius, still only about 9 scale chains in 7mm scale, which would carry a speed restriction and almost certainly a continuous check rail in reality, neither of which were common on most main lines; viewed from inside the curve, I fancy it is not too bad.

But even with what might seem unlimited space available, the curvature problem is still there. This is a 25ft radius curve (12 scale chains) in Gauge 1 with my ten coach 'Merseyside Express' on parade. This would certainly be acceptable on the main line (probably with a speed restriction) but although it looks quite reasonable, that train encompasses at least a 60° arc of the circle and that cannot be said to be typical of most British main lines. The high level view exaggerates the effect, of course, and there are only a few prototype examples of this kind known to me; but I have four similar bends on my Gauge 1 layout, so we are still in the realms of compromise.....

Plate 61: Sometimes we may get away with it. This is a view of No.809 (see also Plate 60) crossing the River Rawthey at Marthwaite on Kendal Mk III. In the foreground is a far better model of the real packhorse bridge than was attempted in 4mm scale at Marthwaite (Plate 28, Chapter 3), the showman's road engine (a commercial model) also adding, or so it might be supposed, a nice degree of verisimilitude to the period scene. The trouble is that, despite all appearances to the contrary, this particular traction engine is quite modern, not having been built until some two years after the railway locomotive was scrapped. I did not know this when I acquired the road engine model and since it looks 'right' to me, I leave readers to decide the issue......

---

select the most favoured historical period and try to develop the model accordingly. We can then, if careful, add in a few historical and/or geographical anachronisms - but not to excess. To illustrate this form of approach, I can only quote my own present solution, arrived at in the late 1970s after 20 years or more of experimentation.

The space available to me, given that I have chosen to remain with 7mm scale, meant that a '100% main line' idea (my preferred choice) was a non-starter. I was therefore forced to adopt a secondary 'main line-cum busy branch line' solution, which actually went a long way towards my ideal - I was thinking along the lines of the LNWR's double track Windermere branch from the West Coast line at Oxenholme,

but with Midland overtones, of course. I could reasonably include models of older engines, carriages and wagons, along with much newer items, provided I confined things to the c.1930 period, which was also an interesting time in LMS history with a lot of transitional livery changes to add to the visible interest.

This was generally fine - I could have lots of older engines, mostly painted red, I could concentrate on fully panelled and fully lined carriages (always favourites), and all wagons would have big company letters on the side and/or be finished in some of the many colourful private owner liveries of the time. The only residual problem, therefore, was how to reconcile this decision with my continuing wish to operate both Stanier engines and pre-1923 prototypes - I had neither the time nor the engineering skill to contemplate all these in the garden live-steam mode.

In solving this one, I took the example of my late and much beloved friend Gavin Wilson. He was a respected Highland Railway modeller, but he loved his 'Duchesses' (on which he had worked as an engineering student in 1938) and 'Royal Scots'. So he built a model of the Edwardian Highland Railway in superb fidelity, basing most of his stations on real places - he had the space. But (and it is an important 'but'), hidden out of sight was the 1937 LMS 'Coronation Scot' and the 1938 LMS Royal Train and 'Royal Highlander'. When he felt like it, out they came for a trip or two round the layout. The latter always evoked the Highland in its prime but on it, he could run

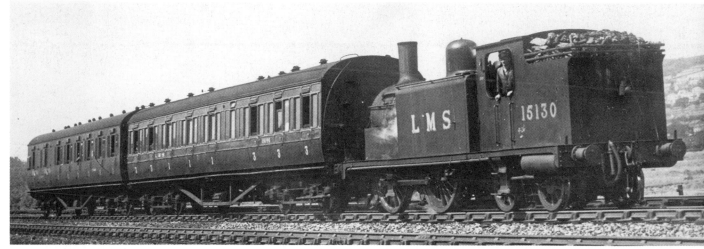

Plates 62-64: The Real Period Factor. *I first became aware of the genuine 'period' problem when I made a model of a Caledonian 0-4-4T in 4mm scale from a white metal kit. I had heard that some of these had migrated to West Yorkshire after the grouping so, given the limited availability of kits at the time (mid-1960s) and my wish to model the Yorkshire scene, it seemed like a good idea to add one to my 'fleet' at modest cost. But my period was early, and I had also read (via a so-called highly authoritative source which I shall not quote!) that one of them (No.15151) had been painted red, so what more natural than that I should get my model painted accordingly - oh dear, what a mistake.*

The appended view of No.15130, taken at Marley Junction, near Keighley, c.1947, shows what these engines probably looked like when they came to West Yorkshire and the second view shows what I did to give my model an earlier style of livery on my Marthwaite layout - so far so good. But what I did not know at the time was that a whole host of ex-CR 0-4-4Ts had actually been given red livery after the grouping and that 15151 was to a totally different design anyway. Needless to say, it did not take long for the armchair experts to tell me how wrong I was and make me feel foolish and inadequate.

Needless to say, the engine was renumbered (15224) and honour wa satisfied. But the most important fact arising from this episode was to distrust the so-called experts without further investigation. The upsho was that my friend Bob Essery and I set out upon a whole investigatio of LMS engine liveries (subseqently published and now regarded a definitive), so this original mistake on my part had happy results.

Plate 65: Squaring the impossible circle. Very early in my 7mm activities, I realised that I could never hope to run all my favourite trains in a single setting as far as period was concerned. I later resolved some of these difficulties in the Gauge 1 garden context, but prior to that time, I had also decided to adopt the 'out of period' or, as my very dear friend Gavin Wilson called it, the 'funny train' approach, in consequence of a problem first made manifest when I obtained a lovely 7mm model of a late 1890s MR Johnson 4-4-0 from another friend and realised that it could never run alongside my LMS models, having been rebuilt long before the main period of my line. I therefore built a period train for it to haul (four Midland 12-wheelers c.1897) and this is seen here running round my garden as early as 1986 on the Kendal MkII layout.

charge of one of the two original 'Patriot' 4-6-0s, a typical 1937 Settle-Carlisle through freight with a brand new Stanier 8F 2-8-0 in charge and (copying Gavin) the 1937 LMS Royal Train behind *British Legion*.

It has to be said that if you want to do this sort of thing, then you may have to plan rather more storage space for the 'hidden secrets' than you would need for normal operations. In turn, this may add complications to the track layout and cause site and space complications of the kind which, in my case, forced 32mm fine scale rather than S7, a decision mentioned above. But above all, it shows how all these compromise factors, which I have done my best to separate out for discussion, all interlock together at the end of the day. And there is still one more to consider.....

his 'funny trains' as he called them, without destroying the realism of the basic setting.

I have followed this idea almost to the letter. My present layout is firmly based on a substantial double track branch line from the Settle & Carlisle across the fells to Kendal - a fictional idea based on the real, but unfulfilled proposal to build a branch line from the main line to Dent and Sedbergh c.1878. It is a sort of Midland equivalent of the LNWR Windermere line if you like, and all items normally to be seen are in period with the 1930 date. Out of sight are a Midland 12-wheel clerestory express of 1897 with a slim boilered Johnson 4-4-0, the West Coast 2pm 'Corridor' in all its 1908 12-wheel glory behind a 'George the Fifth' LNWR 4-4-0, a full length mid-1930s Settle-Carlisle Anglo-Scottish express in

The operational factor

I have come to the conclusion that there are two basic kinds of railway modeller: those who like to build and/or collect models in their own right and those, like myself, who like to operate them as well. But, as always, there is a snag.

A former close colleague of mine at the NRM during the period we were setting up the 7mm scale display, once gave as her opinion that the movement of model trains destroyed the illusion, given that they were the only things which *did* move. The people did not walk, the road vehicles did not move and the grass did not wave in the wind. She could accept the reality of the static scene - a three-dimensional picture 'frozen in time' so to speak - but was not convinced that the movement of the locomotives and rolling stock *only*, contributed much to the total 'believability' of the scene.

This point of view had never occurred to me before but it seemed, on reflection, to reveal a considerable depth of perception. There is, after all, something faintly absurd in wanting to see the trains move when everything else is static - think about it for a moment and you will see what I mean. Yet, taking the opposite view, it seems an awful shame if we can make some of the models move realistically, not to let them do so. But be in no doubt, the operation of a model railway in any form currently practised is of itself a *total* compromise with reality, no matter how good the model!

My own view, for what it is worth, is that there is little or no purpose in building a layout simply to be looked at (save in the highly specialised case of an educational or museum diorama), or to enable a locomotive and its train aimlessly to orbit an otherwise static scene in a sort of conceptual limbo. It will, for a while, re-create a pseudo-realistic vision of a train in motion, but that's about all; and it soon loses its appeal for me - unless it happens to be a genuine live steamer and you (as driver) are fighting to maintain boiler pressure: at that point it can get very realistic....

Nevertheless, I do believe it possible to achieve the kind of mobility in model locomotives and trains which (save for human movement) can re-enact the vast majority of the most interesting operational aspects of the real railway. To do this demands that the historical modeller knows and understands the operational nature of the real railways. In other words, the model should look as though it could be operated in a realistic manner even if we simply indulge in 'tail chasing'.

What is certain is that if the layout really is to be operated realistically as far as pure train movements are concerned, then not only should it look the part, but should also be designed in such a way that the control systems we instal will permit such activity. But here, we are moving out of the realms of design

compromise into the more practical matters which I shall leave until later chapters.

Conclusion

This has been a long and complex analysis of the matter of compromise. But when reduced to its basics, I think it must, as so often, reflect our individual attitude, combined with our perception of the sort of compromises which we can accept - and if anyone tells me that you can build a 'no compromise' model railway, I still don't believe it.

Meantime and when complete (it is already nearly there), my final layout will hopefully encapsulate those aspects of the historical railway scene which most appeal to me after a near-lifetime of study. It will be as accurate as I am capable of making it (of course), but it will also compromise in many aspects of its creation, largely because I am now well into my seventh decade and want to see the trains I have made over the last 20 years or more running through a reasonably realistic setting before the great reaper beckons.... And even were time not a constraint, I would still need convincing that a minute examination of how many rivets were present at 'location X' in 'year Y' gets us very far in terms of the main picture as far as I am concerned - which, I hope, is the only 100% biassed comment I will offer in this review.

Happily, I have no missionary aspirations, so am not at all concerned whether a modeller uses coarse, fine or super-sophisticated standards. All I know is that I have gained such pleasure from indulging in this hobby since the early 1950s, that such writing skill as I possess (communication is, after all, my profession!) have, I hope, mostly been motivated by a wish to share this delight with others. Above all, I do not think we should allow ourselves to be over-influenced by the often well meant blandishments of others if that is not what we most want. Ultimately, the greatest satisfaction lies in doing that which pleases us most - and to hell with the rest. ⬛HRM

CHAPTER 5

Research

Research: Diligent and protracted seeking of facts or principles;
laborious or continued searching after truth; investigation; to search again; to examine anew;
an endeavour to discover new or collate old facts &c. by the scientific study of a subject
or by a course of critical investigation.
Dictionary definitions

I OFTEN THINK, when reading some of the letters sent to me and my friends, not to mention the many and varied pleas for information in the model magazines, that these correspondents may have read some or all of the dictionary definitions quoted above and decided that research is too hard or too boring to justify their own efforts. Instead, they seem to imagine that by simply waving a magic wand, the fruits of research can be made 100% available for the price of a stamped addressed envelope - sometimes without the stamp! It's not quite as simple as that, however, and I never quite know how to answer the letter which, in effect, says: "Please let me have all the information you have gleaned about 'Subject X' over the last 20 years or so", since almost any truly objective reply to such a query would appear either rude or inconsiderate.

Yet I do understand the dilemma and if (as is sometimes the case) I can detect the style of a genuine beginner starting out, rather than that of an older correspondent who is simply too lazy to do the work for him/herself(!), then I do want to help. So, before going on to the practicalities of implementing some of the ideas I have already discussed, I thought I would end this part of the book by trying to explain the business of research as I see it. It is neither as soul-destroying nor as tedious as some might imagine - indeed it can often be very satisfying - so, hopefully, I may be able to encourage at least a few would-be historical modellers to have a go for themselves.

The main point to bear in mind is that research is primarily a 'means to an end' in the context of historical modelling, by which I imply that the main need is to set objectives of a reasonably practical nature and then only do such research as is necessary to turn these objectives into an end product. Of course, it is possible (which was very true in my case) that, once started, research can become of such absorbing interest that it extends well beyond the immediate requirements of the specific model project - but this need not happen if we do not so wish. Fortunately, many research workers (modellers and non-modellers alike) have dug deeply into the many archives (and sometimes their pockets!) and presented their findings in published books and articles which are well worth seeking out for your chosen theme. I have found great personal pleasure and satisfaction in conducting such research, quite outwith my model interests, but I need not have done so, nor need anyone who wishes to make historical models.

That said, however, since it is highly unlikely that we shall be able to get everything we need at second hand, I shall use the rest of this chapter to break down the subject into its main categories in order to make life simpler. To do so, I shall mostly make use of prototype pictures with extended captions to illustrate the methodology which I have found most useful, confining the running text (as with most of this first part of the book) to some of the fundamental 'principles of procedure' which I have found to be most productive.

The importance of first hand knowledge and experience

If a model railway is to satisfy, then it must be an individual creation and it can never be this if it merely copies, however well intentioned, the work of others. By all means let us take our inspiration from fellow modellers (as I have often done), but let us never slavishly copy them. Our initial interest may well have been triggered by a well known name in the hobby, but sooner or later, it needs to be reinforced by first hand knowledge and experience, so let me give a personal example to demonstrate the point.

Many times over the last 30-40 years or so, I have received letters from individuals who 'want to model the Settle and Carlisle'. I am, as you may imagine, flattered if my work has fired their imagination; but I am worried when the letters come from two or three hundred miles away, for the first essential requirement is to go and have a look for yourself. Nothing, repeat nothing, can substitue for personal familiarity with your chosen prototype. You have to get a 'feel' for the place, its character and atmosphere, and this, I suggest, is where you might do worse than to start.

In my case, I have visited those high fells so often that I feel I know them as friends. I have basked in the sun picking wild strawberries at Dent Head (almost missing my last sight of an operational ex-LMS Class 4F 0-6-0 in the process!), I have seen steam engines turning on the famous stockaded turntable at Garsdale, I have run for shelter from a squall into the platelayers' huts, I have been showered by an over-enthusiastic

Plate 66: The record picture. *At its most simplistic level, a good historical photograph gives firm evidence as to fact and can be of crucial value if we want to know exactly what our chosen prototype looked like at a specific time. This fine Eric Treacy study shows a familiar LMS locomotive type, Patriot Class 5XP 4-6-0 No.5514 at Edge Hill, but he does not tell us when. Closer examination of the original print reveals a shed code plate 8D (Widnes) on the smokebox front, which may be of help. But the insignia on the engine are of a type not introduced by the LMS until late 1937 (yellow with bright red shading) and the engine was named Holyhead in 1938. Now Treacy is known to have 'put his cameras away' during winter ("No sun, no picture" he is reputed to have said) and the paintwork, though good, is not pristine - ie the engine is not fresh from works. It therefore seems most likely that this picture was taken in the Spring of 1938 shortly before the engine was named - which information may be just what is needed in the model context.*

Now I cannot impart the knowledge which will allow this sort of interpretation to take place and 40 years ago I would not have been able to offer it anyway; but I have used this quite simple picture to demonstrate the value of such images once we have a degree of basic background information to help us. It is all 'out there' for those who seek it and if I can find it, so can others!

---

fireman taking water too carelessly at Garsdale troughs, I have frozen to the marrow at Batty Moss in mid-January waiting for the right moment to take a picture of Ribblehead (the resulting picture was one of my best!) and I have camped near the line to an accompaniment of an endless procession of steam-hauled night-time freight trains. I have yarned for many hours with signalmen in the remote fastnesses of Blea Moor and Dent and ridden the line both behind and on the footplate of steam and diesel and personally visited every single station.

And all this in the name of 'research', be it noted.......!

Sadly, this sort of thing is no longer possible in the context of the traditionally operated railway as my generation knew it - and the 'Hampstead Heath' atmosphere of the preserved lines (valuable though their contribution is), or on the main line when occasional steam specials go by, is no substitute for the real thing, come to that; but do not despair, the places are still there and this can do much to help our understanding. Indeed, as recently as the late 1990s, even though I had much valuable historical railway data, 'on file' so to speak, from more than 30 years earlier, I was well pleased to re-visit my old haunts to take pictures of the landscape and older vernacular buildings in the context of my latest model - and very enjoyable it was too - ask my wife!.

So my first advice to all those who wish to make historical models is to visit the area of choice: no matter how much it may have changed in recent years, there will still be something of historical value to the seeing eye. This way you will make a positive start and it is as true of the Somerset & Dorset and the West Highland as it is of the Waverley Route and the fearsome banks but always picturesque environment of the South Devon stretch of the old GWR - or whatever other theme may interest you, come to think of it. It is not as easy as it once was since many desirable lines have closed; but all railways had a sense of 'place' and the places are mostly still there. So seek them out, get immersed in them and, when enjoying your evening pint or glass of wine, simply remind yourself that 'this is research' - for it truly is!

At this point, if inspiration is maintained, you can start the more mundane search for prototype information: that essential knowledge to which I have several times referred. You may be lucky or you may have to work hard; but I venture to suggest that it will prove more rewarding and enjoyable than you ever imagined. So...... where does one start?

Plates 67/68: First Hand Knowledge. *Once I decided to base my modelling mostly on the Settle and Carlisle, I made many lengthy and repeated visits to the area to get the 'feel' of the line. But I wanted to model it at least a generation earlier than when I did my own reconnaisance, so I was always looking out for older pictures and these two are exactly what I found most useful. They were taken by a close friend from a generation before mine, the late Norman Wilkinson, fellow Yorkshireman and Settle-Carlisle 'nut'(!), and show the southern approaches to Blea Moor tunnel when he was doing his own survey in 1938. The lack of trains is no hardship (it is not too hard to find out what they looked like) but the infrastructure detail is fascinating.*

The first picture, looking south, shows the magnificent sweep of the line across Ribblehead viaduct at the head of Ribblesdale (it also shows how impossible it is to model this railway - sic!) but what really interested me was that double sided distant signal - a typically Midland feature and proof (along with evidence in other views) that the LMS had not made any serious changes in the pre-WWII era. I later found that most MR signals remained 'in situ' until c.1947 on this line and although I did not envisage a double sided distant on my model, what I did find of interest is that the 'up' arm is on the outside of the bend - "where the b....y drivers could see it, of course" was the signalman's explanation - clearly not at all convinced by the later siting of the new upper quadrant signals to the left of the running lines. I used this fact to good effect with the up starter at Garsdale Road, by the way.

The second picture shows the north end of the lay-bys at Blea Moor box, along with the familiar Midland water tower. Note the provision of a water column on the down lay-by for freight engines held waiting for a path (there was a similar one out of shot on the left for up trains) and the fact that the signal box was on the opposite side of the line to its later wartime LMS replacement, when the lay-bys were converted to running loops. It is such pictures as these which can tell us much about the nature of the railway and they are well worth seeking out for your chosen prototype. You may not wish to copy them as such, but they will give you ideas, and that is what really matters.

References and source material

I am, by nature, somewhat lazy and can see no point in re-doing work which someone has already tackled. Therefore, the starting point must always be, to quote the Book of Common Prayer (sic!) to 'read, mark, learn and inwardly digest' any and all of the published material on which you can lay your hands.

Your local public library is a good start and ought to be able to produce copies of the more important published works. You could also do a lot worse than to ask the library (if it does not already have them) to get hold of a copies of George Ottley's *Bibliography of Railway History* (and its supplements), the real 'Bible' of published railway literature, together with a more recent title *Railway Records - A Guide to Sources* by Cliff Edwards and published by the Public Records Office.

Armed with this valuable information, you can try and find for yourself those items of special interest. Once again the public library could help - and don't be shy of making demands of the service; after all you are paying for it in some way or another! If you have the cash, you could also write to the many railway publishers for their current lists to see what is still in print and build up your own personal library of sources which will help your efforts - over the last 40 years mine has risen to well over 1000 books and papers. On the same theme, read the 'small-ads' section of the many railway journals to try and locate second hand book dealers and write to local magazines inviting readers to offer information. I well recall that many years ago, a short letter to *Dalesman* magazine produced a welter of interesting information about the Settle and Carlisle which was of great value to my own researches.

Plate 69: Peripherals. Sometimes, we come across pictures which, even though not immediately germane to our modelling needs, can help to fill in the background. This is Arnside (ex-Furness Railway) in 1952, probably not too different from the pre-war era I wished to model save for the upper quadrant signal (late LMS/early BR?). The lineside details (sleeper stacks, point rodding, telegraph poles, protection boards over the linkages in front of the signal box, &c.) were much as might be found anywhere and I had no intention of modelling the place anyway.... But in the context of my layout operating scheme, where some trains do, in imagination, head for Arnside, I have found this picture invaluable in terms of envisaging what is going on 'off stage', so to speak.

If you live close to your chosen prototype, then the local County Record Office(s) may have suitable information and, on a national scale, the railway archives at the Public Record Office, Kew, the Scottish Record Office in Edinburgh or the library of the National Railway Museum, York may be able to help; but do be as precise as you can in making requests of any public bodies - they do have vast records which can be hard to find if you only offer a vague 'What do you have about....?' sort of question! The more specific your enquiry, the more likely it is that you will find a satisfactory response - and it will also allow you more time to study the available data when you get there. As far as I am aware, all these public bodies operate on a prior appointment system and the more precise your needs, the more they will be able to help.

A further fruitful source of accurate data is to be found via the many facilities of the Historical Model Railway Society (HMRS), not to mention the more specialised individual railway societies - too many to list here, but well worth searching out: most pre- and post-group systems are covered. Some have 'open' membership (ie available to all who are willing to pay the annual dues) while others are, in effect, 'closed' groups of active research workers. In the latter category (eg the LMS Society of which I am proud to be a founder member), the research output is mostly made available by way of published books and articles or can be obtained (if the information is known at all, of course) by courtesy of a couple of stamped addressed envelopes to the secretary, once again stressing the point that, as with public bodies, the request should be couched in precise enough terms for the reply to be contained within the space of a single letter.

Finally, in this particular context, bearing in mind the ever-changing nature of the modern era, those of you with access to the Internet might do worse than spend an evening 'surfing the net' to see what is out there. Many of the above societies have Web sites and these are usually quite helpful, albeit differing in style - I have looked at most of them and I am very happy to endorse their efforts even though it is not quite my own way of working. But please take note that the genuinely worthy stuff from these reliable sources must be differentiated from a mass of fairly useless and inaccurate garbage which is also on offer from a variety of origins! As always, 'caveat emptor' is the watchword even in our cyberspace age......

Coming back to the more traditional methods, back issues of model magazines and the journals of such organisations as the above mentioned HMRS, Stephenson Locomotive Society and the Railway Correspondence and Travel Society can also offer much of value. In the latter case, the RCTS Journal is an especially valuable source of information regarding matters of operation, locomotive movements, duties and allocations from c.1928 onwards - I have found it most helpful when deciding which particular engine to model for my own favoured area.

Model railway exhibitions (usually advertised in the model press) can often be valuable in drawing attention to special interest activities in the hobby. Many specialist societies take part on a regular basis and, from my experience, are only too willing to help genuine 'seekers after truth', so to speak! Moreover, at these self-same exhibitions can often be found the protagonists of specific modelling scales (as opposed to the afficionados of one particular company) and by combining the virtues of discussing matters with experts in these two separate approaches to the subject, the potential historical modeller can often 'kill two birds with one stone' by the simple expedient of showing some form of enlightened interest in both! It is also at such exhibitions that the potential historical modeller may find the best array of currently available published literature and/or collections of valuable historic photographs.

Where should the effort be directed?

There are numerous ways by which the research effort may be commenced. How far it is taken is very much down to the indvidual but, sooner or later, all research workers will encounter an area about which there is, apparently, no useful published data at all and they are on their own. I am tempted to comment that this is the point which usually sorts out the men from the boys - but this would be unkind, since whether or not you find that you have to get into the realms of investigating basic source material has little or nothing to do with the desire to make or own models: success or failure of your searches in this area is very much a lottery!

That said, however, it is my experience that most successful historical modellers are not always those with the greatest practical skill in modelmaking, but are more often to be found in the ranks of those prepared to do that 'little bit extra' by way of research, and thus make themselves knowledgeable in those specific areas which are particularly relevant to their own field. Once again, I hope I will be forgiven if I quote a personal example to make the point.

Many years ago, I realised that while most serious historical modellers of my acquaintanceship were very knowledgeable on such things as locomotive history and the detail variations thereof (and were quite keen on making freight stock and operating authentic goods trains), their passenger trains were not quite as I recalled them from my youth. This spurred me to investigate the passenger train more closely, for in model terms, it seemed to me that for most of them, any appropriately coloured 'box' on a pair of bogies would suffice.

In due course, this started me on a line of research into LMS coaches, followed later by those of the LNWR, WCJS, LYR, MR &c., until, without realising it, I became branded, for want of a better phrase, as a 'carriage expert'. It even spun off into my full-time work at the National Raiway Museum, where I became much involved with the on-going restoration work on the many historic carriages in the collection. This was not my original intention at all, though I am not complaining at the unexpected and thoroughly enjoyable opportunities which this situation offered - I just wanted to make better models! But it had a practical benefit in that I soon found myself making carriage models for friends in exchange for other items which I needed but which they could make better than I!

However, reverting to the main theme of this discussion, the amount and nature of research undertaken by the historical modeller will vary according to specific needs, personal inclination and the amount of information already available. There are no hard and fast rules and we have to face the fact that we may have to expend money or time (sometimes both) in order to obtain the information we need - in model railways as in most areas of life, what we get out is a measure of what we put in, even though some try to prove the contrary!

I therefore thought I would conclude this particular part of the chapter by listing those areas where, in my view, research will (or may) be necessary to provide the historical modeller with enough data on which to base subsequent efforts:

a) The geographical, geological and human environmental characteristics of the area to be modelled, including buildings, landscape &c.

b) The specific distinguishing visual characteristics, if any (eg architecture, lineside ephemera &c.), of the chosen

railway - ie additional to the obvious matters of locomotive and rolling stock design and livery.

c) The individual operating peculiarities (track layouts, loading facilities, passenger handling, disposition of buildings &c.) of the chosen railway.

d) The appropriate locomotive class(es) for the period in question, their particular detail/livery variations and, where possible, the individual members of the types asociated with the chosen area.

e) The traffic (passenger and freight) likely to be suited to the period/area chosen and the most appropriate railway response in terms of vehicle type, style, livery and quantity

f) The correct (or near-correct) provisioning of such ancillary equipment (platform 'furniture', road vehicles &c.) as is needed to reinforce the overall picture and thus likely to enhance 'believability'.

g) The authentic operational characteristics of the chosen railway at the period in question.

Now this is quite a list, but if one can accept that the criteria are reasonably logical and all-embracing, then it should not be too difficult for the modeller to direct the research effort into those areas which seem less well covered. This will, at least, reduce the likelihood of duplicated effort. It will not, of course, guarantee that all the required answers will be found but it should enable the modeller to make an informed guess as to the likely situation where hard evidence is lacking. Putting it another way, let me simply say that I refuse to be diverted from modelling the Settle and Carlisle c.1930 because I do not know how many cattle wagons were shipped from, say, Settle or Appleby on any one occasion, what kind of livestock they

Plates 70-72: Prototype help for the space-starved. One of the more obvious forms of assistance to the historical modeller is the way in which the British built their railways. Locomotives, carriages, wagons and even modes of operation may change but the fixed infrastructure was set at an early stage and, as I have said in the text, the 'places are mostly still there' for those who seek them out. Moreover, because of the crowded nature of our island state, the real railways often had to adopt quite tight structural solutions which are of self-evident benefit to those of us (maybe the majority?) who are seeking to cram a 'quart into a pint pot'. I have therefore looked out three pictures, very widely separated in time, to show what I mean.

The first dates from 1911 and shows Cudworth station approach on the Midland Railway which, for some reason, was made the subject of this official view. Not only does it show much valuable detail, but it also indicates that the railways would not hesitate to spend money on quite substantial engineering if lack of space and economic circumstances so demanded. My own picture of Settle (1962), showing a Class 5 4-6-0 storming up the hill with a freight train, offers much the same sort of thing in the context of getting a main line railway (committed to its long climb to a summit ten miles or more distant) through some restricted town territory. But it is not that different from the final picture of a preserved scene on the Severn Valley Railway, taken by Barry Lane in 1983, showing a constricted site for the railway at Bewdley which was adopted long before preservation was ever contemplated.

carried or whose particular design of cattle wagons they may have employed for that matter. But my researches have given me sufficient data to be able to say 'It is likely that....' - which, for me, is near enough for all practical purposes.

In the realm of historical research, it was never more truly said that 'The best is the enemy of the good' and I feel sorry for those who fail to start their modelmaking simply because they have been unable to cross the final 't' or dot the last 'i' to their own counsel of perfection. I have met a few such folk in my time and, despite their many undoubted qualities, they usually seem to me rather sad (may I be forgiven for so saying) and, in consequence, many have quit the scene totally unfulfilled.

Research and the personal factor

Although I believe that research is a matter of personal inclination in terms of how far down the road we may chose to go, I do not believe that a successful historical model can be tackled without at least a modicum of such input, no matter from whence it may have come. And this is probably the best point at which to see where other folk and their ideas can help our evaluation. Here, in terms of both knowledge and ideas, I have drawn much valuable inspiration from yet another of my long term 'gurus', my now good friend and well known railway modeller Ken Payne. He is a far better model engineer than I shall ever be, though in some respects, rather less obsessed with the historical minutiae than I can sometimes be. But the vital point which Ken stresses in his writings (and displays in his modelling) is that consistency of approach with which I opened my first chapter and have been pleased to try and copy.

He is firmly of the view that everything should be tackled to a broadly equivalent standard of presentation so that nothing

Plates 73/74: Changes over time. One thing we do need to sort out if models are to convince is the nature of the detail changes within a more or less fixed set of operational criteria and although I am not a Southern expert, I offer these two pictures by way of example: those more knowledgeable than I can doubtless fine-tune the historical detail.....

They show up-market Continental boat trains to the Channel ports on the South Eastern and Chatham route in pre- and post-group days respectively and probably doing much the same job of work. But they are additionally interesting because the later view offers a Maunsell Southern Railway Class E1 rebuild of the original Wainwright Class E 4-4-0s, one of which is seen in all its pre-group glory in the first image, the engines being SE&CR No.736 (sister to the preserved No.737 at the NRM and in the same external state) and SR No.A67. They are hauling Pullman style trains (as might be expected) but the first of them (dated 1908 on the print) carries SE&CR markings on the cars (built for the original 'Hastings car train', later assimilated by Pullman?), whereas the SR view shows umber and cream Pullmans of rather later vintage. The cream painted panels above the windows and the 'A' prefix to the engine number indicate a probable pre-1929 date, after which time the upper panels of the Pullmans became umber and the engine lost its Ashford letter prefix; but they are less than a generation apart despite their obvious differences.

seems out of place or inconsistent with the whole - and in that, respect, like another of my idols, Peter Denny, he succeeds right royally. But the really interesting fact about both these fine modellers (and I trust they will forgive me for saying so should they read this) is that although both of them practice consistency of approach - and have certainly done the research to ensure that they succeed - their layout concepts are totally different: Ken likes to watch highly accurately modelled trains travelling through an aesthetically harmonious setting; and though it is set in no fully defined geographic location, it

nevertheless displays a railway infrastructure more firmly grounded in prototype reality than most I can think of. But it does not run to any defined timetable(!) - whereas Peter (at heart a genuine impressionist I reckon), prefers to run an operational model railway set in an identifiable part of the country which has, over the years, developed a very distinctive personality thanks to his efforts.

In my case I think I may fall somewhere between the two of them - but I have certainly found inspiration from both and it is up to others to form their own conclusions as to how far I

Plate 75: Study the detail. Sometimes, a picture taken for one reason later becomes valuable in a quite different context. In this view, taken at Berry Brow in June 1949, ex-LMS Class 7F 0-8-0 No.49596 passes through with an afternoon Hillhouse to Clayton West goods train. Half a century later, we can use it to confirm, via the two shades of pale grey on the face of the board, that the LMS style 'Hawkseye' signs (right foreground) had black letters on a two-tone support (yellow for the name itself, white for the background board) before being either repainted or replaced in BR days. Also noteworthy in the left foreground is the turnout straddling the coal drops - a nice detail touch which would look good on a model. (B.C.Lane collection)

may have succeeded. But what seems to me to fall out of this brief digression into other approaches is that no matter how inspirational they may be, it is unwise to rely totally on the work of other people. No two modellers (or railway historians for that matter) have the same outlook on the subject and it is essential that our research, be it prototype or model based, should be directed towards our own specific needs.

At this point, unexpected aspects can intervene at times with our efforts, if only because we may need to go back to a further appraisal of our own skills in terms of the many available and attractive options which research may now be suggesting. This could even force a major re-think of such matters as space, standards, costs and spare time. I have already covered some of these topics and indicated that it is

often hard to separate the various strands of our thinking: research is another such consideration to add to the pile!

By the time I came to this stage in my own thinking, I had also visited Jack Ray's splendid Crewchester system and come up with a whole new raft of 'matters arising', as it were. In this case, I saw, for the first time, the operational potential which could be achieved in a huge area (by my standards), simply by working within the sort of modelling parameters wherein some of the more esoteric and, let's admit it, often boring and time-consuming technical problems simply do not exist - Jack will forgive me for saying this simply because, as a result of this visit, we are now very great friends, to which more than a few French vineyards bear ample witness - the 7mm fraternity is rather like that, thank the Good Lord......

Plates 76/77: Non-standard survivals.
It is always worth rummaging round the archives to see if there is anything a bit out of the ordinary which might add something different to the main scene. These two examples from well into the BR era show that not everything, even at this late stage of the traditional era, was a vast sea of standard procedures and monotonous hardware.

In the first view, former Lancashire and Yorkshire Railway 2-4-2T is seen as BR No.50651 in charge of a two coach push-pull set of LMS standard carriages, c.1955; but note that they are not the usual non-corridor types as might be expected at the time. The rear vehicle is an early (1933) Stanier corridor brake third converted for push-pull work, while the nearer carriage is an open third of the mid-1920s which has not only been altered for push-pull work but has also had an extra centre door recessed into the side paneling, including additional steps. There were not too many of these conversions but they did exist and a bit of further devilling might even turn up their running numbers...

Even later in time (1960) one could see the last survivals of the old Caledonian Railway's short-term pre-group flirtation with Pullman catering cars as an alternative to building its own dining cars. Not surprisingly, the LMS would have nothing to do with this and did not renew the contract, though it did have to honour the existing arrangement and take delivery of a few new cars after the grouping. It later bought the cars from Pullman and numbered them into its own (composite dining car) fleet. Being of the usual substantial Pullman style, they lasted a long time and not only served for many years in LMS colours, but also lasted long enough to receive both the BR red/cream and later maroon liveries. Here is Sc217M (built as Meg Dods in 1923 and numbered in the LMS dining car series ten years later), being attached to an Inverness train at Helmsdale in May 1960 - surely a nice idea for modellers..... (B.C.Lane Collection - 2)

Plates 78/79: Prototype curvature. These high level views of Jack Ray's Ravensmoor station on his 7mm scale Crewchester layout and the Midland Railway's one-time Peak Forest route at Cromford share one important feature - a beautiful sweeping reverse curve into the distance. For most of us, this can only be done outdoors, if at all; but when it is tackled on a model, its effect is remarkable and can often supervene all else. Jack's line is to earlier so-called coarse scale running standards (arguably better in an outdoor context) and he tells me that this picture was taken after a long period of unavoidable non-maintenance of his lavish system - but the effect is still there: a classic example of the whole being better than the sum of the parts......

Likewise, I had also observed the efforts of my equally dear friend and long-term writing colleague Bob Essery in the form of his pioneering attemps at the other end of the Gauge '0' spectrum in S7, albeit via the sort of layout which, if I am to be true to myself, was not quite what I had in mind. But nor was Jack's concept for that matter as far as I was concerned, the personal pronoun is quite important in this context.

Thus it was, largely as a result of conducting my research in its broadest sense, that I finally chose 32mm fine scale as being the only solution in terms of what **I** wanted to do - again note the emphasis - and the real point of all these digressions into the work of others is to emphasise the relationship of all aspects of research to our specific and personal needs before we start to do anything. I can only draw attention to the areas which have seemed to me to be both relevant and interesting, but I would never wish to claim that my ideas should ever be seen as anything more than 'thought inducing' stimuli.

I would, however, counsel any potential historical modeller to be very careful to distinguish between the 'essential' and the 'amusing but irrelevant' information which research will turn up, whether it be it by way of archival sources of prototype matters or simply by the careful study of another person's approach to the subject. No matter how fascinating they may be in themselves, such by-ways may well serve to distract and could, in extremis, contribute little to the attainment of *your* ideal. There is, of course, no great harm in allowing yourself to be distracted in such ways, provided you accept that some of your (precious?) time may well be taken up in acquiring a fair amount of quite useless and probably irrelevant information - no matter how interesting it may be in the absolute sense. We have all done it, believe me!

This, of course, is the fascination of railways, the research into their history and the historical modelling thereof by many dedicated folk. There are no hard and fast rules and if you, the reader, feel that I have taken many thousands of words to make this not very startling point, I can only apologise. What I have tried to do in this and the preceding chapters is to analyse a fascinating but compex situation as I see it and, as far as I am able, point out that there are no people with some sort of 'God-given' solution to the many issues which may arise.

Railway modelling, like painting, music or any other art form is, above all, a personal thing - and I do not in any way apologise for using the phrase 'art form', because I truly believe that good modelling is an art in every sense of the word. Who, when contemplating the work of Peter Denny and the late John Ahern, not to mention Roye England of Pendon fame, or even my far less well-known but much loved friend Gavin Wilson and many others (some of whom I have referred to in these pages), could seriously deny that in their efforts, no matter how humble, is also to be found true artistry in the best sense of that word? The fact that they, I am sure, had no such thoughts in their mind when making their contributions, makes it all the more meritorious. Indeed, there is a praiseworthy sub-conscious element to all their efforts which is apparent to anyone who is prepared to let imagination take full rein.

But what I hope I have managed to convey in the last few pages is that although much success and artistic merit may have been achieved by many fine practitioners, they did not get there by mere chance - 'there is no such thing as a free lunch' as someone far more distinguished than I once said! You have to work on it - and this means some sort of research - but it need not be a chore, nor is it vital that we all travel the same route to reach our goals.

I have, therefore, and summing up not only the matter of research *per se*, but also the whole of the first part of my story so far, tried to expound, to the best of my ability (mainly in philosophical terms, I guess), many of those ideas which I have found to be most helpful in tackling a very complex but highly rewarding activity. I have tried to do so in terms which are often overlooked as we seek ever more perfection in our modelling of specific items; but at the end of the day, I reckon I can still only act as a catalyst to thought.

And at that point, I could almost be tempted to conclude my efforts; but since my broader brief is to offer a fully rounded exposition of the whole nature of historical railway modelling, I now need to consider the practical implications of the ideas I have already offered. This I shall try to do in Part II.

The value of research - 1

When planning my 7mm layout, it was important not to have engines which would be inappropriate to the main theme - a waste of time and money. I also wanted to hint at the period I was modelling and these two types were determined at a very early stage. The Horwich 2-6-0 (aka 'Crab') was an obvious choice for a powerful mixed traffic type such as might operate the better trains and its running number (13004) was also chosen before it was built. These engines came out in 1927 and the first 100 were painted LMS crimson which was an additional 'plus'. When I discovered that 13004 remained in this style well into the early 1930s and was based in the NW, this seemed the right choice. The model itself was a fortuitous acquisition, engine and tender having been purchased separately as cheap unattributed job lots (with coarse scale wheels) at two separate auction sales. But they both turned out to be by the famous

James Beeson and a set of fine scale wheels plus a decent paint job soon got me exactly what I needed. (Larry Goddard)

The Patriot too (LMS 5971 Sir Frank Ree) was a deliberate choice and I show it unpainted, the better to reveal the detail. It is one of only two examples built in 1930 (just in period with my model), both of which entered service without the later smoke deflectors and with large centre-boss LNWR driving wheels from the Claughton Class 4-6-0s of which they were notionally, rebuilds - they were actually mostly new engines. I later discovered that 5971 went to Leeds when new, so the final choice was obvious. It is in period for the normal operating mode for the layout but usually heads a display set representing a typical Settle-Carlisle express of the early 1930s. The model was made by Peter Everton, who also rebuilt 13004. (Ron Prattley)

The value of research - 2

I offer these two delightful models (which I can thus describe because I made neither of them....) by way of contrast with the predominantly LMS flavour of much of this book. I wanted to have a through LNER excursion train from the Northallerton area (via Hawes) with a typical ex-NER 4-4-0 in charge, and when I discovered via my good friend Peter Everton (who built the model) that the two 7ft 7in driving wheel 'racing' 4-4-0s of Class Q1 (LNER Class D18) had been put 'out to grass' in the Yorkshire Dales during the 1920s, this seemed to be sufficient reason for having a model of this very handsome type. Since it also seemed unlikely that any manufacturer would offer a kit for such a type, its relatively unique status as a model (I have never seen another one) was a modest bonus. Of the two prototypes, we chose No.1870 as being the only one to remain green (pre-1928 LNER style with all

insignia on the tender) until it was scrapped (1930) - again helping to set the period of the layout.

The second view shows a dainty little Midland and Great Northern two-coach train headed by one of the celebrated Beyer-Peacock 4-4-0s built for this route. The models are additionally interesting in having been researched and built by yet another of my friends, Lawrie Loveless, from kits which he also designed and marketed. Having seen this train, and knowing that Lawrie also made kits for GNR articulated stock of the type which would be just right for my excursion train behind No.1870, above, it did not take long for me to add a pair of Lawrie's fine models to my own stock, rather than hand build them myself. For once, I could use someone else's research in the sure knowledge that it would be right. (Larry Goddard; Ron Prattley)

PART II

GETTING DOWN TO PRACTICALITIES

CHAPTER 6

Fundamental considerations

"The nicest thing about this hobby is that we are our own general managers."
The late Jim Russell - in conversation

IN PLANNING this second part of the book, notwithstanding the King of Hearts' quoted remark at the head of Chapter 3, the best starting point was difficult to decide, conventional wisdom suggesting that one should move from layout planning to final operational considerations, all of which matters I shall cover in due course. But like the themes I have addressed in Part I, the practical aspects of the subject also tend to interlock with each other, even though I have tried to separate them out into reasonably specific chapter headings. In the end, Jim Russell's remark (above), offered to me almost 40 years ago when I first visited his famous EM Gauge 'Little Western' layout, provided the essential clue.

Jim's logic was simply that no matter how you approach the building of a model railway, what really matters is that the end product should be as close as possible to that which you hold most dear and that you and you alone hold the key to success. It therefore follows that the best place to start is by first considering what the final end product is intended to be; only then can we plan and execute the rest. This is difficult to do on a purely theoretical basis - we are all different - and I do not propose to try, but there is a *sequential strategy* which I believe we can all follow. I shall use (mostly) my own current indoor layout scheme in the next few chapters by way of explaining this strategy and hope that as I go along, some of the ideas I have found useful will be of wider application. That said, of course, it will be up to the reader to judge whether or not my own specific solutions are consistent with the ideas I have and shall be expounding.

I shall work through the various factors, more or less in the order in which I tackled them. Needless to say, I start with the need to establish a satisfactory *raison d'etre* for the whole project - reminding readers that I am thinking in terms of a 'total' model railway (see Chapter 1).

The Background Scenario

Underpinning all the really convincing model railway layouts I have ever seen, whether or not they be 'historical' in nature, I can always detect a well-argued rationale and although this is often quite different from that which I have adopted, I would almost hold it as axiomatic that we should place the resolving of this issue at the top of our list of priorities before detailed planning commences. In Chapter 3, I listed those many criteria which I wanted my layouts to meet and explained why I chose the scales I did. But these choices were measured against the fundamental 'story line' which I had always had at the back of my mind since 1962. This too, I have alluded to in Chapter 3, but I now need to 'flesh out the carcass', so to speak, in order to discover, more precisely, where such conclusions are likely to lead in terms of detailed layout planning.

I left the story at the point where I had concluded that the Settle & Carlisle main line *per se* was impossible for me to assay in the context of my own developing likes and dislikes, and that I could get my main line 'fix' rather more effectively by running Gauge 1 live steam in my garden. But if I was to go back to the branch line idea, then it had to be interesting in the operational sense, rather than a simple 'one engine in steam' or 'cabbage patch and brewery' sort of job! In other words, it was likely to display a modicum of main line characteristics.

Other than the Hawes branch - not really very exciting in terms of what I had in mind, either in visual or traffic terms - there was no suitable branch off the Settle and Carlisle, so I took the well documented, but abortive, petition to the Midland Railway in the 1870s by the villagers of Dentdale to build them a line and presumed it had been constructed, an idea I first used on the original 4mm scale Marthwaite layout. But even in 7mm scale I had more space available in my large shed than was ever at my disposal (proportionally) for either Marthwaite or Garsdale Road in the smaller scale. I therefore 'extended' the hypothetical line to Kendal to produce a sort of Midland Railway equivalent to the LNWR Windermere line. It involved some consequential juggling with the real railway geography of the area - nothing excessive - and the resultant revised railway network is shown at Fig.14.

From this, it can be seen that the terminus at Kendal is, in effect, Midland and Furness joint and that routes go to both the Midland main line at Dent Head and the Furness main line at Arnside. I have also imagined a triangle at Natland which comes into its own when devising an operating sequence for the model. Kendal Castle (thus named because it would have been located under the shadow of the old castle in Kendal on the site of the former canal basin) is predominantly Midland in

Plate 80: "...a modicum of main line characteristics".

Much to my surprise, this high level view of Marthwaite on the final 7mm layout, with a local about to depart for Dent Head, seems to offer far more of a main line look than I had ever thought possible in what is, for 7mm scale, quite a restricted space. Even the 10ft radius curve through the platforms seems to be less severe than it actually is.

Fig.14: System map.

This map shows the alignment of my imaginary lines (marked with cross-hatching) in relation to the real railways in the area, save that, for sentimental reasons, the name Garsale Road appears where the real Dent was located......

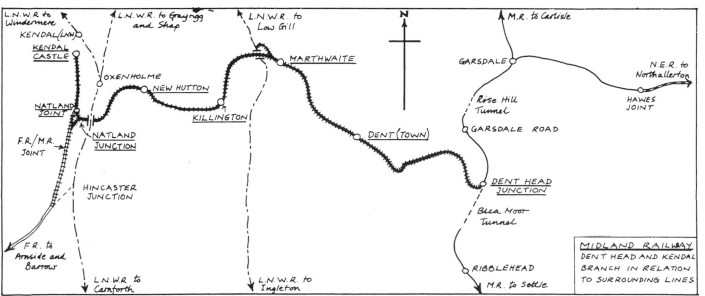

Plate 81: Period and Place. In this view of the outer end of the Kendal platforms, the signal box establishes the fundamental Midland nature of the infrastructure, though there is insufficient background detail visible in this view to indicate the north country. But the ex-LNWR 2-4-0, No.5012 John Ramsbottom *also hints at the fact that some services originate from what, prior to the grouping, was non-Midland territory, It is one of several 'foreign' classes chosen for this purpose and its precise identity stemmed from the fact that its livery can be exactly dated to 1928 - the only 'Jumbo' to have been given the post-1927 LMS insignia with red livery, prior to them all becoming plain black. And it* was *based in the north.*

---

character, it being assumed that the MR would have been the instigator, the Furness settling for full running powers and a smaller financial stake in the enterprise!

So much for the basic story line, whose principles can be adapted *ad infinitum* for any other area of the country, given a knowledge of local geography and a tad of railway history - it just needs a bit of work and lateral thinking.

The next thing to establish, I think, is period. In my case, I had to have the LMS (of course) but since I wanted to convey a Furness element to the finished scene, I felt I should go for a period before all the FR engines had been swept away by the ever-increasing LMS standardisation. I also have a preference for the fully lined LMS crimson lake livery (suppressed on most engines from 1928 onwards and the full lining on coaches from 1934), not to mention favouring the aesthetics of both pre-group and pre-Stanier LMS carriage stock (ie all built

before 1932), despite the superb passenger amenities of the latter. On this totally subjective basis (Have I not many times said that this is what it is really all about?), the 1928-30 period more or less 'fell out of the woodwork' and I felt that this relatively short time span was not too much at odds with the ideas I have already developed and offered in Chapter 4. It also happened to be a very interesting transitional period in terms of livery changes as far as the LMS was concerned - ie giving yet more scope for a bit of creative modelling......

In practical terms, what it meant (in the 'purist' mode) was that no prototype built after 1930 should be seen on the layout; while the liveries adopted would be a mixture of pre-1928 and post-1927 styles so as to hint at the time of changeover. Of course, I could have opted for a purely pre-1923 display (I would still have Midland Red to satisfy childhood memories) but this would have denied me the very attractive carriages built by the LMS from 1923-30. It is also true that the lovely little Furness 4-4-0 'Sharpie Seagulls' and the well known '990 Class' Midland 4-4-0s, of which I have fine models, were both scrapped before 1930; but in my imaginary world, it is not stretching the bounds of possibilty too far to presume that one or two of these engines were kept going for a year or two more to work the Kendal-Dent Head and Kendal-Arnside trains! After all, who is to say precisely what subtle differences might have taken place had the LMS inherited a line such as I have envisaged? This is the beauty of Arthur Whitehead's 'just supposing' principle, provided it does not stretch the bounds of credibility too far, of course.

This, then, was the background against which I designed my last three 7mm scale layouts. Typically, trains would be quite short (passenger and freight) but a real line 24 miles long would develop some main line characteristics (as did the Windermere branch), so it seemed not unreasonable to assume a fair amount of mineral traffic from intermediate quarry sites which might have been opened up by the arrival of a new line, along with one or two rather more impressive passenger trains, especially in summer (analagous to the 'Lakes Express' on the Windermere line). It also seemed likely that the gradients on such an imaginary line would be justification enough for at least a few bigger engines.....

So how do we put such thoughts into practice?

As ever it is simply a matter of taking action in a logical sequence and I offer below the order in which I tackled things; the rest of this chapter will cover the first two of them:

a) Analyse the traffic patterns, passenger or freight, to be reproduced and devise an appropriate timetable (or at least a train movement sequence) which will meet these needs.

b) Determine the *least* amount of station and running line provisioning which will allow matters to be achieved, not forgetting to include servicing facilities (eg locomotive sheds, carriage sidings &c) if, but only 'if' they would be needed in reality.

c) Work out the appropriate quantity (and types) of rolling stock and locomotives (in that order!) which will be needed to handle the traffic, not forgetting such things as correct train formations.

d) Devise an operational system which will allow the whole scheme to work in a realistic manner.

Traffic patterns and timetable planning

At first glance, this may seem a strange way to start the whole process of layout design, but it follows on logically from the establishment of a convincing story line, because it is the only way I know which will enable us to find out if we can achieve a satisfactory end product within the constraints of our own situation. For those with long memories (or a good reference library), studying the gradual evolution of Peter Denny's famous Buckingham layout and/or Frank Dyer's 'Borchester Saga' will give two classic examples of something very close to what I have in mind.

Real railways were built to fulfil real needs and for a model to convince, it should look capable of handling the sort of traffic which is offered. Facilities should not be too lavish (this would not get past the shareholders on grounds of expense), nor should they be inadequate (traffic would be lost or delayed, thus reducing revenue). Consequently, the detailed design of the track plan should be undertaken against the known or likely traffic to be handled. I shall return to this theme later in the chapter, but before we can do even this, we must first try to envisage the sort of traffic patterns which our putative model will try to replicate. And the great value of this sort of exercise is that it will usually apply to any subsequent layout you may design, as long as the underlying theme does not change. Thus, I found that the principles I worked out in advance of my first 7mm layout in 1976 were applicable without any significant change to my second and third 7mm scale attempts to meet the same sort of wishes.

However, I should perhaps stress that this sort of detailed

Plate 82: A bit of modeller's licence. Midland 4-4-0 No.809 (originally 999 until the LMS renumbered it in 1927), although the last of the 990 Class to be withdrawn (in 1929), is technically incorrect for the 1930 date which I originally chose for my layout, as is Furness 4-4-0 No.10133 (seen elsewhere in other pictures in the book, eg Plate 107), also withdrawn too soon. I therefore temporised at 1928-30 (see text). But in the context of the overall presentation, neither seems wildly out of place to any save pedantic rivet counters - and I can manage without them....! The train is an up local for Dent Head: three square panelled Midland clerestories with, respectively, twelve, eight and six wheels and displaying a mixture of gas and electric lighting.

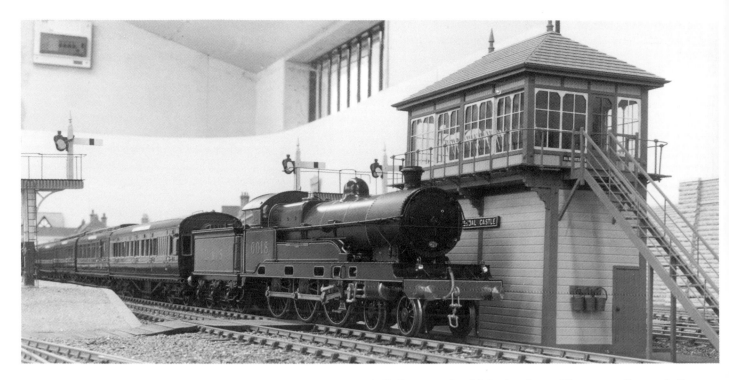

Plate 83: Traffic Patterns - 1. In order to emphasise that the Kendal branch had some main line pretentions - it is, after all, 24 miles long in theory and also double track - it seemed perfectly reasonable to insert a few through workings of a more imposing kind, analogous to those on the LNWR's Windermere line from Oxenholme. The vital thing was not to make them look too imposing, so I settled on a sort of 6-7 coach length. This is the summer 'Lakelander' working to various northern cities about to leave Kendal behind ex-LNWR Claughton Class 4-6-0 No.6018 Private W.Wood VC *in immediate post-1927 LMS red livery. The leading brake composite, an early LMS standard type, is for Bradford while the main train for Leeds consists of four ex-Midland clerestories. Two more brake composites for Liverpool and Manchester are at the rear and, in imagination, the train reverses and changes engines at Dent Head, where it is augmented by a few further carriages working through from Hawes on the Wensleydale branch.*

---

preliminary scheming usually only applies if the model is to be operated in the semi-purist mode. If all that is wanted is a display circuit on which to operate favourite trains, such as my Gauge 1 garden system, then you might just as well get down to layout planning and tracklaying as soon as possible.

The all-essential point to remember about devising traffic patterns for an operational layout is that they should mirror reality as far as possible. Real railways are economic arteries and trains are not operated just because they look nice or because it is 'a long time since the last one.' Consequently, the first and over-riding need is that the pattern of traffic should make sense in relation to the geographcal realities of the area modelled, real or imaginary. Given this, then it is logical to suppose that we can select the appropriate mix of stock and prime movers to create the impression we desire.

In other words, we should *not* start by picking engines, carriages or what have you and then tailor the traffic to suit.

Rather, we should devise the traffic pattern first and discover what we really *need* to have. That is how the real railways did it and in model terms it can save an immense amount of time and money if we do not buy or build that which we do not need. Of course, this 'hard-line' approach may well exclude some of our personal favourites from consideration, which is why I (and many others) elect to have a few 'out of period' favourites hidden from sight. So where do we start?

If you are modelling either a real station or an imaginary line based on a connection with a real railway, then the best starting point is almost always the timetables for the period in question. This immediately tells you what sort of trains were operated and how many. The public passenger timetables are not too hard to find from such sources as offered in Chapter 5, though the working freight timetables might be more elusive. However, freight patterns were often more static over quite long periods, so it is not absolutely essential to have the same year for both - and you could, *in extremis*, probably make do with the passenger workings only and fit the goods trains round them in a coherent way.

In my case (see Fig.14), I looked up the times at which the real trains passed or stopped at Dent Head and Arnside (pass times only at Dent Head - there was no real station there, of course), confining my attention mostly to stopping passenger and pick-up freight services. I argued that the bulk of branch services would be related to this type of train rather than the expresses and long distance main line freights. This exercise suggested that some six to eight daily passenger services along each route would connect with most main line stopping trains. This would give about 15 or so local passenger arrivals and departures at Kendal, which seemed about right.

To these I then augmented the Kendal-Dent Head traffic with a daily through service from St Pancras via Leeds and

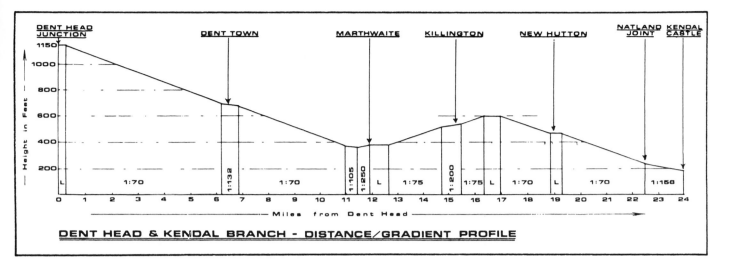

DENT HEAD & KENDAL BRANCH - DISTANCE/GRADIENT PROFILE

Fig.15: Gradient profile. This is a more refined version of the original Marthwaite given at Fig.1, Chapter 3. It is mostly self-explanatory, but it may be worth noting that since real railways tried to ease gradients through the station sites where possible, I have tried to copy this idea. On the model, the entry to Kendal is on a slight up grade, the station itself being level. Arguably, a real railway might well have done something similar.

two summer only workings, one from the industrial areas of Yorkshire and Lancashire (amalgamating at Hellifield) and the other from the North East via Wensleydale, the latter to be operated by the LNER using its (real) running powers over the LMS beyond Hawes Joint station. I also felt that some form of connection would be needed from Marthwaite to the LNWR Low Gill line (possibly a steam railmotor shuttle) and that a few overnight carriages between London and Kendal (to be detached from a principal express at Dent Head) would not be out of the question.

On the freight side, a morning and afternoon pick-up on each route would serve adequately for local traffic, to be supplemented by the occasional cattle special and the regular mineral workings to and from the various supposed lineside quarries *en route*. In this connection, local knowledge of the area in question is invaluable for determining any non-routine traffic such as timber, steel and so forth - ie the province of the special purpose wagons so beloved by we modellers! For the most part, however, there would be nothing too exotic, it being safe to assume that local freight would follow typical patterns and employ very ordinary sorts of vehicles. Such traffic would include coal for the local merchants, general merchandise and spasmodic movements of livestock (one or two wagons) if a special cattle working is neither feasible nor appropriate.

This sort of thinking gives a basic service pattern to be attempted and, after satisfying ourselves that it is likely to sustain interest, the next stage is to evolve a series of train movements which will reproduce these features.

Here, we first need to assess how long it would take real trains of the type envisaged to traverse the full length of the route in real time and distance terms. Study of old timetables

(which usually give distances as well) will generally give some idea of elapsed time in relation to distance and this can then be modified, if need be, for favourable or adverse gradients. Thus, for example, on my mythical branch line, for which I prepared a gradient and distance profile (Fig.15), I reckoned it would take stopping passenger trains some 65 minutes to go from Kendal to Dent Head and some ten minutes less in the opposite direction. Expresses stopping only at Marthwaite would be quicker, while pick-up freights would not only take longer between stations than either of them, but would also spend some time at each station to shunt the traffic.

From this, the next process is to establish a 'public' timetable for the route, ideally using a train graph (below), which must be taken to completion - in other words it must include all possible passenger trains, including those which only run on certain days. In my case, this involved three principal routes (Kendal-Dent Head; Kendal-Arnside/Barrow and Dent Head-Arnside direct) plus the additional Marthwaite-Ingleton railcar service. This can then be converted into a quasi-official timetable, part of which I offer at Fig.16.

There was one more aspect to resolve in my case; it is very unlikely to affect most folk but does serve to explain some of the peculiarities of my train graph which might otherwise be confusing. In my final scheme I originally intended that trains leaving Kendal for Arnside and/or Barrow would simply go to the hidden storage roads and be seen no more (see track plan Fig.9, Chapter 3), but I then realised that because of the triangular junction at Natland (Fig.14), they could actually go through Marthwaite as if they had come *from* Arnside/Barrow.

This 'change of identity', was actually forced on me with the first two 7mm layouts (see later) and had already been plotted on the graph. These trains were given fictional times to and from Dent Head so that when they finally returned from Dent Head, they got back to Kendal as if they had originated from Barrow or Arnside. The same reasoning could also apply to some goods trains too - all very subtle!. As a result, when I came to plan the final version, I found I could use the existing train graphs and timetables virtually unchanged.

							(SX)	(SO)	(SO)						(SO)					
KENDAL CASTLE	12a15	6b40		7 30		9 02	11 10		12d 32			2 20		4h15	4j33	4 40		7b10		10 30
Natland Joint	—	6 45		7 35		9 07	11 15		—			2 25		—		4 45		7 15		10 35
ARNSIDE			6 32		8 c 06			11 56	·	12e31	1f40		3g09				5k05		7 56	
Sandside			6 38		8 c 12			12 02		12 37	1f44		3g14				5k10		8 02	
Heversham			6 42		8 c 16			12 06		12 41	1f48		3g18	The Dalesman			5k14		8 06	
Sedgewick			7 00		8 44			12 14		12 49	2 14		4 02				5 29		8 14	
New Hutton	—	6 54	7 05	7 44	8 49	9 16	11 25	12 19	—	12 54	2 19	2 34	4 07		—	4 54	5 34	7 25	8 19	10 44
Killington	—	7 02	7 12	7 52	8 57	9 24	11 32	12 26	—	1 02	2 27	2 42	4 15		—	5 02	5 42	7 32	8 27	10 52
MARTHWAITE	12a45	7 10	7 20	8 00	9 05	9 33	11 40	12 34	12d54	1 10	2 35	2 50	4 23	4h37	4j55	5 10	5 50	7 40	8 35	11 00
Dent Town			7 35	8 15		9 48	11 55	12 49		1 25		3 05	4 38			5 25	6 05	7 55	8 50	
DENT HEAD JUNCTION	1a10		7 55	8 34		10 08	12 14	1 09	1d 19	1 45		3 24	4 57	5h03	5j21	5 44	6 25	8 15	9 10	

Fig.16: Timetable. This fictional timetable is not strictly necessary in order to arrive at a logical sequence, but I enjoy the mental exercise and have prepared similar versions for the Kendal-Arnside and Marthwaite-Ingleton services. After this timetable was prepared, the Leeds express was named 'The Lakelander', while for those interested, the train graph (Fig.17) starts, effectively, with the 9.55am arrival at Kendal from Dent Head. In accordance with the standard LMS custom, a vertical line between the hours and minutes column denotes pm times.

a   Through carriages and sleeping cars to London (St Pancras). Sleeping car passengers may join at Kendal from 10.30pm.

b   Steam Railmotor - third class only.

c   Change at Sedgewick.

d   Dining Car express to Leeds (Wellington). Through carriages to Bradford (Forster Square), Liverpool (Central) and Manchester (Victoria)

e   From Barrow (dep. 9.56am)

f   Change at Sedgewick, runs 10 minutes earlier (SO).

g   Change at Sedgewick, runs 5 minutes later (SO).

h   To London (St Pancras). Dining car service terminates at Derby. Through carriages to Bournemouth (Central) and Bristol (Temple Meads).

j   To Newcastle (LNER) via Northallerton. Conveys through carriages for Middlesbrough and York

k   Runs 2 minutes earlier (SO) and change at Sedgewick (SO)

Only after the passenger services have been included is it possible to find 'paths' for goods train workings (from the same train graph), after which one can then produce a full sequence of arrivals and departures (passenger and freight) at terminal points, along with their passing times (or shunting periods) at intermediate locations. At this point, those readers who are familiar with gradient profiles and train graphs may wish to skip the next part altogether, but for those coming to it for the first time, I thought it would help if I explained the processes in slightly more detail.

Plate 84: Traffic Patterns - 2. I use non-Midland engines to differentiate the workings onto what was once the Furness part of the system and although a Furness goods engine would have been equally suitable, I aleady had this model of ex-Lancashire & Yorkshire 0-6-0 No.12345 which was also fitting, given the post-grouping migration of many former LYR engines into ex-FR territory. In this view, the engine is about to leave Kendal with the daily pick-up freight to Arnside.

						(SO)	(SX)		(SO)				(SO)						
DENT HEAD JUNCTION	3a50	7 45		9 00			10 25	10d55	12 55	1 15	2e35	2f43		4 16	5 00		6 45	8k30	9 10	10 20
Dent Town	—	7 55		9 10			10 35		1 05	1 25	—			4 26	5 10		6 55	8 40	9 20	10 30
MARTHWAITE	4a10	8 05	8 10	9 25	9 45	10 05	10 45	11d10	1 16	1 36	2e50	2f58	3g16	4 36	5 20	6j30	7 05	8 50	9 30	10 40
Killington	—	8 14	8 19	9 34	9 54	10 14	10 54	—	1 25	1 45	—		3g25	4 45	5 29	6j39	7 14	8 59	9 39	10 49
New Hutton	—	8 25	8 30	9 45	10 05	10 25	11 05	—	1 34	1 54	—		3g36	4 56	5 40	6j50	7 25	9 10	9 50	11 00
Sedgewick		8 29				10 09	10 29				1 58		3g40	4b23			7 29		10 00	
Heversham		9b14				10 17	10 37				2b35			4b23	6N07		7 37		10 08	
Sandside		9b18				10 21	10 41				2b39			4b27	6N11		7 41		10 14	
ARNSIDE		9b24				10c27	10 47				2b44			4b35	6h16		7 47		10 18	
Natland Joint	—		8 36	9 50			11 11	—	1 41					5 46	6j56		9 16		11 06	
KENDAL CASTLE	4a35		8 40	9 55			11 15	11d32	1 45		3e10	3f20		5 50	7j00		9 21		11 10	

(Branch stations Sedgewick–Arnside served via "The Dalesman".)

a Through carriages and sleeping cars from London (St Pancras). Sleeping car passengers may remain in their berths until 7.30am. Sleeping car passengers for Marthwaite may travel to Kendal and remain in their berths until 6.30am, returning at 6.40am.

b Change at Sedgewick.

c To Barrow (arr. 11.20am).

d From Leeds (Wellington). Conveys dining car from Leeds. Through carriages from Bradford (Forster Square), Liverpool (Central) and Manchester (Victoria).

e From London (St Pancras). Dining car service from Derby. Through carriages from Bournemouth (Central) and Bristol (Temple Meads).

f From Newcastle (LNER) via Northallerton. Conveys through carriages from Middlesbrough and York.

g Runs 5 minutes later (SO).

h Change at Sedgewick and runs 4 minutes later (SO).

j Runs 2 minutes later (SO). Steam Railmotor - third class only.

k Steam Railmotor - third class only.

Gradient Profiles and Train Graphs

If you are modelling a piece of the genuine railway, then it is not too difficult to locate a distance and gradient profile from the sort of reference sources already mentioned - I suggest you first try the NRM; they have a lot. But for a 'might have been' such as my own, more work is needed - and it can actually be quite a lot of fun while, at the same time, helping you absorb some of the realities of building a real railway.

The starting point is the relevant large scale Ordnance Map for the area in question - you may need more than one. For the unreconstructed adherents to imperial measurements, the old 1" = 1 Mile series (the final 7th Edition is one of the classics of British map making) is the ideal choice and for a historical model, the older it is the better, since it will show more railways and give the extent of the built-up areas at a time closer to the (supposed) period when the imaginary railway was built. But as with newer maps, it is still worth doing a bit of 'devilling' to discover precisely where and when towns and villages grew in size. Even using the oldest map available, you may find that you can route your line through what is now a housing estate but which was open country in Victorian times.

If you are forced onto modern maps, then the nearest to the old 'One Inch' series is its modern 1:50,000 successor - now known as the 'Landranger' series and probably familiar to all in its pinkish-red covers. These are nice and clear, often having the old railway alignments marked as such. But in more recent years, an even better choice has presented itself for those who cannot get hold of the (preferred) older maps. These are the new full colour 1:25,000 (2.5" = 1 mile) series in the 'Outdoor Leisure' (Yellow covers) and 'Explorer' series (Orange covers).

Plate 85: Out of town. When I came to design the final 7mm layout, I realised that Marthwaite would, inevitably, be sited some way from the town it supposedly served. This offered the chance to give the station the slightly remote character of many of the real Settle and Carlisle locations where most man-made features were almost wholly of railway origin with little else within close range. Therefore, tempted though I was to insert a couple of late-Victorian grand houses in the space behind the station and the associated stationmaster's house (there was room), I finally left it as shown here.

These are quite magnificent and beautiful examples of the map making art and although not yet (2001) available on a fully Nationwide basis, the range is expanding all the time.

The next stage is to use a soft pencil (you will do a lot of rubbing out) and mark the route of the imaginary line on the map. This needs doing with some care and must take account of physical features *en route* by way of detour, tunnel, viaduct &c. The economic nature of the supposed route (Chapter 2) may well determine how much civil engineering is justified and this too must be thought out as the line is 'surveyed'.

Stations should be positioned as near to settlements as the lie of the land will permit, bearing in mind that no real railways would make use of unnecessarily tortuous detours or over-steep gradients, simply to get a few hundred yards closer to the settlement, though if it was a big enough place, some adjustment might be reasonable. On the other hand, if you are modelling a main line concept, bear in mind that the prototype often made no compromise at all for the smaller places - how

often did the GWR resort to 'XXXX Road' in its station names rather than divert from the best route, for example? Likewise, the ex-Midland station at Kirkby Stephen on the Settle-Carlisle is two miles from a quite substantial town - any nearer would have steepened the ruling gradient for many miles of main line; and mention of gradients brings us to the next item to resolve, particularly that of the maximum permissible value.

The concept of 'ruling gradient' is most often related to the economic importance of the line. There are, of course, many fearsome gradients on real main lines, but it is generally more likely that the lesser routes will take more detours or accept steeper gradients than the main line (sometimes both) to cut down on civil engineering costs. I thus decided that in my case, although the main line was built to a ruling 1:100 (better than this wherever possible), the Kendal branch could perhaps have a ruling gradient of 1:70, or thereabouts, with some slight easing through intermediate stations as in prototype practice. This figure was arrived at largely because of the considerable vertical fall between Dent Head and the valley floor at the supposed Marthwaite location. Even so, adopting this steeper value still produced quite a number of detours from the direct line from Dent Head to Dent Town and between Marthwaite and Kendal (see Fig.14).

Plate 86: Approach to Kendal - 1. Because of the physical site constraints, the final approach to Kendal had, perforce, to be fixed at 1:70 in order to give sufficient headroom for the hidden trains below the station itself. This view, taken from a position not available to the naked eye, shows the end of the ascent into the station, the gradient actually continuing through the double slip in the foreground. It works well and, in the case of heavier trains, has the advantage of slowing them down anyway, prior to their entering the station. The fully working signal gantry is directing the approaching railcar into Platform 3.

Plate 87: Approach to Kendal - 2. Four platforms may seem a bit generous for a station of this type, but they are all essential during an operating session. Here, Scottish 0-4-4T No.15051 (Highland Railway this time - shades of the 4mm scale Marthwaite, Plates 62-4 - but see Chapter 7 for the reasons for its presence in 7mm scale!) propels the overnight sleeping car set into the carriage sidings from Platform 1. In the foreground can be seen the tandem turnout which allows access to the goods yard from Platform 4 which (again see text) is mostly used for freight traffic. The crowded nature of the goods yard itself, along with its arguably too short sidings, is shown on the title page double spread.

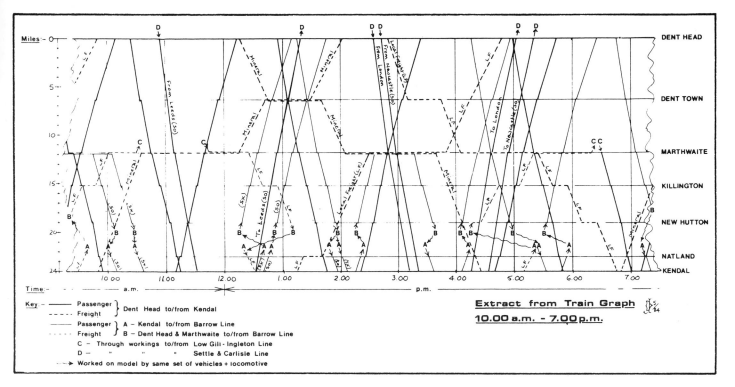

The graph contains the following labels:

Vertical axis (left): Miles:- 0, 5, 10, 15, 20, 24

Vertical axis (right, stations top to bottom): DENT HEAD, DENT TOWN, MARTHWAITE, KILLINGTON, NEW HUTTON, NATLAND, KENDAL

Horizontal axis (Time): 10.00 a.m., 11.00, 12.00, 1.00, 2.00, 3.00, 4.00, 5.00, 6.00, 7.00 p.m.

Key:- ——— Passenger } Dent Head to/from Kendal
- - - - Freight }
——— Passenger } A – Kendal to/from Barrow Line
- - - - Freight } B – Dent Head & Marthwaite to/from Barrow Line
C – Through workings to/from Low Gill - Ingleton Line
D – " " " " Settle & Carlisle Line
~~→ Worked on model by same set of vehicles + locomotive

Extract from Train Graph
10.00 a.m. - 7.00 p.m.

Fig.17: The Train Graph. *This extract from the train graph I prepared for Kendal MkII in 1984 stood the test of transition to Kendal MkIII over ten years later. I show the trains which 'change identity' (see text) by a wavy line with arrowhead. It may seem complicated, but in model terms, all that matters is that the train should not arrive at the second station (in real time) before it leaves the first. It does not matter if the difference is only a minute or two on the 'real' timetable, because there is no need to assume 'correct to prototype' transit time between Kendal and Marthwaite if the train on the model is intended to represent a different prototype working at each location..*

Having established what seems like a plausible route on the map, it is not difficult to measure distances along the 'line of railway' to arrive at the length of the route; but the gradients themselves need a little care. The contour lines give a good lead (check first whether they are given in metric or imperial measures), but it may be necessary to allow for hypothetical embankments or cuttings and it is unlikely that you can allow for the more subtle gradient changes exhibited by the real railway (eg 1:100; 1:110; 1:90 in quick succession). I usually find that averaging over a mile or two of route is satisfactory and here, the old One Inch maps with 50ft contour intervals are a godsend. A drop of 50ft in one mile is a real gradient of c.1:100 (105.6 to be precise) and 100ft per mile is 1:50 for all practical purposes.

At the end of all this, the final gradient profile can be made; but this is not so that the model can be given correct values, though it can if you so wish. Rather, it is to allow a realistic calculation of times between stations when preparing the train timetable from the graph, to which subject we must now turn.

Train graphs can be confusing and complex (see Fig.17 for part of my own version), but if the modeller is prepared to spend time in their preparation, they can not only improve the 'believability' of the model, but also help develop insight into the problems of the real railway in terms of line occupation and possible 'choke' points where shunting takes place.

To prepare one, the first need is to obtain a very large sheet of graph paper to take a full day (hours and minutes) along the horizontal axis; this need not be 24 hours unless your services so demand. The vertical axis represents distances between the stations; any suitable scale will do but stations must be at the correct scale distance apart and I find it quite useful to have a vertical axis on both left and right hand edges of the sheet. The

trains can then be plotted in, starting with passenger services. I also find it helpful to use different coloured pens for each type of train, having first put them all in with a pencil.

The process is easier to do than to describe and I find it far simpler to plot all trains in one direction first. Start at the departure time opposite the station in question, mark it on the graph, then mark the arrival time at the next station and join the two together. The line then runs horizontally to represent the period of the stop and the process is repeated for all the remaining stations and trains - then do the same for the other direction. The steeper the line on the graph, the faster the train, while trains in the opposite direction slope the opposite way.

Having got the passenger trains plotted, this will reveal where a sufficiently long interval exists for a slower moving goods train. It will also show where, say, a passenger train can overtake a freight train (shunting &c.) and will certainly show all cases where trains pass each other in opposite directions. If these are relatively few, then with a bit of juggling, it may be possible to contrive them so that they always take place at a station, thus suggesting that a single track main line will be sufficient - no real railway would lay a double track if a single line with passing places could handle the traffic, though there

101

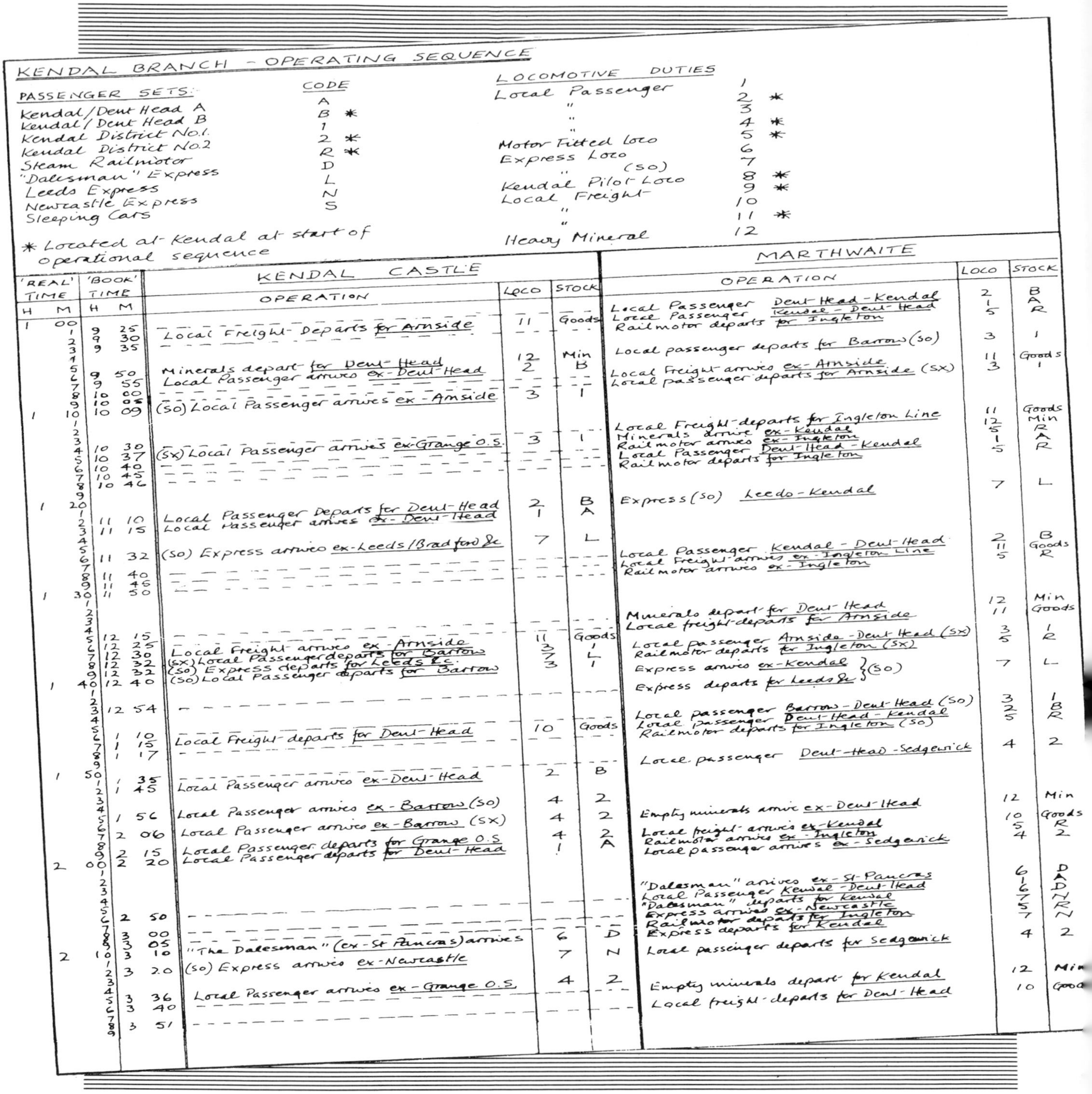

KENDAL BRANCH — OPERATING SEQUENCE

PASSENGER SETS:	CODE		LOCOMOTIVE DUTIES	
Kendal/Dent Head A	A		Local Passenger	1
Kendal/Dent Head B	B *		"	2 *
Kendal District No.1	1		"	3
Kendal District No.2	2 *		"	4 *
Steam Railmotor	R *		Motor Fitted Loco	5 *
"Dalesman" Express	D *		Express Loco	6
Leeds Express	L		(SO)	7 *
Newcastle Express	N		Kendal Pilot Loco	8 *
Sleeping Cars	S		Local Freight	9
			"	10 *
* Located at Kendal at start of			"	11 *
operational sequence			Heavy Mineral	12

'REAL' TIME		'BOOK' TIME		KENDAL CASTLE			MARTHWAITE		
H	M	H	M	OPERATION	LOCO	STOCK	OPERATION	LOCO	STOCK
1	00						Local Passenger Dent Head — Kendal	2	B
	1	9	25	Local Freight departs for Arnside	11	Goods	Local Passenger Kendal — Dent Head	1	A
	2	9	30				Railmotor departs for Ingleton	5	R
	3	9	35				Local passenger departs for Barrow (SO)	3	1
	4			Minerals depart for Dent Head	12	Min	Local Freight arrives ex-Arnside	11	Goods
	5	9	50	Local Passenger arrives ex-Dent Head	2	B		3	1
	6	9	55				Local passenger departs for Arnside (SX)		
	7								
	8	10	00		3	1			
	9	10	05						
1	10	10	09	(SO) Local Passenger arrives ex-Arnside			Local Freight departs for Ingleton Line	11	Goods
	1						Minerals arrive ex-Kendal	12	Min
	2						Railmotor arrives ex-Ingleton	5	R
	3	10	30	(SX) Local Passenger arrives ex-Grange O.S.	3	1	Local Passenger Dent Head — Kendal	1	A
	4	10	37				Railmotor departs for Ingleton	5	R
	5	10	40						
	6	10	45						
	7	10	46				Express (SO) Leeds — Kendal	7	L
	8								
	9								
1	20	11	10	Local Passenger Departs for Dent Head	2	B	Local Passenger Kendal — Dent Head	2	B
	1	11	15	Local Passenger arrives ex-Dent Head	1	A	Local Freight arrives ex-Ingleton Line	11	Goods
	2						Railmotor arrives ex-Ingleton	5	R
	3			Local Passenger arrives ex-Leeds/Bradford &c	7	L			
	4								
	5	11	32	(SO) Express arrives ex-Leeds/Bradford &c					
	6								
	7	11	40				Minerals depart for Dent Head	12	Min
	8	11	45				Local freight departs for Arnside	11	Goods
	9	11	50						
1	30								
	1								
	2								
	3						Local passenger Arnside — Dent Head (SX)	3	1
	4						Railmotor departs for Ingleton (SX)	5	R
	5	12	15	Local Freight arrives ex-Arnside	11	Goods			
	6	12	25	(SX) Local Passenger departs for Barrow	3	1	Express arrives ex-Kendal } (SO)	7	L
	7	12	30	(SO) Express departs for Leeds &c	3	L	Express departs for Leeds &c }		
	8	12	32		3	1			
1	40	12	40	(SO) Local Passenger departs for Barrow					
	1						Local passenger Barrow — Dent Head (SO)	3	1
	2						Local passenger Dent Head — Kendal	2	B
	3	12	54				Railmotor departs for Ingleton (SO)	5	R
	4								
	5	1	10	Local Freight departs for Dent Head	10	Goods	Local passenger Dent Head — Sedgwick	4	2
	6	1	15						
	7	1	17						
	8								
	9								
1	50	1	35	Local Passenger arrives ex-Dent Head	2	B			
	1	1	45				Empty minerals arrive ex-Dent Head	12	Min
	2								
	3			Local Passenger arrives ex-Barrow (SO)	4	2	Local freight arrives ex-Kendal	10	Goods
	4	1	56	Local Passenger arrives ex-Barrow (SX)	4	2	Railmotor arrives ex-Ingleton	5	R
	5						Local passenger arrives ex-Sedgwick	4	2
	6	2	06	Local Passenger departs for Grange O.S.	4	2			
	7					A			
	8	2	15	Local Passenger departs for Dent Head	1				
	9	2	20						
2	00						"Dalesman" arrives ex-St Pancras	6	D
	1						Local Passenger Kendal — Dent Head	1	A
	2						"Dalesman" departs for Kendal	6	D
	3						Express arrives ex-Newcastle	7	N
	4						Railmotor departs for Ingleton	5	R
	5	2	50				Express departs for Kendal	7	
	6	3	00					4	2
	7	3	05	"The Dalesman" (ex-St Pancras) arrives	6	D			
	8	3	10		7	N	Local passenger departs for Sedgwick		
2	10	3	20	(SO) Express arrives ex-Newcastle					
	1								
	2						Empty minerals depart for Kendal	12	Min
	3	3	36	Local Passenger arrives ex-Grange O.S.	4	2	Local freight departs for Dent Head	10	Goods
	4	3	40						
	5								
	6								
	7								
	8	3	51						
	9								

Fig.18: Planning Charts.

a) This diagram is part of the master planning chart for the operating sequence, its main function being to ensure that activities at all the modelled locations dovetail nicely together. This was again prepared for Kendal MkII and the only change when Kendal MkIII came along was to eliminate one of the local passenger sets for the Barrow Line (explained in more detail in Chapter 7), so I did not prepare a new one;

it would have taken time to compile, being hand-written, and seemed to be superfluous given the few changes, so the original was merely amended: its revised form is not shown here - too untidy!.

b) For the operators, an expanded version of the master chart is desirable (applicable to one location only), including, ideally, supplementary information regarding shunting &c. This can be done on a typewriter or word processor and a typical example from the current layout is shown here. It is easy to prepare individual 'flip over cards' from this type of document if that is preferred by the operators. I tend to use both......

KENDAL BRANCH: REVISED OPERATING SCHEDULE

NOTE: Each line space represents five minutes of <u>real</u> time - ie to indicate how much time is available between scheduled moves, thus allowing operators to plan accordingly. 'Remarks' are confined to offering hints as to what should happen (ideally!) before each scheduled move and are short enough so as not to affect the vertical scale. 'Real time' is in the LH column for convenience, not to be asssumed as the time when operations should take place save where printed **in bold for scheduled moves.** All operations start at a notional 4.05am (real time)

MARTHWAITE, SHEET 1

TIME	SCHEDULED OPERATION	REMARKS
04.05		
04.10		
04.15	**Sleeping Cars: Dent Head to Kendal**	
04.20		
04.25		
04.30		
04.35		
04.40		
04.45		
04.50	**Mineral train from Dent Head**	
04.55		1. Train stops at home signal, detaches the Barbon and
05.00		Marthwaite 'empties' to their correct locations and then
05.05		returns to rest of train in down platform
05.10		2. Balance of mineral train into down lay-by
05.15		
05.20	**Parcels and/or L.E. from Kendal**	
05.25		Spare engine spots vans to yard
05.30	**Mineral train departs for Kendal**	Spare engine spots wagons for Kendal to up platform
05.35	**Local goods from Dent Head**	Train stops at home signal
05.40		1. Spare engine draws Dent Head wagons to up lay-by
05.45		2. Train engine spots Marthwaite wagons into yard
05.50		3. Train engine collects Kendal wagons from up main
05.55		4. Re-formed local goods to down lay-by
06.00		
06.05		
06.10	**Local goods from Kendal**	1, If necessary, train stops at home signal until down
06.15		goods has finished shunting and is in down lay-by
06.20		2. Train engine collects wagons for Dent Head from
06.25		spare engine in up lay-by and replaces them with any
06.30		wagons for Marthwaite
06.35		3. Re-formed local goods to <u>down platform</u> to allow up
06.40		passenger train to pass and railcar to arrive/depart
06.45		4. Spare engine shunts Marthwaite if necessary
06.50		
06.55		
07.00		
07.05		
07.10	**Railcar from Kendal to up platform**	
07.15	**Railcar to Kirkby Lonsdale from up platform**	
07.20	**Local Passenger, Arnside to Dent Head**	
07.25	**Local goods to Kendal**	
07.30		Local goods from down platform to up starter
07.35	**Local Goods to Dent Head**	

are examples where initial provision was made for an eventual double track (bridges, &c.) which never materialised.

In my case, there seemed rather too many places where trains would pass in the country (especially on the steep banks), so I decided that the branch would need to be double track for much of its length, certainly between Kendal and Natland and probably for most of the Midland line to Dent Head, though the Furness line to Arnside could safely be left single track. This conclusion could not be determined without the train graph and although almost all these routes are 'off stage', so to speak, this preliminary exercise was very relevant to the actual detailed planning of the stations themselves.

All that then remained was to translate this information into a series of working instructions for each modelled location and I offer a typical extract at Fig.18. But before going into more detail in later chapters on this side of things and the stock planning to meet it, the final stage in the preliminary work is to ensure that the concepts can be realised in the physical space we have available.

Site considerations and the layout plan

I have been very lucky in that both the second and third 7mm layouts could be planned, with but very little change, so as to accommodate the patterns I had originally devised for the first effort, no matter how awkward the site. Indeed, the 'change of train identity' notion (above) first came to my mind during the building of the first and second layouts where all departures from Kendal simply had to go through Marthwaite (Figs.6 & 7, Chapter 3) before they could reach the fiddle yard. This very necessary modification to the programme translated happily to the third and final version to even better and more realistic effect and it was this fact which made me realise, as I have already stated earlier in this chapter, that a sound scheme is often independent of a specific track plan.

Nevertheless addressing this complex mixture of thoughts also re-activated yet another fundamental which I considered in Chapter 4, that of size and scale. Had I not had the space in which to create this sort of traffic pattern in 7mm scale after my 1981 house move, then I would have been on the 'horns of a dilemma', as they say. I did not want to go back to 4mm scale after I had enjoyed the many virtues of the larger size between 1975 and 1981 (not to mention building quite a lot of new models in that time) and although I never had to 'face the unfaceable' in this respect, I suspect that had things been different, I may well have remained with the 7mm option and tried to design a less complex scheme. I cannot be sure, of course, since it would still have to be operationally interesting, this being the objective of all my efforts - which leads me nicely into the final funamental which needs to be addressed: the factors affecting the layout plan itself.

I shall return to a general discussion on layout planning in Chapter 9, along with offering a few possible ideas, but this seems to be the appropriate moment at which to address some specific principles which have to be born in mind when providing trackage to meet the needs which the above kind of analysis presents, using my own layout scheme as usual and starting with the particular problems of terminus design.

Fig.19: Platform Occupation - Kendal Castle. Making this chart revealed the need for four platforms at Kendal. For much of the time, two or three would suffice but it clearly drew attention to a few places in the proposed programme where an extra platform would help - see text.

I have never found it easy to design terminal stations. My first EM gauge effort (Marthwaite), a small country terminus in its first incarnation, went through two major rebuilds before I got it close to my liking (Fig.1, Chapter 3). The embryonic Kendal was even worse. The difficulty was that which may well have faced real railway builders - how to get all the required traffic facilities into a restricted urban space. Those readers who remember Leeds Central station (ex-GNR/LNER) will recall what a cramped place it was and how short its platforms were in relation to the important trains which used it. Kendal Castle has, in the event, turned out to be rather similar in principle if not in strict complexity of scope.

The essential need, therefore, is to establish the minimum requirement and hope it can be fitted in. For example, if the timetable reveals that as many as three passenger trains will arrive at the terminus before any of them leaves, it may be necessary to provide three separate platforms. Alternatively, it may be better to provide extra sidings into which stock can be shunted - this decision is down the the individual. But it is only at this point that we can really determine whether a proposed layout is too lavish or too limited. I therefore decided to produce a 'platform occupation' chart based on my proposed timetable (Fig.19). Study of this revealed that while, with some slight adjustment, two platforms might just suffice at a pinch, a third would be very desirable if possible.

This would give a marginally surplus platform capacity for some of the time and would also allow for some flexibility of operation. And in my own specific case, since I did not have the lateral space for a fully separated but wholly essential 'goods arrival/departure' line, I actually designed a four platform terminus wherein one platform is almost exclusively used for goods trains - not unprototypical, by the way. It was signalled for passenger operation *in extremis* and as things have transpired, it sees one passenger arrival (though not its subsequent departure) at the busiest time of the day.

Similar thought processes applied to the planned freight services and locomotive movements will also give a clear idea of how many sidings (and what type) will be needed in the goods yard, along with establishing the minimum facility for locomotive handling. In my case, the former could (just) be contrived in terms of the number of sidings (albeit shorter than

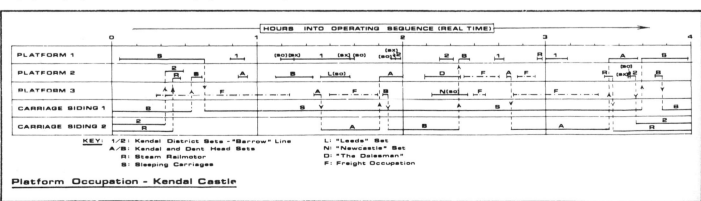

104

Plates 88/89: Kendal MPD. *Most modellers like to have a motive power facility and it was fortunate that the operating pattern of the layout justified reasonable provisioning at Kendal. These two track level views (taken in opposite directions from behind Platform 1 and its approaches) show the bulk of it. There is a bit more scenery to tackle, mostly by way of adding detail behind the coal stage, burying much of*

the track in 'sludge' and increasing the amount of grime.....

The shed is based on the real Midland structure at St Albans, but rendered in stone finish, while the working miniature Midland signals serve to release engines to the main line. They are interlocked to some extent with the track sections - see Chapter 8 - and are still finished in MR 'livery', it being argued that the LMS had not yet repainted them.....

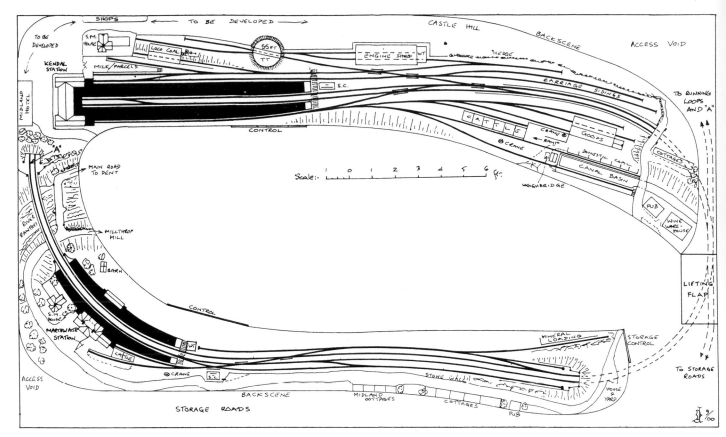

Fig.20 Kendal Mk III - final version: 1999 onwards. *I have include this second plan of the final 7mm layout, partly to make this part of the text simpler to follow without excessive back-reference to Chapter 3, but also to show the final changes to the locomotive yard around the turntable at Kendal (fewer dead-end roads), together with the slightly enhanced siding facilities at Marthwaite (c.f. Fig.9, Chapter 3). The addition of the single slip on the down main line, plus the mineral siding, much reduced the need to shunt forward via the tunnel (which involved seeking prior permission from the next forward section), so as to get into the down layby with most normal length freight trains.*

I would have liked), while the latter revealed that at least six engines (plus the railmotor) would need to be stabled overnight at Kendal, thus requiring a proper locomotive depot rather than a mere servicing facility, which reminded me, *en passant*, how often we provide engine sheds on a layout simply because they look nice - in my case, I actually needed one! The final arrangement is shown at Fig.9 (Chapter 3), its earlier versions being given at Figs. 6 & 7 in the same chapter.

In like manner, a similar line of approach will also reveal the maximum occupation of any hidden storage sidings and/or concealed running loops, thus indicating how many will be needed. Obviously there must be enough for each train or, if two trains must occupy the same storage road (perhaps for reasons of baseboard width) one must consider whether one or two storage sidings might be long enough to accept two trains, always provided that the order in which they leave is in reverse of that whereby they arrived.....

A quite different (and often more difficult) problem can be encountered with passing stations. Normally, on a typical British double track line, they would have two passenger platforms, a main station building (with offices) and some form of freight handling facility, however rudimentary. How much elaboration there should be on this basic theme is very hard to assess - even the Midland got it wrong on the Settle and Carlisle at times, where some stations were clearly over-provided with facilities in relation to the traffic which was eventually on offer.

In my 7mm efforts, where Marthwaite is transmogrified into a through station compared with its 4mm scale role, site space determined the final solution in all three cases and this caused a bit of philosophical head-scratching in the final two versions. As I have already indicated, Marthwaite represents the real market town of Sedbergh (I simply changed its name to that of an adjacent parish with a nicer name!) and, as such, would probably merit the sort of facilities which, on the real Settle and Carlisle, would be of the Settle, Appleby, Kirkby Stephen &c. degree of complexity. This was actually achieved on the first 7mm layout (Fig.6) and looked very promising before an essential house move forced a change. It may now be seen (shorn of its Settle and Carlisle architecture) forming the main through station on the NRM's 7mm scale display layout for those interested.

Subsequent attempts have been rather more difficult. I never really solved it to my satisfaction on the second attempt (Fig.7) and on the third and present layout (Fig.20, but see also

Attention to detail

Several years ago, as part of my publishing activities, I commissioned my friend, Ron Prattley, to take pictures of two of the finest layouts I have seen and have been pleased to re-use some of these pictures in this book. Here are two more which encapsulate much of what I have been trying to convey. They scarcely need captions but, for the record, they show a Marylebone express behind a Great Central 4-6-0 leaving the terminus at Buckingham on Peter Denny's famous 4mm scale layout and a Midland semi-fast entering Lonsdale from the south and passing the LNWR locomotive yard on Neil Corner's impressive 7mm scale layout which I helped to design and is explained in more detail in Chapter 9.

Stretching the imagination.....

When I started in this hobby, the area beyond the layout, no matter how good the backscene, if, indeed, such was present at all, was usually left entirely to the imagination; but with the advent of computer technology, all sorts of tricks can be played. These pictures were taken by another friend, Tony Garner, not a railway enthusiast but a retired professional photographer who showed interest in the models and asked if he could use the layout by way of conducting experiments with his camera. I did not know what to expect but these images took my breath away. Kendal goods yard has now been given a proper Lakeland background while at Marthwaite, the scene has been enhanced by a magnificent skyscape, the foreground being extended into what is, in reality, the floor of my 'train shed'.... By some strange quirk of fate, the latter picture is the only one I have of the daily mineral empties, with appropriate 'Settle Limes' wagons, arriving on the scene behind ex-LNWR 0-8-0 No.9090.

Plate 90: Congestion at Marthwaite. *For reasons explained in the text, the layout at Marthwaite is only barely adequate at busy times. In this view, two local passenger trains are present at the same time, the railcar is in the bay and the tiny goods yard is almost full to capacity. It only needs a goods train in one or both of the headshunts to give the operator a real problem.....*

Fig.9, Chapter 3) I did not have quite enough length or width available to create a full facility. However, when planning the latter, I discovered, quite by chance, that the site would permit an exact re-creation in 7mm scale of the old Garsdale Road track plan, which seemed somehow serendipitous, given that it was not only my favourite but also undoubtedly the best of my 4mm scale efforts - so it had to go in. But how could I justify the reduced facilities for such an important town?

I have to admit that the final explanation is a bit contrived. I explain the present rather simple station by pointing out that it is some distance from the town centre for reasons of local geography (true) and that the real life station at Sedbergh on the LNWR Low Gill line, which preceded the Midland's entry to the town, had already taken much of the traffic, which would probably be true had 'my' line ever been built. I could also argue that there was no space at the chosen location for a proper goods yard (again true) and that this facility was therefore located beyond the tunnel at the Kendal end of the station - Knaresborough on the NER was such a place if you want a real-life equivalent. But even then, in the light of operating experience, I had to modify (by slight enhancement) the track layout at Marthwaite to enable it to cope with the

traffic pattern I had devised. This took the form of an extra slip point on the main line and a new mineral loading facility which is also shown on the revised plan at Fig.20.

It will therefore be seen that when it comes to the practical realisation of even the best thought-out schemes, there is either insufficient space to produce trackage for the desired operating pattern or, alternatively, that the optimum operating pattern is too restricted to justify the type of track layout envisaged or desired - it will usually more often be the former and it will be rare if you get it right first time! On balance, however, I think it is better if the envisaged layout is too complex for the traffic on offer. It is easier to simplify the layout and this, by way of bonus, may have the wholly desirable effect of enhancing the spaciousness of the scene - something which my good friend Jack Ray discovered when converting his famous Crewchester garden line from clockwork to electric power many years ago.

Nevertheless, and despite the many interesting, albeit often very frustrating problems which this approach to pre-planning of the fundamentals may throw up, I still consider that before expending precious time, cash and energy in actually building a layout, some form of preliminary attention along the lines I have advocated will usually serve to clarify your priorities in quite a number of associated areas. I am not saying that any or all should go to quite the degree of detail which I have done, unless they so wish, but I do think it to be worth a bit of thought, after which, we are probably ready to decide what sort of trains we might need......

CHAPTER 7

Train formations and stock planning

"Yet the order of the acts is planned and the end of the way inescapable."
Boris Pasternak

REGARDLESS of the (usually uninformed) comments on the current railway system (2001) by many practitioners in the modern media, the prototype railway has always been and still is a highly regulated affair with an enviable historic reputation for safety and sound organisation. It therefore follows that if our models are to convince, especially in the operational sense, they should not only look the part to the best of our ability, but also give the impression of the underlying order and precision which characterised the prototype. Nowhere was this more true than in the realm of the trains themselves, which, even in their simplest forms, were run to a far more elaborate pattern of both locomotive allocation and rolling stock provision than is often supposed.

If we are to re-create this sort of impression in believable form in our models, then long before we think in terms of the 'hardware' which we might want to replicate, we first need to know a little more of the way in which things actually worked. I shall therefore begin this chapter by looking first at the matter of train formation and marshalling, which seems to me to be one of the areas where many folk may be confused, not least those recent converts to the hobby who never experienced the traditional railway in its prime at first hand. It is one thing to be able to work out how many and what sort of locomotives, carriages and wagons are needed in strictly numerical terms, but we then need to study the way in which trains themselves were made up and operated in the steam locomotive, vacuum braked age - likely to be the commonest choice for most potential railway modellers of the historic British scene. I have always found it easier to plan my trains once I had worked out, as carefully as I could, what their precise roles would be.

The principles of train make up

If we consider the c.1900-1970 period (give or take a few years at either end) as being likely to embrace the majority of potential historical railway models, then the modeller should be aware of the basic principles which govern the way the trains should appear and, curiously, this has nothing to do with ownership or livery. My good friend Bob Essery (well known modeller and ex-fireman with much experience of the ways of the 'traditional' railway) has often made the point that the

essential *modus operandum* of the railway altered but little from late Victorian days for three-quarters of a century or more: only the rolling hardware and colour schemes changed. In a strange sort of way this is very re-assuring, for it means that, within broad limits, we can make our choices from a very broad spectrum of possibilities, provided that we know how they were operated; the basics are not hard to understand.

There were, of course, rule books to follow on the real railway - and a copy of the relevant rule book can be a most useful document for the historical modeller if he/she can find one, see Chapter 5 - but a few more general matters can be identified in terms of train make-up, types of vehicle, order of marshalling and so forth. From these and with a little effort, it is often possible to make intelligent and informed 'guesses', in the absence of anything more positive, when we try to make up our model formations.

Let us therefore turn first to passenger trains, where the only vital factor, apart from a continuous automatic brake throughout (commonly vacuum in Britain during the period I have in mind, though there were several companies which adopted the Westinghouse air brake alternative), is that there must be at least one hand-braked vehicle in which the guard would ride - he must not only have somewhere to base himself but also have access to an emergency hand brake. There would also be luggage and, maybe, parcels or other such facility (ie extra to that provided in the passenger carrying areas), and this was typically combined with the guard's and brake provisoning in the commodious 'van' portion of a hand-braked vehicle. This could vary from a full brake (with no passenger seats) to a carriage almost wholly composed of passenger carrying areas with but minimum provision for the guard/handbrake/luggage facilities. Whether or not such vehicles had side corridors, lavatories or other such exotica was totally subsidiary to their main guard/brake function.

Any train of more than two or three coaches would often have two hand-braked vehicles and it was normal to have these at the outer ends of the formation, brake ends outwards. But there were many exceptions such as 'inside out' brakes and what were often called 'swingers' - ie carriages without any handbrake marshalled to the rear of the brake vehicle proper, although their automatic braking systems would, of course, be

Plates 91/92: Basic trains, prototype and model. These images indicate that the fundamentals of passenger train operation did not change for several generations. The first picture, two of the late Jim Richards' fine 7mm scale models of LNWR prototypes (now on display in their entirety at the NRM) show what is, for all its minimum status, a proper train of late-19th Century vintage. The second view taken over 50 years later (at Dillicar troughs on the old LNWR line through the Lune valley in 1949), shows a similar basic one coach operation of inspection saloon plus locomotive. They can be properly described as trains because both coaches contain guard's accommodation with its essential hand brake apparatus. *(Ron Prattley; Eric Treacy)*

connected properly to the rest of the train. Ideally, on the LMS at all events, no more than eight axles (ie two four-wheel bogie coaches or their equivalent) would be found to the rear of the brake-equipped carriage, but there were many exceptions.

In modelling terms, this means that one handbrake-fitted carriage will *in extremis*, do for any train up to about five carriages, provided it is placed somewhere in the middle of the train. But that said, it must also be mentioned that in the final locomotive-hauled BR 'Inter City' trains of the pre-HST (and later) era, there was often but one brake-ended vehicle - and it did not seem to matter whether it was front, back or centre!

Thus, the simplest passenger train (excluding single unit railcars) could consist of a prime mover with one carriage,

provided that the latter had space for the guard, &c. It is therefore perfectly proper to operate a locomotive and full brake and call it a 'parcels train'. Generally, however, more than one carriage was usually involved, containing more than one class of passenger accommodation. In this respect, a quite useful rule of thumb is to keep first and third class in proportions between 1:3 and 1:6, depending on the nature of the area modelled. Here, it may be worth mentioning that the traditional second class in Britain, already abolished by many companies before that time, was abandoned almost entirely in 1912, save for a few minor exceptions, some of which lasted until 1956, thus perpetuating the curiously British 1st/3rd division for over 40 years. The modern situation, wherein we

Plates 93-95: The archetypal 'local'. *The short local passenger train is an obvious and deservedly popular choice in terms of modelling. The close study of contemporary pictures is recommended, for the variety was enormous and tempts the conclusion that we do not need to have the same trains as everyone else on our layouts. These three are typical:*

The first picture, taken at Hellifield at or just after the turn of the 19th/20th Centuries, shows an original Johnson 4-4-0, No.238, rebuilt with 'H type' boiler, on a typically short set of Midland clerestories: brake composite and luggage composite (both with lavatories and near-identical save that only one has guard's accommodation) plus a six wheel brake at the rear. It has not yet been put into the passenger platform; the exact working is not known. (B.C. Lane Collection)

Next is a typical LMS 'Inter-District' semi-fast working from the 1930s at Marsden on the Huddersfield to Manchester line: two brake thirds plus composite, all with lavatories for at least some customers. An interesting point to note is that the central composite is of LNWR design, the flanking brakes being to LMS standard pattern. Two LNWR design bogie vans bring up the rear. Pedants may like to note that the engine (Stanier 2-6-0 No.13248) bears a post-1935 12B shed plate on the smokebox door (Carlisle, Upperby - sic!) but still carries its pre-1934 running number; it later became No.2948.

The last view, an Eric Treacy 'classic', shows former Great Eastern Class E4 2-4-0 No.7416 with a three coach train of former North Eastern clerestories leaving Penrith (ex-LNWR) with a cross-Pennine train via Kirkby Stephen and Stainmore, probably bound for Darlington. The E4s were drafted into the area by the LNER and given bigger cabs for the protection of the crew on this exposed route. Note that the leading third class carriage is 'outside' the two brake ends which are not identical: only the trailing example has a lavatory. The train may even be third class only - details not quite clear.

112

are seen as either first class or 'standard' can safely be ignored!

Coming back to the real thrust of this analysis, it is worth commenting that excursion trains would be predominantly third class (maybe wholly so), as would be the now long-vanished workmen's trains. Business expresses would often have more first class (proportionally) than, say, a cross-country local; but a Saturday only 'extra' would have far more third class than its mid-week equivalent.

In terms of marshalling, the first class areas were, wherever possible, put close together, either somewhere in the centre of the train or exclusively at one end. A favourite LMS practice (copied widely by BR and its latter day successors, especially in the fixed formation trains on most main lines) was to put the first class at the 'London' end and separate this area from the lower orders by way of the catering facility. On the historical railway (and this gives reason for quite a bit of imaginative carriage modelling when it comes to express trains), this was often a lavish facility for both classes but sadly, in our more 'enlightened' modern era, it is usually proper diners for the first class but buffet facilities only for the 'riff-raff.' They call this progress, of course, but small wonder that so many of us elect deliberately to 'wind the clock back' in modelling terms if only to remind ourselves of how things once were and could still be - sermon over!

Plate 96: A different sort of local. *For those whose interests in the traditional railway favour a somewhat later period than the mid-1930s, it is well worth recalling that some local passenger trains were made up from gangwayed stock, not infrequently with rather more imposing motive power than might be expected for such workings. This example at Beattock, taken by Eric Treacy in the early 1950s is not untypical. The train is a Carlisle to Glasgow 'stopper', entirely 'LMS' in concept if not in livery. The four carriages comprise a three-coach 'Inter-Corridor Set' of Stanier stock (two brake thirds and a composite) plus an extra corridor third of much older (c.1925) design 'outside' the rear brake van - note that the leading brake third is 'inside-out'. The engine is a rebuilt Royal Scot No.46112* Sherwood Forester *which, on examination, reveals a Leeds (Holbeck) shed plate on the smokebox door. The engine was probably commandeered at short notice at Carlisle for some long-forgotten reason, Leeds engines normally working through to Glasgow via the old Glasgow and South Western route on genuine express trains.*

Nevertheless, all prejudice apart, this brief and arguably biassed digression from the main theme does serve to indicate how much more variety there was in the historic railway; and in terms of passenger operations there is much more to add, all of which can enhance the operating potential of a model. Some of it depends on the specific nature of our layouts but several further possibilities are well worth mentioning.

Plate 97: Express Passenger. The formation of express trains is often difficult to determine from prototype pictures alone and if you wish to model a real formation, further research may well be needed - try the NRM library for marshalling details. But an understanding of the governing principles can be just as helpful if you wish to 'invent' a reasonable train - and just to show that they need not be especially glamorous, I have chosen this Eric Treacy picture, taken at Bangor in the early 1950s; it was, in fact, the inspiration for my own five-coach 'express' on the original 4mm scale Marthwaite layout, even down to the use of a Stanier 2-6-4T - see Plate 27, Chapter 3. The prototype view shows Bangor-based 2-6-4T No.42617 with an unidentified train carrying the express headlamp code. The first carriage is a wood panelled corridor composite (built in 1930) still in LMS colours and behind it is a Stanier corridor third. Not until the third vehicle is reached do we have a brake-ended carriage (see text), in this case a brake third. The exact length of the train cannot be determined but it is unlikely to have had catering provision and the probability is that behind the brake third came the rest of a routine three- or four-coach 'Inter Corridor' set.

If an express train consisted of two or more sections (eg but not exclusively the LMS 'Royal Scot' with its Edinburgh and Glasgow portions), then it would not be at all unusual to find duplicated catering facilities within the one train. Equally, and here the Southern Railway 'Atlantic Coast Express' is a classic example, one might well find so many independent parts that the whole train represented a veritable cornucopia of carriage types, many of which would be one or two-coach portions and destined to be attached or detached at intermediate locations - a wonderful excuse for a few exotic carriages, even on a modest branch line layout. I have certainly 'milked' this idea to full effect in my own modelling activities.

In addition to this, it is well worth bearing in mind that the 'passenger' category embraced all manner of other vehicles, ie parcels vans, milk vans, horseboxes, special cattle vans, Post Office vehicles and the like. These were collectively referred to by that wonderfully vague, somewhat ambiguous yet fully understood and all-embracing term: 'Non-Passenger Coaching Stock' - NPCS for short. They offer a marvellous opportunity in the model context, since all that really mattered was that the vehicles were 'passenger train compatible' in the running sense (ie automatically braked and capable of running at reasonable speed) and that they reflected, as far as possible, the needs of the area in which they operated. They could be added to or detached from passenger trains, more or less 'ad lib', and must surely commend themselves to modellers. And at the opposite end of the operating spectrum, there were even special rules relating to the odd occasion where non-automatically braked vehicles might (just) be permitted on passenger trains.

On the freight side, all that was necessary was a prime mover and a goods brake van to accompany the cargo carrying vehicles. The brake van was almost always at the rear (there were rare occasions when a goods train could be propelled brake first along the main line) and, until almost the end of the 'traditional' operating era (say after 1970 or so), the question of automatic braking of all vehicles from the engine itself rarely arose. The engine could brake itself and the guard applied the handbrake in the guard's van to control the train. The wagons themselves had handbrakes (often only on one side, however) which were mainly used as parking brakes in sidings after shunting; but at the top of steeper gradients out on the line, handbrakes could be applied ('pinned down') on some or all of the wagons to add extra brake power. An appreciation of this

Plates 98/99: Express Parcels. *Parcels trains were often given much the same sort of priority as express passenger types and can be a fine source of inspiration for the modeller; and they do not have to be quite as big as this pair to look authentic. They were taken by Eric Treacy on Shap bank and at Dillicar troughs, respectively, both heading north. Although separated by at least 15 years (c.1938 and c.1954) they are* almost identical in style with a typical assemblage of fully braked vehicles. Although the majority of the latter cannot be identified with precision, the fact that both trains contain many fitted four-wheel vans is self-evident. Note that the pre-war example is headed by an express passenger type (Class 5XP 4-6-0 No.5674 Duncan), *the BR example being in charge of Class 5 4-6-0 No.45048*

During the traditional era, the most common long distance main line freight trains carried the 'one over one' headlamp code of the 'Through Freight', the only real criterion being that they ran (officially) over 15 miles without stopping. They were many and various and these three examples are quite typical of the variety which could be seen. Albeit longer than most layouts could accommodate, they offer many ideas, some of which I was happy enough to copy with my main line ventures in 4mm scale.

The first picture, taken in May 1940 at Baron's Wood on the Settle-Carlisle by Norman Wilkinson, shows a nicely random set of vehicles behind ex-Midland Class 3F 0-6-0 No.3231, a not unusual type for this sort of job - they were tough little engines and popular with the men, often more so than the later Class 4F 0-6-0s. The latter, in the shape of Skipton-based No.4222, was photographed by Eric Treacy in the Aire Valley near Keighley c.1946-7 on a train of mostly open wagons, some of which are sheeted down, not always tidily. The third picture, also by Eric Treacy, shows a vast train of empty coal wagons near Mytholmroyd on the four-track Calder valley main line of the old LYR behind LMS standard Class 7F 0-8-0 No.49674. Of one thing we can be certain: there were no fitted wagons on any of these trains.

Plates 103/104: Fitted Freight. *The head lamp code carried on these two trains denoted what was still something of a rarity even in the BR phase of the steam era - a fully fitted freight. Even so, these relatively uncommon trains only had to have 'at least one third' of their vehicles properly fitted to qualify for superior status. The first view, taken by Eric Treacy at Scout Green on the climb to Shap in the early 1950s (note the banker), indicates that like parcels trains (Plate 98), fully fitted freight could also be in charge of express types, in this case un-named and unrebuilt Patriot Class 4-6-0 No.45542. The second picture shows Class 5 No.44943, storming through Kirkby Stephen in 1962. As can be seen, both trains consisted mostly of covered vans. These were the most likely, though not exclusive, vehicles to be given automatic brakes since they generally carried more valuable and/or more vulnerable loads. 'En passant', the same head code was used for 'Empty Coaching Stock' trains, but the latter were 'belled' differently between the signal boxes.*

near-primitive prototype situation is vital if our models are to have any historical believability.

As automatic brakes began to be fitted to goods vehicles, a few additional rules began to apply - and these do affect model train marshalling. On the main line, express freight trains with a proportion of wagons fitted with automatic brakes would have all such vehicles immediately behind the engine, their brakes being connected to the locomotive and applied by the driver. This was known as the 'fitted head' of the train and even if it only consisted of a few vehicles, it could considerably enhance the brake power available and allow the train to run at a greater speed.

It should, however, be pointed out that automatic brake-fitted wagons were very thin on the ground and generally confined to those which carried perishable or valuable cargo: fish, fruit, meat, dairy produce &c. In consequence, a 'fully fitted' freight, which could run at an even greater speed than a part-fitted version, was a very rare creature indeed until well after World War II, and not all that common afterwards. But since fitted wagons allowed trains to run at higher speeds, the railways tended to concentrate their often meagre supply of such stock into fully or partially fitted trains to speed up the traffic flow and several categories of freight train arose in consequence - usually reflecting the number of fully braked wagons which, in turn, determined the speed at which they could run. Timetables were planned accordingly and the best freights could be given a similar sort of priority to the passenger workings, sometimes greater.

The 'pick-up' freight, however - the train which merely collected or delivered wagons from intermediate stations to take them to or from marshalling yards - was often operated by a locomotive not even equipped with automatic vacuum brake. In this case, fitted vehicles were treated like any others and often added to the train at random. But a few vehicle types, even when running 'loose-coupled' (ie no automatic brake in use) were usually located in specific places wherever possible.

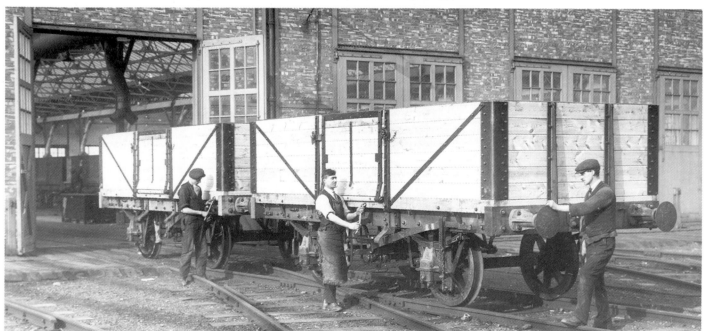

Plates 105/106: Axleboxes. *The first view shows a typical array of coal wagons with grease axle boxes, being unloaded at Kildwick & Crosshills station between Keighley and Skipton on the Midland main line north of Leeds. The wagons seem very new (the paint is abnormally glossy for a coal wagon which had seen much use) and are but four planks deep, which suggests a sort of late 1890s/early 1900s date. The LNER official picture shows a pair of new wagons with oil axleboxes emerging from Darlington (Faverdale) works in the 1920s. The wagons are bigger but technology has not moved on very much (nor had it on the other railways either): note that wooden underframes are still used. (Peter Whitaker Collection, courtesy B.C. Lane - 1)*

Loaded cattle wagons, for example, were marshalled next to the engine (to lessen the risk of injury to animals in the see-saw motion of a freight train), whilst gunpowder wagons and petroleum tanks tended to go towards the rear (but never next to the guard's brake van) for obvious reasons. In fact, it was quite common to place a few empty wagons (usually known as 'runners') fore and aft of a rake of 'inflammable cargo' vehicles if they would otherwise be next to the engine or brake van.

Similar runners would also be placed adjacent to any wagon with an overhanging load at one end - eg timber and the like.

At the main marshalling yards, the wagons from the various pick-up freights from outlying areas were sorted by destination into outgoing express or through freight trains. Here, the fitted vehicles (if present) would form one group at the head of the train, the non-fitted stock coming behind them. Additionally, when full or part fitted trains became more common and train speeds increased, the railways began to consider the matter of axleboxes rather more carefully.

In steam days, there were two sorts of freight axlebox, those lubricated with grease (almost solid when cool) and those lubricated by oil. Grease (or 'fat') boxes were the older standard and relied on the friction of the axle rotating within the axlebox to warm-up and melt the semi-solid grease and thus lubricate the bearings. Oil boxes were much better in that the oil was always liquid, thus giving better lubrication and allowing the wagons to run at higher speeds. This difference did not matter too much when all freight was slow speed and unfitted, but as automatic brakes came into use on even a few vehicles, the consequential higher speed of the train could cause grease boxes to run too hot and *in extremis* sometimes catch fire! As a result, the railways began to exclude grease box wagons from their better freight trains and, as a rough rule of thumb, it would not normally be prototypical to operate, on a model, a main line freight with a fitted head *and* unfitted grease box wagons to the rear, though I have no doubt that it *did* sometimes happen in real life.....

Additional ramifications were caused by 'through pipe' wagons - vehicles having a vacuum pipe running from one end to the other but without their own automatic brakes. This then allowed the continuous vacuum to be maintained between fully braked wagons on either side and they could go in the middle of the fitted head, sometimes even on passenger trains, subject to strict rules, of course. Cattle wagons were particularly common candidates for a through pipe since it allowed them to be placed in the preferred position at the front of the train without destroying the fitted head and thus able to enjoy faster transits. Through pipe vehicles - a typically cheap British response to a fundamental problem on which the railways were not prepared to spend real money (sic!) - were sometimes referred to as 'partially fitted' in the operating instructions, &c.

It is for the modeller to try and assess the likely nature of the freight trains on the layout and run them accordingly. In general, main line trains will have their wagons arranged by destination, as will inward bound (usually loaded) local good trains. The precise order of marshalling for each destination will depend on the siding layout to be shunted and whether or not this is best achieved from the front or back of the train, the principle being to minimise shunting moves.

Outward bound pick-up freights, save for single cargo types (eg cattle trains) would present a somewhat random mix until they reached the next marshalling yard and the daily pick-up would itself do the least amount of shunting possible, partly to save time and also because constantly reversing the locomotive can be hard and tiring work for the crew, who also have to work the train along the line as well - train engines always did their own shunting at intermediate places along the route.

Finally, it should be pointed out that when it comes to specific wagon types, the modeller would do well to avoid almost all the more exotic varieties. Common or garden coal and merchandise wagons would be the norm, the majority of the latter being of the open type, often with their load protected by a tarpaulin sheet. Covered vans were always a minority type (be they fitted or not) during the heyday of the steam railway. The specialist vehicles tended to be seen most often on the main lines in connection with specific traffic flows, regularly running between a few fixed points only and rarely being seen off their well-established routes.

It will thus be see that in a definitive historical model there is considerable scope for operational subtlety in terms of authentic movements and marshalling and the subject well repays close study via archive photographs, rule books and the like. So, having established how best to operate our trains, we can now turn to the matter of how to plan them in model form. This is a twofold process, consisting first of defining the trains themselves and then working out how many and what sorts of vehicles might be needed. I shall cover them in this order and again use my own latest layout to exemplify some of the ideas.

Establishing the train types

With any luck, all the above mentioned planning, both in this chapter and the last, may well have begun to establish in the modeller's mind a sort of 'character' which the finished system will hopefully display; for it is not as academic and sterile as it may seem. In fact, during one of many such sessions, I got so absorbed that it struck me that if I was not careful, I would have the set-up so well worked out in my mind that there may perhaps be no need to build any models at all! Perhaps all I needed was a good track plan, a vivid imagination and a large number of coloured pins to represent the trains, locomotives and so forth - actually, the latter is not a bad idea in terms of evaluating an operating layout. But the real next step is to translate the pattern of traffic into trains, locomotives &c., and this is where the real fun begins.

First and foremost is to evaluate the types of trains which will most accurately reproduce the workings required and the first essential is to establish 'how many?' I shall analyse the precise rolling stock implications later, but meantime, in my context, I soon discovered that the passenger train requirement was likely to be as follows:

a) For the Kendal-Dent Head local service: two non-corridor local sets.

b) For the Kendal-Arnside (Barrow) services: one local non-corridor set, two not being out of the question.

c) For local 'shuttle' services: one steam railcar or push-pull driving trailer.

d) For the overnight service: between two and four through carriages, including sleeping car(s).

e) For the principal London service: one main line corridor set of some five to seven vehicles, including dining car.

f) For the summer only through trains: two sets (one LNER) of about six, mainly corridor vehicles, possibly with dining or buffet facility in one of them.

- plus, possibly, one or two spare carriages and a reasonably representative selection of NPCS (see previous section).

It will be noted that the Dent Head-Arnside service is not included. This is because of the 'change of identity' situation outlined in the last chapter. Set (b) will therefore serve for this duty too; but a second 'Barrow' set would give more flexiblity when the higher priorities are met.

A similar analysis of freight working suggested that the following trains would be needed, though here I am thinking in terms of 'engine and brake' combinations; the wagons would, of course, vary from day to day, unlike the passenger sets:

a) For the Kendal-Dent Head local pick-up workings: two engines and brakes

b) For the Kendal-Arnside pick-up service: one engine and

brake, though two could be considered - see remarks above about the Barrow line passenger trains.

c) For cattle workings: one engine and brake.

d) For mineral workings: one engine and brake.

- plus one or two spare brake vans.

Having sorted out this situation, we can then consider the locomotives, by which I mean the minimum number needed *in reality* to run the service. No real railway would provide much more than was essential, least of all on the sort of secondary line which I and many others choose to model. From this, I soon concluded that I would need three each in the 'local passenger' and 'local freight' categories, three engines for the through passenger trains, one 'mineral' and one 'cattle' engine plus a railcar or push-pull engine. It also seemed likely that Kendal might need a resident 'pilot' engine given the amount of traffic it would be handling - which has turned out to be true.

To these, I added my out of period trains which, I reckoned, would number about four or five. I had planned space for them and they would be introduced 'as and when' so to speak - ie usually when I felt like making them in a single 'hit'.

And so, having deduced the right sort of trains, the final phase is to decide what they should look like. This can also raise the matter of precise vehicle quantities, especially in the field of freight operation, but I think this is easier to do as a later and separate exercise, so I will follow that approach.

Choosing the prototypes

I guess I am not alone in having my personal favourites, and it is at this stage in the process that we can first find out if they are likely to be relevant to our concept. There is much freedom of choice as far as the prototype is concerned, even within a strictly defined set of parameters such as I have suggested, but we need to make sure that it does not get out of hand. By this I mean that if choices are too far divorced from what might have happened in reality, then the illusion we are trying to create is at risk of being destroyed. So let us see how these thoughts turned out in my own case, dealing with them more or less in the order given above.

In terms of passenger trains, close scrutiny of many pictures from the late 1920s/early 1930s revealed an almost 'anything goes' situation as far as carriage styles were concerned on rural LMS services. Their types, however, were far more consistent and formed up much in line with the principles I have outlined. A fairly common feature was their relative shortness (two to four carriages) and their use of modest sized engines, albeit in some variety. This offered practical modelling advantages in terms of train length related to layout size and formed quite a contrast with the generally longer stopping trains found in suburban areas, usually made up from far more consistently styled stock. This gave me the perfect opportunity to indulge several of my own preferences without things looking out of place, so the following trains were planned, this time associating engines with carriages:

a) The Kendal-Dent Head locals: These were decided as three-coach sets, one of which would be Midland clerestories, so I built a six, eight and twelve-wheel example to get some

variety. One of them has lavatories (not essential but not uncommon) and there is only one brake; and it is in the middle. The second set is an ex-LYR LBL formation (Leeds, Bradford, Liverpool), arguably the tidiest train on the line. I could have used early period LMS standard stock but it is only 1928, so I presumed that these rather older carriages (built c.1908) had been relegated to the country from their one time urban haunts. They also presented an interesting model challenge with their inward tapering brake ends. Handling these trains are ex-MR 4-4-0s and I chose quite beefy ones because of the gradients. One is a Class 3 'Belpaire' No.773 and the other is '990' Class 4 No.809, renumbered from 999 by the LMS in 1928. When first built, these latter engines were mostly intended for the Settle and Carlisle line and the renumbered presentation is a modest touch to hint at the date.

b) The Kendal-Arnside set: Here I wanted something rather old fashioned and I had both the data and the parts available to make a trio of former Glasgow & South Western 43ft low roof bogie coaches - a little off their beat but it is post-grouping and they look very similar to Midland types. They are augmented by a genuine Midland low roof six-wheeler. Ideally, there ought to be one or two Furness carriages in this set and these may be substituted one day. To handle this train, I have two diminutive engines: Ex-Furness Sharp Stewart 4-4-0 No.10133 and ex-LNWR 'Jumbo' 2-4-0 No.5012 *John Ramsbottom*. Their non-Midland origin serves to further differentiate the train from the two Dent Head sets and the two engines allow the 'identity change', though the carriages remain the same. One of these two engines also works the cattle train as part of its roster and No.5012 is painted in a unique livery which dates it precisely to 1928

c) The 'Shuttle': This is a kit-built model of an ex-LNWR steam railcar which was withdrawn c.1930, again helping to date the line.

d) The overnight carriages: This is a motley assortment consisting of an ex-Midland clerestory full brake, a similar vintage clerestory side corridor composite, a venerable ex-LNWR clerestory first class sleeping car and a brand new LMS standard third class sleeping car of the type introduced in 1928. To these I have added a Newspaper brake van from the LNER (presumably sent from Leeds, York or wherever) and the train is handled by one of the two Midland 4-4-0s as part of its daily roster.

e) 'The Dalesman' Express: This, the principal London train, consists of a five coach main portion (with dining cars) plus individual brake composites from Bristol (LMS stock) and Bournemouth (SR stock). Like the real LMS 'Lakes Express', which had several parts, this train is presumed to be the major element of a larger formation which has already had some of its coaches detached for elsewhere (Grassington and Hawes in my case). It has a mixture of pre-group and early post-group coaches and is in charge of a red-painted LMS standard 2-6-0, No.13004, one of almost 100 of the celebrated 'Crabs' to receive the red livery when new.

f) 'The Lakelander' Express: This is the LMS summer only through train and is almost wholly pre-group in terms of stock.

Plate 107: The 'Furness' invasion. *The idea of having a two-company story line and moving the period back to the late 1920s, did not really emerge until I moved to 7mm scale and extended the fictional line to Kendal: this is one of the first fruits of that decision. It features dainty little Sharp Stewart 4-4-0 No.10133 (ex-Furness Railway) in pre-1928 LMS livery and entering Marthwaite with a train of elderly arc-roof stock, ostensibly from Arnside and Barrow to Dent Head.*

The main four coach Midland clerestory section (with diner) is from Leeds, with three separate brake composites originating from Bradford, Manchester and Liverpool. It is in charge of ex-LNWR 'Claughton' Class 4-6-0 No.6018, *Private W.Wood V.C,* painted in early post-1927 style. Some of these engines were transferred to the Midland Division of the LMS after the 'Royal Scots' came into service in 1927-8 so this choice again emphasises the transition period I am trying to represent.

g) The LNER through train: This six coach train, intended to represent a predominantly third class excursion working from the Newcastle area, is mostly non-corridor with a mixture of GCR, NER and GNR stock. It is the sort of assemblage which might have been put together at quite short notice in reality and there are no catering facilities. It is hauled by the ex-NER Q1 Class 'racing' 4-4-0 No.1870, one of two 7ft 7in driving wheel engines which were put out to grass in the Yorshire Dales area during the 1920s. The engine carries the pre-1928 green livery in which it was withdrawn as LNER Class D18 in 1930.

I have gone into some detail on the passenger trains, mainly to demonstrate the approach I have taken. It may seem rather tedious but it has two great virtues. Firstly, it can further emphasise the 'mental' image of the type of railway which will emerge and secondly (arguably more important), it serves to indicate quite clearly what sort of models should be tackled; this can be critical on several grounds

From the outset, it can indicate whether the building or acquisition programme is likely to be too ambitious in relation to the cost and/or time scale envisaged. As a corollary, it can also draw attention to areas where purely modelling problems might arise. These could vary from a lack of information about the prototype, via a realisation that there is a lack of suitable component parts for scratch buiding, to the onset of panic at the modelling challenges involved! In the case of the modeller working from a 'ready-to-run' or kit-based approach, it can reveal gaps in the offering from the trade or the total non-existence of an acceptable alternative. Whatever effect it may have, however, it will soon point up any potential difficulties. And even if it forces a few consequential changes in plan and philosophy, it should save a lot of time and expenditure in terms of acquiring models which then turn out to be irrelevant.

The same line of reasoning can be applied to freight patterns and traffic but here, I have adopted a slightly different form of approach, concentrating on the nature of the workings and the engines which will be needed, rather than the specific wagon types - the latter would be mostly fairly ordinary as I

Plate 108: Goods congestion. This lively scene at Liverpool (Great Howard St) goods yard (LYR: August 1913) gives a vivid example of just how much freight traffic was handled by the railways at the peak of their activity, even in very constricted spaces. Apart from the layout ideas it might suggest, what can also be distinguished is the preponderance of open wagons, albeit that the old LYR had proportionally more large covered vans than many railways. Note too the very sharp curves on some sidings and the lack of any obviously special purpose wagons at all. (B.C.Lane Collection)

---

have already explained and all that really matters is to make sure that they offer a correct balance of types and that none of them are too modern for your period. On this basis, I arrived at the following conclusions, again making sure that every engine had an allocated task.

a) The 'Midland' line local freights: These simply had to be in charge of ex-MR 0-6-0s and although I like variety, this time I decided on two near-identical types. For the type of trains envisaged, two of the vast army of Class 2 engines would be a logical choice, but mindful of the amount of 1:70 gradients, I again decided (as with the passenger trains) on the equally common Class 3 0-6-0s in their rebuilt Belpaire boiler form, both from identical kits. I have given them detail variations between each other, as per prototype, and painted them one

each in the pre-1928 and post-1927 liveries to add variety.

b) The 'Furness' line local freights: Two more 0-6-0s seemed appropriate here (this wheel arrangement was by far the most common freight type during most of the steam era), but of non-Midland origin for much the same reason as my choice of passenger engines for this route (above). A genuine ex-Furness 0-6-0 would have been nice, and may well appear one day, but I lacked sufficient prototype information when I started out on this scheme so I settled for one each of ex-LYR and ex-LNWR origin in the LMS Class 2 power range. Unsurprisingly, they have appeared in the form of the classic Aspinall type (I could not resist the real LMS No.12345; I had a picture....) and one of the celebrated LNWR 'Cauliflowers'. The latter were much associated with the Lake District and many ex-LYR engines went onto the old Furness system after the LMS was formed. The presence of the two engines allows the above mentioned 'identity change' to take place on freight workings too and as with the ex-MR types, one of them is in pre-1928 livery and the other post-1927.

c) Mineral workings: These were likely to be the heaviest freights on the layout so a bigger engine was relevant. The LMS (or ex-MR) standard Class 4 0-6-0 would be the obvious choice, but yet another 0-6-0 seemed a bit unenterprising so I sought a reasonable alternative. My attention fell on that considerable number of ex-LNWR 0-8-0s which, during the 1920s, were at an intermediate stage of rebuilding prior to all becoming Class G1/G2/G2A in the 1930s. A bit of research soon turned up LMS No.9090, originally a B Class 2-8-0 compound, but later rebuilt to Class G, retaining its original 'piano front' casing below the smokebox. It was paired, rather unusually, with a former Webb tender, which added to its appeal, and had a curious transitional late 1920s LMS livery with LNWR lining retained on the tender; and this settled the matter - of such inconsequential ephemera can our final choice sometimes be determined..... It was in LMS Power class 5, by the way, so that was appropriate to its planned task.

d) Other locomotives: It soon became clear that although the train engines did most of the shunting out on the line, the level of planned traffic at Kendal, combined with the need to turn and service the train engines themselves on arrival, would make a 'station pilot' more of a necessity than a luxury, so an open cab ex-MR 0-6-0T was added to perform this role. It is one of only two tank engines on the layout, the other being a diminutive ex-HR 0-4-4T, acquired on pure impulse simply because I liked it. I did need a spare engine at Kendal for the planned programme and the little Highland tank does have work to do, especially since it is vacuum fitted (the station pilot is not), but an ex-MR 0-4-4T would perhaps have been a more appropriate choice. My story is that the Highland engine came south (for evaluation) in exchange for a former Midland Kirtley design 2-4-0, which really *was* sent to Inverness for such purposes soon after the grouping.....

Rolling stock - how much should we have?

I think I should start by saying that the absolute minimimum number of locomotives and rolling stock to run our system can be quite small, without affecting the operational side of things. It is perfectly possible to shuttle one set of carriages (or one engine and goods brake for that matter) to and fro so as to represent as many different trains as possible, but realism is sacrificed almost from the outset and even the most modest of operational sequences soon reaches its limits if based on this premise. Even so, it can get us up and running quite early in the day and has much to recommend it for that reason alone. I did it myself on my present layout when evaluating the final programme, using any engines and stock available to represent all manner of trains, including one occasion when a 4-4-0 of 1897 (from my 'hidden' trains) was pressed into service to simulate the railcar workings before the railcar itself was built..... If nothing else, it revealed that a bit of adjustment to the operating programme was needed.

However, for full realism, we need to establish how many sets of vehicles and engines would be needed in reality to run the service. If one set of carriages could shuttle to and fro along the line and cope with all the booked workings, then that is what the real railway would do, with maybe the odd extra carriage or two at busy times. This is equally the case with freight trains in terms of the utilisation of engines and brake vans. And the easiest way to determine this sort of thing is via the train graph.

Plates 109-111: Wagon Loading. *Wool, wheat and bran are the loads on this trio of pre-group wagons, all photographed officially, presumably to demonstrate loading procedures for bale and sack traffic, though the Midland example might, conceivably, be showing how not to do it; I am unqualified to judge.... Under some circumstances, these loads might well be covered with a large tarpaulin sheet to protect the cargo. Note too the 'ordinary' nature of the wagons, a useful point to bear in mind when deciding what sort of stock we may need because by using detachable loads to aid the illusion, we can often reduce the number of wagons needed - see text. (B.C.Lane Collection - all)*

123

Using this method, I soon realised that for a line such as mine, the 'Midland' part would definitely need two sets of local passenger stock and two local freight engines - hence the logic behind the choices listed earlier in this chapter. But I could get by with only one mineral engine on the basis that it did two trips daily. Moreover, all five engines involved (with their associated trains or brake vans) would end the day where they started - a desirable situation to aim for otherwise there will be non-revenue empty stock or light engine movements to plan. The real railways did this, but not unless they had to.

I also discovered that one passenger set and one dedicated freight engine for the Furness line would actually suffice (I had originally planned for two of each and acquired the engines), as long as one or two passenger workings were handed over to the care of the steam railcar. This turned out to be possible, thus freeing off one of the planned 'Arnside' engines for cattle train duty and also enabling me to offer the 'change of identity' (above) for both types of train, simply by changing engines 'off stage' when relevant.

My more exotic through passenger trains from elsewhere on the system were added as and when I built the stock. They are not 100% essential to the basic pattern of traffic and would probably have been mostly left out had I had less space at my disposal. As it was, I simply ran the engines with but a few carriages (so as to validate the programme) until all three trains were fully complete - and so it goes on.

But there remains one area which I have not yet explained in detail - the actual provisioning of freight vehicles. In steam days, freight represented well over half the revenue of our railways (some two thirds in the case of the LMS and LNER) and I believe that an authentic historical model (save, perhaps, for the more passenger-orientated Southern Railway - the one exception) should try to reflect this fact. It presents both problems and opportunities and I shall try to deal with both, starting with the problems.

It is hard to realise today, with block trains, intensive working and a general change in emphasis of freight vis-a-vis passenger working, just how many freight vehicles were in use on the old railways - well over a million of them at the peak of activity. Moreover, a goodly number (probably numbered in hundreds of thousands on a nationwide basis) were not actually moving at all. Local merchants would frequently use coal wagons and the like as 'free mobile warehouses' until such time as the railways insisted on having them back and as a rough rule of thumb, for every vehicle in a train there would be at least as many if not more similar types standing idle. This had incredible ramifications in terms of siding provision and the modeller should try and provide as much siding space as his site will allow and not mind too much if they get filled with vehicles: have a look at some old photographs if in doubt.

But that is simultaneously the problem for most of us - we do not usually have such spaces and I have already pointed out that although Kendal probably has the right *number* of sidings, most of them are far too short compared with a real situation. But there is a sort of solution which I have found helpful and this is where the 'opportunity' arises.

I suspect that the usual trouble for most people in this field of railway activity is a lack of detailed knowledge of the prototype realities of freight movement in the old days, not least because they recede ever further into the past, often well before our own personal recollection. I am no exception, but many years ago, I was able to examine comprehensive traffic statistics for the Settle & Carlisle line and the archives I used - along with many similar - should still be accessible via the Public Record Office at Kew. This gave me some very useful insights into the probem and I still tend to use this knowledge, almost 40 years later, whenever I consider the situation. It tends to focus on the two areas of most interest to modellers, namely the type of traffic handled and its quantity.

As far as type is concerned, modellers must make their own choices depending on the real or imagined geography of the area in question. Within limits and depending on historical period chosen, the railways have, in their time, handled just about every form of traffic from circus animals to aeroplanes. Provided the traffic makes economic sense and the loads do not fall foul of the structure gauge, there is no good reason why modellers cannot be as exotic as they please, provided that it is not overdone and that the 'bread and butter' trade (coal, general merchandise, &c) is properly represented.

In my own case, I felt I could justify heavy mineral traffic, a limited supply of specialist timber traffic for a hypothetical paper works or pencil company (eg 'Cumberland' pencils) and a little more livestock traffic than usual. This would add some variety to the otherwise very orthodox traffic envisaged.

The matter of quantity is more difficult to appraise. In the case of general purpose traffic, the amount is closely related to the population of the community served and this should not be too hard to discover. In my case, I reckoned that Marthwaite and Kendal, albeit both slightly larger places, would generate traffic somewhat akin to Appleby and Settle, whose statistics I had available. In both cases the LNWR was there prior to the arrival of 'my' line and would have 'creamed off' at least some of the traffic, thus making it illogical to provide massive freight facilities even had I the space - the LNWR goods yard at Kendal was very big, for example. Using this as a basis, I arrived at the following conclusions for the two taken together:

Livestock: Some 1-2,000 wagon loads per year.

General Coal: some 10-20,000 tons per year.

Loco Coal (Kendal): 6-8,000 tons per year.

Outgoing Milk: Likely to be churn traffic (my line is pre-milk tanks!) and sent by passenger train; operated daily though exact quantities difficult to appraise.

General freight: 5-10,000 tons per year.

Timber: Somewhat flexible (to choice) but likely to be many wagon loads per week, especially given the timber transhipment facilty from canal to rail which I had planned at Kendal, some of which would be imported uncut timber for the furniture trade which could form a balancing load for incoming sawn timber.

In addition, I calculated that the quarries along the line (exact locations unspecified - they are not modelled) would generate an annual output somewhat similar to the Horton-in-

The railwaylike approach

These two fine portrait shots were taken by Jack Ray when the Gauge 1 layout was just finished and the 7mm scheme hardly started. They show two specialised aspects of what I refer to as 'railwaylike' in Chapter 9. The first is a superb scratch built model by Geoff Holt of my favourite Stanier engine, the original taper-boilered member of the LMS 'Royal Scot' Class No.6170 British Legion. It is modelled in its original (1935) state and although inappropriate to the main theme of my 7mm layout, has always been on my personal 'wish list' in both 4mm and 7mm scales. It normally functions in the out of period display mode as my Royal Train engine. Its quite excellent livery was applied by Larry Goddard, who has painted the majority of my 7mm scale locomotive and carriage models, many of which are featured in this book.

The second picture shows an equally fine representation of another favourite type, the Aster Gauge 1 live steam model of the celebrated Pennsylvania Railroad Class K4 4-6-2 No.5475 in its very attractive decorated green livery, an unusual form of treatment for an American steam locomotive type at the time the prototype was built. The original 5475 was the first PRR K4 to carry the famous 'Keystone' emblem on the smokebox door and is seen running 'right hand road' in charge of my model of the 'Broadway Limited' during the 'Heavyweight' carriage era.

River crossings

Until recent years, Gauge 0 has been something of a 'Cinderella' scale in most cases as far as scenic backgrounds are concerned, the latter being often seen as more a characteristic of the smaller scales. Happily, this is now changing as, hopefully, these views may show. In the first, taken by Ron Prattley, Ramsbottom LNWR 2-2-2 No.531 *Lady of the Lake* (a fine Peter Everton model) has the 'all clear' as it crosses the River Lune with a northbound train of six-wheelers on Neil Corner's Lonsdale layout (see Chapter 9), while the second picture shows my own kit-built ex-Midland 4-4-0 No.809 about to cross the River Rawthey at Marthwaite with a local train for Dent Head.

Both scenes feature the work of that fine scenic modeller and track-builder extraordinary: Norman Solomon. When I first met Norman and saw his work during the early stages of Lonsdale, on which he laid most of the track and created almost all the scenery, I was very impressed - he does, after all, make his living from this sort of thing - and was happy to commission his help at Kendal when a nasty brush with ill-health prevented me from doing much of the work, especially the heavier stuff, which hitherto I would have tackled myself. We often worked as a 'duo' as the layout progressed and the river crossing at Marthwaite is very much a combined effort, myself making the basic buildings and civil engineering structures with Norman doing most of the 'twiddly bits'. I was happy to study his methods and he was kind enough to show me some of his secrets so that I could continue on my own when he had returned to deepest Somerset....

Ribblesdale or Ribblehead areas and I put in 100-150,000 tons per year for the branch as a whole, including some transfers at Marthwaite of quarry produce from the Low Gill branch - see Fig.14. Operation of the layout itself soon revealed that it would also be useful to have a mineral loading facility at Marthwaite from an 'off stage' location, analogous to the real equivalent at Long Marton on the Settle-Carlisle main line.

Now I must stress that these are not precise figures, but they are based on real values from real places and neither excessive in scope nor under-played. And I consider that this sort of exercise is not beyond the scope of most of us if we are so-minded. Moreover, if things are done this way, it is not too difficult to turn such figures into daily wagon needs on the basis of normal average loads at the period in question. I took c.8 tons for minerals and coal and c.2-3 tons for general goods. It is essentially a matter of arithmetic and I give the following daily approximations for the two locations I have modelled, bearing in mind that in most cases, these quantities would be augmented by the needs of the non-modelled locations:

Livestock: 6-7 wagon loads daily, probably operated two or three times weekly as a cattle special.

General Coal: 6-10 wagons daily.

Loco Coal (Kendal): 3-4 wagons daily.

Outgoing Milk: 2-3 vans daily.

General freight: 10-12 vehicles per day.

Timber: Averaging 1-2 vehicles per day but maybe consigned twice per week as a 'block' load.

Minerals: Some 50-60 wagons per day, mostly from places other than Kendal and certainly needing two trains per day.

Obviously, not all the wagons would be seen on the layout at any one time. Some will be in transit (ie the 'fiddle yard' in modelling parlance) and others lying idle as I have already indicated. But although it is possible to work out the total wagon fleet to be modelled in an ideal situation, most of us do not live in this sort of world and this is where we can use the fact that the vast majority of the wagons most appropriate to this sort of operation were very ordinary looking. A loaded van looks identical to an unloaded one and a sheeted down open wagon bringing in one sort of load will not look too different when it departs with a different sheeted load, so it is quite feasible to allow some 'doubling up'.

Genuine open vehicles (mostly coal and mineral) are best given detachable loads (not difficult to do) to simulate the different traffic flows, and you may need a few more of these in consequence so as to have enough of them lying about in your goods yard(s) in one state or the other. But it is my experience that for most of these 'anonymous' wagons, it is by no means essential to stock the layout with the full quota needed. I have found that I can usually get by with about twice the total number of vehicles which are likely to be found on any one local freight train and often far less.

To give an example, I will take the mineral trains on the layout where the thought of building 50 or more wagons (even allowing for the existence of suitable kits) was not greeted with any degree of enthusiasm, nor had I the space on the layout for such extravagances. I therefore argued that with the

gradients I have postulated (Fig.15), a single daily train would be out of the question and that two per day would be far more likely. And since some of the wagons on these trains would be added or detached between Marthwaite and Dent Head, there was no real need to model more than the dozen or so which would reach the modelled part of the layout in any one train. And since they would all look very similar, save for 'anoraks' who like to record wagon numbers (hmm....), why not trip the whole lot in and out on a twice daily basis? This is a perfectly reasonable solution, provided I made sure that the detachable 'loads' (above) would differentiate the incoming from outgoing wagons. And by doing it this way, I could also add 'loco coal' and timber wagons to the train, it being perfectly legitimate to add such items to a train running under 'mineral' headlamps - the rule book says so!

Needless to say, and in spite of all the above, when I finally came to evaluate the operation of the layout after more than 20 years of building carriage and wagon stock against the final requirement, I found that I had far more wagons than could possibly be used in a fully realistic mode, so what should I do? It seemed a pity to sell or give them away but I then realised that the one thing I could not do on my layout was to run a genuine main line express freight train of the type which so characterised the real Settle & Carlisle. It did not take long for me to realise that I could solve this probem by adding such a train to the 'out of period' fleet, so I removed the more modern stock from the freight collection (thus enhancing the historical 'look' of what was left), added a later vintage brake van and built a model of a Class 8F 2-8-0 (a favourite Stanier type but totally inappropriate to my main theme) to head up the train.

And that more or less sums up this part of the story, save that mention of the 8F does raise the question of my 'other' trains, thus far mentioned only *en passant*. They are not really relevant to the main thrust of my argument, though the thought behind them may be of some help, but since some of them are quite likely to feature pictorially in this book, the text being prepared ahead of the picture selection, this may be the right time to offer a concluding note.

The 'Funny' trains

I use this heading in memory of my very dear friend, the late Gavin Wilson, whom we have met before and whose company I still miss after more than 25 years. I have already explained (Chapter 4) how he prompted the idea of having a hidden collection of favourite 'out of period' models so as not to dilute the historical impression which his main layout theme offered. He called them his 'funny' trains - a typically self-deprecating comment - and I have been glad to follow his lead.

I have mentioned the 8F and its train (c.1937 is the period represented by this formation) which was actually the last to take its place in my plans. But prior to that, bearing in mind my specific interest in building carriages, I had already settled on a quartet of passenger trains which by no stretch of the imagination would ever be seen at the period of my choice, nor, come to think of it, on the Settle-Carlisle at any time in

some cases. They mostly reflect my personal historical interest and so - purely for the record and reasons of completeness - I offer their rationale as a conclusion to this chapter, again adopting a listing process:

a) <u>Midland Railway 1897</u>: Like many folk, I have a great affection for the Midland Railway at the turn of the 19th/20th Centuries. This period is not appropriate to my main interests, but it was so elegant in terms of external presentation that I could not resist the idea of modelling a typical example and the acquisition of a fine model of an original Johnson 4-4-0 was all the spur I needed. I chose the very first full clerestory formation (the St Pancras - Manchester express of 1897, a nice four-carriage train of 12-wheelers) and although its building diverted me from the main theme, I have no regrets.

b) <u>West Coast Joint Stock '2pm' train, 1908</u>: Despite my generally Midland predilections, I was fully aware that the LNWR, along with its Caledonian Railway partner, had always offered a faster and more convenient route to Scotland. What is more, they had also overtaken the much vaunted Midland in terms of both carriage quality and passenger amenity during the Edwardian era, no more so than in the famous 1908 mid-day train of elegant 12-wheelers, probably the finest carriages ever offered at normal fares (ie without supplement) to the travelling public. I simply wanted a model of this famous train, so I finally made one, headed by an example of perhaps the finest inside-cylinder 4-4-0 type ever to run in Britain, the LNWR 'George the Fifth' Class. I chose No.1595 *Wild Duck*, a well known example in its own right but also the original *Mallard* when you think about it.

c) <u>Settle and Carlisle Express, c.1932</u>: This train is a bit like the freight train headed by the 8F - ie an example of the sort of thing which my layout in its 'pure' mode could never justify. I have elected to model the mid-day working with LMS coaches (Glasgow via the G&SWR line) and LNER types (Edinburgh via the ex-North British 'Waverley' route). The train engine is

one of the first two LMS 'Patriots', No.5902 *Sir Frank Ree* in its original 1930 condition (ie no smoke deflectors) when it first went to Leeds. As such it is (just) in period with the main theme of the layout and can be used accordingly if desired.

d) <u>The LMS Royal Train c.1937</u>: This is another unashamed tribute to my old friend Gavin Wilson who did the same thing in 4mm scale and whose model now resides at the NRM. It also gives me the excuse to have my favourite Stanier engine on the layout - a rebuilt 'Royal Scot' in perhaps its prettiest form as No.6170 *British Legion*, the 1935 doyen of the class. As I write (2001), the train is not fully finished, though some of its carriages are complete and all of them are started. It will be the last of my funny trains, partly because I am running out of space, partly because it is the hardest to make, partly because it is arguably the most irrelevant to the main concept of the layout and thus deferred in priority terms; but mostly because it represents the last 'must have' in my plan and I dread to think what may happen if there is nothing else left to do when I have finished it.......

*   *   *   *   *

The only serious conclusion I would draw from the last few paragraphs of purely private fantasy is that no matter how 'straight and narrow' may be our main objective, the concept of 'funny trains' does allow a great deal of self-indulgence in other interesting matters without too much risk of diluting the overall impression we want to achieve; and it does wondrous things for our sanity whenever we are tempted to get *trop serieux*, as the French might say.... But now, it is time to sum up the whole business so far, by looking at how to make our trains perform as though real railwaymen were in charge.

CHAPTER 8

Model railway operation and control

"He's murdering the time! Off with his head!"
Lewis Carroll, 'Alice's adventures in Wonderland'

THE SIGNIFICANCE of the above quotation by the Queen of Hearts will, I hope, become clear later, but meantime, let me take you back to the scene in the Leeds Corn Exchange in late 1971 where 'Garsdale Road' had one of its last two or three exhibition outings prior to being built into the final EM gauge layout a year or two later. Our operational sequence involved shunting a local freight just prior to the booked 'passing time' of a fully laden loose-coupled mineral train and the trick was to get the local freight 'inside' (ie not fouling the main lines) before the mineral was due. We also had working signals (which were not interlocked by the way) and, to add piquancy to the sauce, my 'back-stage' crew were more than likely to try to embarrass the 'front of house' team by doing the unexpected.

On one occasion, having noted that the local freight was well and truly strewed across both main lines *and* the goods yard as well, albeit all fully protected (visually) by signals, they decided to 'offer' the mineral ahead of time - mainly, I suspect, to see what happened next. Simultaneously (or was this the real reason behind the action of my so-called team?), the onlookers were joined by a pair of footplatemen from the ex-MR shed at Leeds (Holbeck) on their way home - probably even from a trip on the real Settle and Carlisle line.

The minerals were in charge of a converted Hornby 8F and the wagons mostly repainted Triang, such were the highly sophisticated modelling methods of those days(!), but we knew that the 8F was a superb slow runner, so we 'accepted' the mineral and set it in motion from 'backstage' at ultra low speed, about one foot per minute as I recall, leaving all signals at danger; meantime, we continued to shunt the local freight in the sort of leisurely fashion as might suggest that nothing untoward was happening. As we shunted the station, the 2-8-0 gradually crept into view round the corner from the tunnel and approached the up 'home' (still at danger, of course) and we were rewarded by the following conversation from our Holbeck observers:

DRIVER (pointing to the slowly emerging 8F): "Sithee (this is Yorkshire dialect for 'see thou'), he's a cautious b....r isn't he?"
SECOND MAN (he was far younger and since 1971 was well into the diesel age, the word 'fireman' is inappropriate): "But why is he going so slow? Couldn't he simply stop at the home signal and wait for the road?"
DRIVER: "Oh, you young lads know nowt; it's good to see that thou art far too young ever to have worked steam freight

loose-coupled. I've worked that sort o' train many a time and if tha were my age tha would know it's a b....y sight easier to keep it all moving than to stop for owt, unless tha b....y well has to. He's hoping that b....y signal will come off before he has to stop - and I reckon these lads (referring to the Garsdale Road operating team) know that."

Plate 113: Keeping the main line clear - 1. This view is as near as I can get to the anecdote at the start of this chapter in the context of Garsdale Road. Here, the loaded minerals were in charge of LMS standard Class 7F No.9580 rather than the later Class 8F 2-8-0 mentioned in my story, but the effect was much the same. The local goods is in charge of Class 4F 0-6-0 No.3893, an ex-Midland (ie not LMS standard) example of a common class of engine shedded locally at the time. Note the tender 'cab' (a later modification) which was a feature of many Class 4F engines located in the area.

Plate 114: Keeping the main line clear - 2. If there was no headway for a slow moving freight before a faster train was due in the same direction, then it had to be 'put inside' as the saying went. This was done by way of a 'refuge siding' which was either a lay-by (into which the slower train could reverse from the main line) or a running loop with a connection to the main line at both ends which was entered in the conventional way. This highly characteristic operating feature of the steam railway is not difficult to achieve on a model even if the trains are often shorter. This picture shows a loose-coupled train of wooden bodied open four-wheelers standing in the up loop at Blea Moor in the mid-1940s behind Class 8F 2-8-0 No.8177 - note the 'Through Freight' headcode, see Chapter 7. The Blea Moor refuge sidings were converted from conventional lay-bys into running loops during World War II mainly to speed up the operations, it taking much longer to reverse the train into a dead-end lay-by. Note too the water column, provided purely for the benefit of 'freights in waiting'.....

I'm not sure even now whether or not we did; but we subsequently performed the same trick deliberately on the basis that if we had convinced the professionals, we had probably got it more or less right. More important, however - and, indeed, the whole point of telling the tale here - the fact that the train was converted Hornby Dublo heading repainted Triang caused me furiously to think about what we really mean by 'scale modelling'. Could it be that convincing prototypical operation is just as much a 'fine scale factor' (if I may thus put it) as the visual accuracy of our individual models?

I don't know the full answer to that one either, but as far as my modelling was concerned, it dominated my approach from that point onwards, having nothing to do with the actual scale I eventually chose to adopt. Whatever else my layouts did, they simply had to perform like a real railway and the rest of this chapter must be read accordingly.

It therefore follows that I have no wish to model grass meadows which look far better than the Good Lord ever had in mind when he started the process, though I do respect those who gain creative satisfaction this way. Neither am I too bothered whether my models are 100% accurate to the last micron of dimensional fidelity, provided they do not go to the extremes (eg pre-war Hornby Gauge '0') of trying to pretend that *Flying Scotsman, Caerphilly Castle, Lord Nelson* and *Royal Scot* were all identical 4-4-2s, save for livery. I had my reservations about these models at the tender age of four - and still have for that matter, despite the collectors' market!

Even so, though I always want my models to look as correct as I can make them in terms of appearance and pesentation, I cannot accept the elitist hi-fi attitudes which the other side of the hobby sometimes reveals. After all, we still mostly use 'sparks and juice' to make them go, no matter how much 'working' inside valve gear or 'back to back' fidelity we may assay; and the people on our stations never move even though the trains do! But since I can solve one major problem by getting a live steam propulsion 'fix' via the Gauge 1 garden option (which is otherwise rather less prototypically accurate than my 7mm fine scale efforts), my indoor system has deliberately been designed to meet rather different criteria.

All of which may make me something of a philistine, but there is a logic to my ideas which actually underpins this episode of the story, for I reckon that you cannot design a control system for an electrically powered model railway until you have first decided *exactly what you want it to do.* I therefore propose to treat this topic by looking at the question of what I mean by operation in general terms and then try to explain how I tried to evolve the sort of control system which would permit such an outcome on my own layout.

Plate 115: Decide what you want the layout to do. When I built Garsdale Road, the main line flavour of the Settle & Carlisle was essential, so in spite of the limited space, up and down lay-bys had to be provided, even at the expense of many other desirable features which I might have liked to include. Both are seen unoccupied in this view which shows a down parcels train running through with Class 8F 2-8-0 No.8105 in charge. Risking an aside, parcels trains are well worth modelling for those of even semi-main line persuasion, for they offer the opportunity to model rather more of the attractive non-passenger coaching stock types than we might otherwise be able to justify.

The ultimate aim

One of the many official statements to both staff and public by the old Midland Railway in 1903 reads: *"Carriage Trucks and Horseboxes are kept at all the principal stations on the line; but to avoid possibility of disappointment, it is recommended that one day's notice be given at the stations when they are required."* Just about the only thing it does not define is 'principal station', but it represents the railway-like forward thinking which we would do well to follow in the operation of our layouts. Yet, considering that most modellers go to considerable pains to make their creations move under their own power, it remains a constant source of surprise to me how often so little attention is paid to the operational fidelity of the systems on which they run. And for every layout which is operated as though real railwaymen were in charge, there seem to be many more on which movement is unreliable, random or illogical.

If this makes me sound a trifle dogmatic compared with my declared (and, I hope, fairly relaxed) attitudes so far, then I apologise, but as far as I am concerned, the operation of a model railway is that which adds authentic train movement to an already, hopefully convincing, static scene. This seems to me to necessitate operating to the sort of timetable or sequence mode I have tried to expound, rather than indulging in tail-chasing. The latter can be enjoyable, of course, and I often do it myself (usually when testing a new locomotive), but it is not really operating in the sense of increasing the credibility of the scene, so I shall not mention it again.

'Real' operating involves a fundamental understanding of the ways of the railway. For those of us who are old enough to recall the traditional railway, we have our memories and experiences to help (not that we always pay them too much attention...), but for many enthusiasts (probably most of those born in the second half of the 20th Century), it can be difficult to know what to do or where to start. As I have more than once said, this may well be why so many modellers go for scenic fidelity where they are usually on safer grounds.

A copy of the General Appendix to the working timetables of the company modelled is a very useful start and gives a welter of valuable detail; but these books are not as easy to come by as was once the case. Normal libraries are unlikely to have them and many modellers may be unable to get to such places as the NRM where photocopies of the more relevant sections can often be provided at modest cost. It is principally to these folk that my comments in this section are addressed, though I hope that those readers who can recall former days will find something of interest, even if much of it may seem rather obvious to many of them; so perhaps a slight digression will help to demonstrate my reasoning.

Several years ago, my friend Bob Essery told me a story of a model railway exhibition he had visited whereat a young teenager was operating a rather nice little branch line stocked mainly with proprietary items labelled 'LMS'. There was a goodly scatter of private owner wagons and appropriate stock and the young man, who had set his scene extremely well, was shunting the goods yard nicely. He eventually despatched his goods train but forgot, or so Bob supposed, to attach the brake van. On being reminded of this he replied, quite innocently: "What is a brake van?" There was not, in fact, a brake van on the layout and it transpired that the only real-life freight trains which this young man had ever seen were the modern versions, fully braked and without a brake van, so Bob duly explained. But if that young man (who is now probably middle aged and with a family - sic!) ever reads this book, I hope he is pleased that he has provided the inspiration for the next few pages.

The speed and time factors

Before we look at operations proper, I think it is necessary to develop a realistic conception of the meaning of speed in real railway terms. In the modern 125-140mph era, with even the freight trains often racing along at what seem to me to be obscene 70-80mph speeds, it is difficult to realise how slowly, relatively speaking, things actually moved in the steam age. I know that *Mallard* reached 126mph (once only and very briefly), but the railway as a whole at that time was, and only then for the very best passenger trains, a 60-70mph affair in terms of average speed, and often slower. The 'mile a minute' passenger schedule was regarded as so praiseworthy as to merit special articles in the railway press; while normal freight trains (with a few highly favoured exceptions) were doing very well indeed if they managed 20 or 30 miles in one hour.

Local passenger trains occasionally, and briefly, reached the dizzy heights of 60mph if there was enough distance between stations, but the local pick-up goods trains were doing well if they ambled along between stops at 15-25mph. There would even be time for the footplate crew, if they were so minded, to stop and pick dandelions for their rabbits off a lineside cutting before the signalman at the next block post began to show any undue concern about the whereabouts of the train.....

The truth of this was brought home to me forcefully in mid-1983 when I was involved with the operating of Stanier 4-6-2 No.46229 *Duchess of Hamilton* from Carlisle back to York. An immense load (by British steam standards) of some 570 tons was behind the tender and we were making a magnificent 48-50mph attack on the 1:100 uphill stretch from Appleby to Ais Gill. All that one customer could say was that it "seemed a bit slow." The fact that the engine was delivering almost 3000HP at the cylinders and performing better than any single unit BR diesel could possibly offer (save, perhaps, for a 'Deltic' in good order) was completely lost on this chap, arguably brainwashed by 4500HP of HST power cars and 250 tons of lightweight BR MkIII stock on the level sections of the East Coast Main Line!

Thus, the first thing to do in terms of historically authentic operating is to slow everything down. This can be even slower than one might suppose - and the very few layouts which run at what I might call scale speed are often criticised as being *too* slow. However, consider for a moment a few facts. At 60mph

a real train covers 88ft per second which is just under 14in per second in 4mm scale and about 24in per second in 7mm. At 90mph (a very rare speed for most of the time in steam days) the scale figures are 21in and 37in respectively. Alternatively, a characteristic 30mph freight train would cover only 7in and 12in per second in the two respective scales. Next time you operate your layout, try to run at this sort of speed and I will wager that most of you will be surprised to see what real scale speed is all about.

As for shunting, anything above a brisk walking speed (say 5mph) would be very quick most of the time. And if you work out the scale speed for this pace, you will appreciate that *good slow running* is a prerequisite for authentic model operation, from which it follows that we need to have good mechanisms in our (presumed electrically powered) model locomotives. Moreover, it should take just as long to marshal the trains in miniature as it does in reality - which brings me nicely to the subject of so-called 'scale time'; and this is where the Queen of Hearts comes in, lest you had forgotten her - above.

It is often assumed that because we can reduce the physical dimensions of our models, related to reality, we can also lessen the time taken to carry out operations. This is a philosophical nonsense, for if a real locomotive takes, say, four seconds to travel its own length then it must take the same time to do so in miniature - unless we want our models to twitch around like frightened rabbits. In fact, I would go so far as to say that it is impossible to scale the time factor, even though the celebrated Edward Beal himself fell into the trap of advocating something like this in one of his books. In consequence, if you have worked out a 24 hour timetable for your railway then it will take that time to run it, all other things being equal.

However, all other things are not equal as we all know. For one thing, it is unlikely that we shall have scale distances between our stations if there is more than one on the layout and for another, we may have only a few hours at a time in

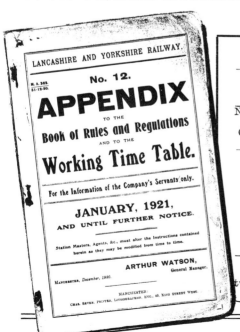

SPECIAL INSTRUCTIONS TO ENGINE DRIVERS—continued.

TABLE TO CALCULATE THE SPEED OF TRAINS.

No. of Seconds in going a Quarter of a Mile.	Miles per Hour.	No. of Seconds.	Miles per Hour.	No. of Seconds.	Miles per Hour.	No. of Min. Sec.		Miles per Hour.	No. of Min. Sec.		Miles per Hour.
15	60	24	37	33	27	0	50	18	1	40	9
16	56	25	36	35	26	0	53	17	1	52	8
17	53	26	35	36	25	0	56	16	2	8	7
18	50	27	33	37	24	1	0	15	2	30	6
19	47	28	32	39	23	1	4	14	3	0	5
20	45	29	31	41	22	1	9	13	3	45	4
21	43	30	30	43	21	1	15	12	5	0	3
22	41	31	29	45	20	1	22	11	7	30	2
23	39	32	28	47	19	1	30	10	15	0	1

900 divided by the number of seconds occupied by a Train travelling between any two quarter-mile posts will give the average speed of the Train in miles per hour.

Plate 116: Express Passenger. The make-up of express trains is often difficult to determine from prototype pictures and we may not always have space to offer the massive rakes which were regularly to be seen. With Garsdale Road I was limited to nine coaches and the 7mm option was even more restricting, so I began to think in terms of intermediate sized expresses commonly to be seen. This view, taken during the early stages of the construction of 7mm scale Kendal MkI - see Chapter 3 - was my first attempt to produce this sort of thing in this larger scale. The formation back from the engine is: brake third (LNWR); corridor third plus open third diner (both early LMS); first class kitchen dining car (ex-M&GSW), corridor composite (middle period LMS), corridor brake composite (ex-LNWR). All six carriages are different and once I had determined this and other formations for the new layout, I realised that I should have to scratch build all of them. An opposite end view of this train is at Plate 1, Chapter 1. (Ron Prattley)

which to operate the system. But although speeding up the clock, as some folk recommend, does not really solve the problem, there is a very useful compromise which I can offer without getting into the realms of metaphysical debate - and it too stems from the reality of the railway.

On a real railway of the type we will usually choose to model - ie not a busy metropolitan terminus or major through station in a large city - much time is occupied between trains when nothing much moves for many hours at a time. Office work is done, vehicles are loaded and unloaded and so on, but the trains do not move - indeed there may be none present. For the onlooker of the miniature system, and the owner too for that matter, to replicate this situation would be about as exciting as watching paint dry. On my models, therefore, I attempt to carry out all the planned manoevres in 'real time' terms but I suppress, entirely, the intervals between separate activities. Thus, for example, if the timetable shows no train action between 2.00pm and 4.00pm, I move straight to 4.00pm and do not get too neurotic about the 'lost' two hours.

In practice, depending on the complexity of the operating programme, I have found that if I allow one minute (real time)

to represent between three and five minutes (prototype time), then I can actually perform the specific movements at realistic visual speeds and absorb all the prototypical 'dead' time in the process. My operational schedule at Kendal starts, notionally, at about 4.35am with the arrival of the overnight sleeping cars (see timetable: Chapter 6 Fig.16) and concludes just after midnight with the departure of the same carriages, say 20 hours in real time terms. My operating team (there are three or four of us) usually get through this quite complex programme in some five to six hours at scale speeds, always provided that one scheduled activity follows immediately after the previous one and as long as we don't get too distracted or have to break off to make an urgent repair to a point tie bar or some such - these latter occurrences being thankfully very rare.

Furthermore, if you don't have sufficient time to work through the programme in one operating session, then simply leave everything *in situ* and resume next time from where you left off. It is not the perfect solution, but it works. What is more, I know of no other alternative which, on the one hand, enables a complete sequence to be operated in a reasonable time envelope and on the other permits physical movements to take place at a realistic pace from the onlooker's viewpoint.

If the logic of the previous paragraphs is acceptable to the reader, then the next stage is to analyse the nature of train operations themselves and I will tackle these in four areas: passenger, freight, locomotive and signalling. At all times I shall be taking as exemplar the typical steam age (and/or early diesel) scenario, which remained very stable for many years.

Passenger train operations

I make no secret of the fact that the subject of passenger trains and their operation is my own favoured area. This is partly because, in many ways, it is the most neglected aspect of the model railway scene but also because I find it fascinating in its own right. Most modellers seem to accept, almost by instinct, that freight traffic demands attention, but tend not to take the

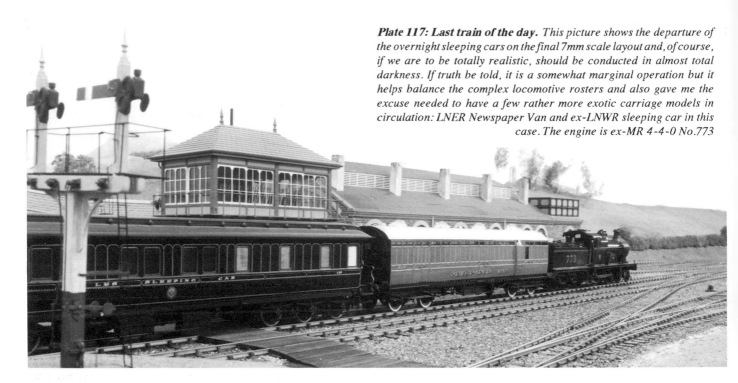

Plate 117: Last train of the day. This picture shows the departure of the overnight sleeping cars on the final 7mm scale layout and, of course, if we are to be totally realistic, should be conducted in almost total darkness. If truth be told, it is a somewhat marginal operation but it helps balance the complex locomotive rosters and also gave me the excuse needed to have a few rather more exotic carriage models in circulation: LNER Newspaper Van and ex-LNWR sleeping car in this case. The engine is ex-MR 4-4-0 No.773

same view with passenger services. All that often seems to happen is that the train arrives, the engine runs round and then departs again - no problem. But the reality is a little different. I have already explained (Chapter 7) something of the nature of the passenger train so we now need to put this information to practical use on the model.

Firstly, all passenger stock is continuously braked, so when dealing with coaches, the train brake pipe has to be made and proved (ie tested for completion and efficiency). This process involves checking the brake pipe connections between all the separate carriages and ensuring that the last one (at the rear of the train) is sealed into its housing. The same is true for the steam heat pipe if fitted. On electrically lit stock, it was also common for plug and socket connections to be made between carriages to allow the guard to control all the train lighting from one point; and for those with long memories, this is why, in daylight hours, the electric lights would mysteriously come on just before the entry to a tunnel. Finally, screw couplings had to be tightened to bring the side buffers into firm contact.

But it did not end there. With a corridor train formed up from coaches with the old British Standard gangways (mostly the LMS and GWR) it was also necessary to unfasten the retaining hooks (which restrained the extending part of the gangways by keeping them fully compressed to the carriage end), thus allowing the bellows to be pulled out to meet the similar gangway on the adjacent vehicle. The two 'free' ends had then to be clipped to each other to avoid accidents to passengers passing through. End boards were then clipped to the outer ends of the formation to seal them off.

With automatic 'buckeye' couplers and 'Pullman' gangways (LNER, SR [mostly], BR and Pullmans themselves, of course), the act of propelling two vehicle together would make the

coupling and seal the gangway, but all the pipework still needed to be connected. But if, for example, a coach with British Standard gangways was connected to one with the Pullman type, then the former had to be fitted with extended 'gangway adaptors' to allow clipping to the wider Pullman version and the buckeyed vehicle had to have its buckeye 'dropped' so as to expose a normal coupling hook (to accept the screw coupling), while its normally retracted side buffers then had to be extended to meet those of the adjacent vehicle. This was done by dropping a 'collar' onto the extended buffer shank to avoid it retracting again.

In practice, a degree of loose coupling of carriage stock was often tolerated in the carriage sidings during the train make-up stage. But before an assembled set of vehicles was despatched to the station for traffic, and certainly before loading any passengers, all the necessary connections had to be made and tested. Needless to say, all these procedures had to be followed when attaching or detaching vehicles to or from any passenger rated trains; and it applied equally to mail and parcels trains and to the fitted head of any freight trains.

These operations always took time to complete and the implication, for modellers, is that this time should somehow be reproduced. The sado-masochists might try to make models wherein all the pipework is properly modelled and connected together - and it can be done - but for most normal mortals, the best substitute is a rational pause between movements.

Thus, to take a simple run-round operation by way of example, the following sequence is correct:

a) The incoming train arrives and stops with a full automatic brake application. The coaches are now braked and even if the brake pipe remains connected throughout, the train cannot move until a new vacuum has been created.

b) Head/tail lamps are removed and if the engine can run round *without moving the train*, it can now be uncoupled, allowing due time to disconnect pipes, unscrew the couplings and maybe easing back the locomotive so as to compress the buffers in order to slacken the coupling. If the locomotive has to move the train before the run-round pointwork is cleared, then time must be allowed to re-create the vacuum in the train pipe and release the brakes, which are applied again when the train is in the correct position.

c) The locomotive, now a light engine, moves up beyond the release crossover and waits until it receives a signal to set back (maybe a ground disc) after the points have been set. This too takes time.

d) The locomotive now sets back and starts the run-round, but it may have to stop before it completes the manoevre if the pointwork at the rear of the train (soon to be the front) is under the control of a different signal box, ground frame or whatever.

e) The locomotive completes the run-round and stops. Again time is needed to change the points and signals and adjust the reverser on the locomotive.

f) The locomotive moves slowly onto the train and gently 'buffers-up'. Remember that in reality, passengers may be boarding so 'softly-softly' is the watchword.

g) Brake/heat pipes are re-connected, along with the couplings, and a new vacuum created and proved. Head/tail lamps are re-positioned, after which the train is ready to depart on receipt of the appropriate signal.

.... all in all, quite a lot of activity for one of the simplest and most common railway routines.

In modelling terms, the only way to reproduce this is with pauses, which is why an unknowing observer may well wonder what on earth is going on, may even think the layout operator is carrying out activities too slowly, and possibly express this view audibly. There's not much one can do about this save grin and bear it, or better still in the exhibition context, try to explain the rationale to the audience. Based on my experience, it is surprising how much this can be appreciated by those genuinely seeking to understand more.

It is, however, well worth noting that one of the reasons why the railways preferred to use fixed 'sets' of carriages as far as possible was to reduce the time taken to 'make and break' the formations, though they did it if they had to rather than lose traffic. We can use this to advantage in our models as well, which is why almost all the carriage sets I described in the last chapter remain virtually unchanged in terms of their major portions. But at Appendix 1, I have offered a facsimile of just a small part of the LMS carriage marshalling books to show how much planning went into the business at all times.

I will not analyse all the other possible passenger operations in similar detail because much of it is common sense once the basic principles are understood. But as part of Appendix 2, in which are offered facsimile reproductions of pages from the

Plate 118: Where Greek meets Greek.... On one occasion during the day, both Midland line locals pass each other at Marthwaite. Here, No. 809 heads for Dent Head with the Midland clerestory set while No.773 approaches with the ex-Lancashire and Yorkshire 'LBL' set - see text.

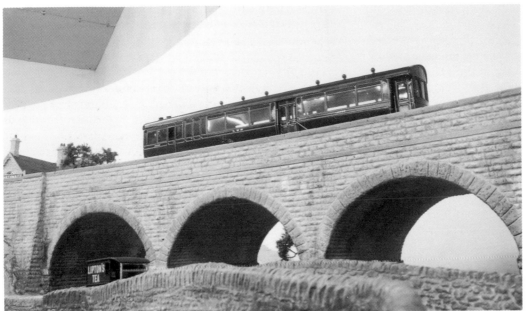

Plate 119: The 'Shuttle'. The idea of a steam railcar was also a relatively late development, influenced by the availability of a reasonable kit. When built, I soon realised that if I could plan a suitable roster for the car, it would eliminate the need for two separate 'Furness Line' passenger trains and reduce the amount of extra stock I would have to make. It never gets beyond Marthwaite station from the Kendal direction in the normal run of things, but I could not resist posing it on one of my favourite bits of the current 7mm layout: the viaduct on the route to Dent Head.

LMS General Appendix, there will be found basic definitions of passenger rated trains in accordance with standard practice in the 1930s; the other companies were similar. It gives quite a lot of other detail too and one wonders how railwaymen of the day ever managed to cope at all; but they did.

Whilst on the subject of fixed formations, it is perhaps worth mentioning that this principle is even more universally applicable on the modern railway, not always to beneficial effect. When did you last see the modern railway add extra coaches to cope with peak loading at busy times, especially Friday afternoons? They will tell you that it is not possible with fixed formation trains and driving cabs at each end, but this is rubbish. It is quite possible (technically) to strengthen a train - even the HST type - and have separate through portions if need be, as they still do on the overnight sleeping car trains to Scotland; but it would seem that the economics of following this procedure on a comprehensive basis are not acceptable these days. Thankfully, we can still do so in miniature and it adds enormously to the realism of our models if we do.

Plate 120: 'Foreign' invaders. Even after the grouping, many of the older types kept to their traditional areas of operation for quite some time. However, on the Furness section of the LMS, in imagination a part-stakeholder on my system, much of the native locomotive stock was given very short shrift at a very early stage by the new LMS management. It therefore seemed to me logical, given that by the late 1920s other rather more numerous pre-group classes had already replaced some of the Furness engines, that this situation could well be reproduced in miniature by a bit of 'selective importation' of non-Midland types - and why not pick a few personal favourites if they are not too wildly out of line? Moreover, being all now part of the greater LMS, they do not need to remain as tightly confined to routes as in pre-1923 days. Here, ex-LNWR 'Jumbo' 2-4-0 No.5012 John Ramsbottom is doing duty on a Midland line local to Dent Head while the ex-LNWR 'Cailiflower' 0-6-0 No.8472 is more suitably rostered to a Furness line local freight to Arnside.

Freight train operation

I explained some of the ramifications of this area in terms of train formation as part of the last chapter and in modelling terms, one of the most rewarding areas of the hobby can be the correct handling of freight trains. But it must be logical.

As part of Appendix I, as with passenger trains, I offer a basic summary of the various categories of freight trains as recognised by the LMS, along with their headlamp and signal bell codes. However, for model purposes I think an equally important aspect of the subject is to ensure that the freight trains themselves are related properly to the geographical realities of the area modelled, again as suggested in the last chapter. Only when this is achieved to our satisfaction does it make sense to look at the rule book to discover what types of train will best fit the traffic on offer and decide how to operate the vehicles on the layout.

In a nutshell, the word is 'purposefully'. At all times, we need to remember that we are striving for an illusion of reality. It might be fun to bang a few vehicles in and out of sidings as often as possible so as to demonstrate the superb slow running capability of our favourite shunting locomotive to our admiring friends; but real railways do not do this. So before looking at the trains themselves, let me start with the business of shunting

137

Plate 121: Recurring Themes - 1. *Once their operational logic is established to my satisfaction, certain themes tend to recur on many of my layouts. This c.1966 view of the 4mm scale Marthwaite shows just two of them. In the background, the cattle special is setting off for Dent Head behind a Class 4F 0-6-0, while left foreground is the LNER Class B12 4-6-0 which we used for the first incarnation of the through train from Northallerton. The engine choice (converted Triang) was rather improbable in the latter case but both ideas are still seen, in rather more refined form, on Kendal MkIII 35 years later.....*

Plate 122: Recurring Themes - 2. *On the 7mm layout, the LNER train is much better thought out than in 4mm days and with a far more appropriate locomotive - former North Eastern Railway 4-4-0 No.1870. It is seen here leaving Marthwate for Kendal, the first two carriages being ex-Great Central non-corridor clerestories. I like to think that this scene is a sort of equivalent of the real life Plate 95 (Chapter 7), the Midland infrastructure in this case clearly indicating that the LNER train is on 'foreign' ground.*

itself, where the object is to get the job done with as few moves and as little effort as possible.

The reason is not hard to seek because in reality the job is hard work. It involves regular reversal of the locomotive itself, a tiresome and tiring job in steam days, especially if it was fitted with screw reverse gear necessitating many turns of the reversing wheel (or handle) from full forward to full backward gear. *(Technical aside for those interested: The screw reverse, being infinitely variable, is capable of much finer adjustment than a lever reverse which has a number of fixed positions, or 'notches'. This makes the screw reverse more appropriate for main line running where a good driver could, along with his use of the regulator, make it 'play tunes' to get the optimum out of his engine. But the simpler lever reverse, a much older idea and generally less sensitive, could be changed from fore to back gear quite quickly, which is why shunting engines, not needing to be quite as sophisticated, were most usually given lever reverse. However, when out on the line, a footplate crew was often faced with shunting the local station with the train engine; and if it had a screw reverse gear - very probable - it was no easy task)*

On top of this basic problem was the regular coupling and uncoupling of vehices with that fearsome instrument, the hand-held shunter's pole, not to mention pinning down handbrakes (or unpinning them) and the making/breaking of vacuum pipe and/or screw coupling connections (sometimes both) if the train had a fitted head. There was also much manipulation of hand-operated point levers, or much to-ing and fro-ing in the signal box if the points were connected to the lever frame. Thus, the less effort expended, the better for all concerned.

In practical terms this usually means working out, before any movement starts, the order in which things will be done so as to minimise effort. I have actually sat in the brake van with a goods guard for ten to fifteen minutes or more, simply to work out movements at the National Railway Museum sidings ahead of starting a complex shunt. It was time well spent and its miniature equivalent is perfectly possible. So let us look at a typical example of a newly 'arrived' freight train, either at its terminal point or a marshalling yard.

Either way, the wagons in the train will be destined to go into several different sidings (or assembly roads in the case of

Plate 123: Recurring Themes - 3. *Dedicated mineral trains have been a feature of all my 4mm and 7mm layouts and one is seen here in its 'middle form' (as part of the main line services) at Garsdale Road (4mm scale) in 1970. The engine (Class 7F 0-8-0 No.9580 - Hellifield based in reality during the 1930s I believe) was only my second scratch built effort and prior to its use on this layout, had given yeoman service for many years at Marthwaite on a similar kind of job. It, along with several more engines from the old 4mm collection, now belongs to my good friend Chris Matthewman who, as well as making quite superb 4mm scale layouts, also helps operate the current 7mm display and, amongst other things, made both the fine signal boxes on the layout which are to be seen,* inter alia, *at Plates 120/122.*

Plate 124: A busy goods yard. *Kendal goods yard can get very crowded in the middle of an operating session, although not deliberately designed to create this effect - see also the main title page. The fact that the sidings are shorter than desirable - see text - makes it vital that best use is made of them and it needs a good operator to make sure that things do not get out of hand.....*

a marshalling yard) and the shunting engine's job is to get them there and it duly takes position at the end of the arrival road. But what it will *not* do is push the first group (or 'cut') of wagons into the first siding, uncouple them, reverse, and then repeat the procedure for all the rest - a procedure which most model layouts demonstrate regularly. Rather, before the first move, the human shunter on the trackside will uncouple the first cut of wagons, set the points for its appointed siding and then give the 'go-ahead' to the locomotive driver who will then start his engine vigorously, give the train a good 'shove' and then stop quickly, leaving the uncoupled wagons to free-wheel into the siding, the trackside shunter accompanying them so as to use their hand brakes to slow them down if need be. This done, the points will be changed, the next cut separated from the train and the whole process repeated.

Normally, this would be done without any need to reverse the shunting engine at all, or at the very least with far fewer

reversals than we are prone to make on our models. And, of course, 'hump' marshalling yards made this process semi-automatic, wagons being pushed over the hump and simply going downhill, cut by cut, as they passed the 'summit' of the hump itself. Either way it saved a lot of time and energy and without doing it this way, it is doubtful if any of our railways could have handled or re-marshalled their freight trains sufficiently quickly to allow any sort of decent service to be offered to their customers.

Now it has to be said that this is difficult to achieve on a model if the wagons are not free running, but it is well worth giving it a try......

When it comes to trains out on the line, it is a bit different. At its simplest, if the train in question is a simple 'pick-up' and destined for a marshalling yard where it will be sorted much as described above, the chances are that the wagons will be added to the train as they come, save for ensuring that any loaded livestock and/or fitted vehicles are properly treated. This sort of goods train was the very life blood of the system, the seed corn out of which the main line services grew, and is the most likely (and arguably the only essential) type of freight we shall need to model. By the time it reached its destination, subject to the officially laid down maximum number of wagons allowed, it could assume either massive and very random characteristics or, on a quiet day, seem hardly worth running at all.

The next complication arises if a goods train is destined both to collect and deliver *en route*. This was usually the in-bound equivalent of the pick-up freight where it would be normal to separate the vehicles which were to be detached intermediately from those which were going all the way - and in the order in which they were to leave the train. Whether these wagons went front or rear of the 'through' element (it could be either or both) would depend on the nature of the sidings to be shunted on the way; but it would usually be organised so as to minimise the inevitable shunting movements, consistent with the over-riding regulations governing the train in question.

This basic operational philosophy can be taken just as far as the modeller wishes and here, it has to be said, our American friends are rather better at it than are we, if truth be told. But at the very least, every wagon in a train should be intended for a specific destination before an operating session takes place and the layout operators should know what this is. This can be as simple as 'go' or 'stay', or as complex as giving a specific destination for each wagon and/or imposing restrictions as to total loads, type of train by which to be consigned, priority handling considerations and so on. I firmly believe that this is where modellers should decide for themselves - I am certainly in no position to predict any individual situation. But what I can say, based on experience, is that if you try to do it this way, the layout will soon develop the 'personality' which is, I suspect, that which we are most trying to achieve.

But talking of 'personality', we can also insert a few more individual touches on an imaginary layout if we are so minded. I have done this by inventing a whole raft of imaginary small businesses whose premises are presumed to be located either along the route or elsewhere for that matter. They all have

Plates 125/126: Wagon handling. *The presence of a goods shed or warehouse on the layout can help in operational terms, there being no need to change the loads of vehicles which may be inside to give a correct impression. But even if the yard is constricted, there needs to be road vehicle access to the shed, a point to which I shall return in Chapter 9. These two views show similar concepts which I adopted at Marthwaite (4mm scale) and was happy to repeat at Kendal in 7mm scale - even to the extent of laying out the yards in like manner. The main difference is that on the new layout, I have modelled stone sets for the road approach, having later discovered that this was a commonplace feature of many goods yards - eg Plates 109-111, Chapter 7.*

their own private owner wagons which appear regularly, and if these wagons happen to bear the names of many of my closest modelling friends, so what? All that matters is that the liveries are appropriately chosen and applied (ie they look much like real PO wagons of the time) and that they are given genuine operational tasks to fulfil. They have already fooled more than a few folk and offer an element of humour as well, especially if the publicity slogans (often found on real PO wagons) are chosen to reflect the personality of the 'proprietors'!

At this point, there only remains the matter of moving the vehicles round the layout itself, where I reckon that the main principle is still to keep it slow. Remember that in reality real men had to perform operations which were highly dangerous if loose coupled vehicles were allowed to career around at high

Plates 127/128: Friends Commemorated. *These two quite deliberately posed pictures (the wagons would never normally be seen all together at one place) represent my attempt to add personality and humour to my wholly imaginary scene. The publicity slogans which may just be readable (some may have otherwise been seen as libellous!), were cleared with their namesakes beforehand but, more to the point, all of these wagons have a quite genuine role to play on the layout.*

speed in an age where many of them were so primitive in their basic technology as to beggar belief. But it does show when a layout is operated against this sort of background, so I will conclude this section with another brief anecdote about my own modelling activities which I hope will bear this out - the first one was at the head of this chapter.

When Marthwaite was on the 'exhibition circuit' in the mid-1960s, we used proper bell codes and a freight train was offered to Marthwaite from the fiddle yard. The operator at the terminus acknowledged the bell code and then did nothing at all! Amongst the spectators were a couple of visitors, one of whom was obviously baffled. He said, audibly, to his friend: "Why haven't they brought that train in yet?" His friend replied: "You silly fool, it's supposed to have set off some five miles down the line. It takes time for it to get here and they are allowing 'time on the block'." We were delighted....

Locomotive operations

It is not by coincidence that I have relegated locomotive operation to third place in the operational story. The job of the railway is to move traffic and only when traffic needs are known can we look at the locomotive requirement and how to deal with it.

I have already discussed the matter of selection of types and the like, pointing out that there is ample scope for modellers to indulge their personal preferences. All I would add here is that the final choices should tend towards those which typify rather than to the more exotic, albeit theoretically feasible types. But since the most unlikely locomotives have appeared on quite improbable trains in their time, it does not do to be too dogmatic and we can be slightly self-indulgent without too much fear of ridicule; provided we do the homework properly.

It is much more important to ensure that locomotive stock and associated servicing facilities are appropriate. We all like engine sheds (or motive power depots [MPD] to use the more correct term - the shed was merely the covered building which formed part of the MPD), and most of us do our level best to include such a feature. But perhaps we should ask ourselves whether our model really needs a full-blown depot; maybe a turntable and water column might suffice. In the case of Kendal, I have already explained how my plan revealed a genuine need for a modest MPD, but when I built Marthwaite in 4mm scale, the engine shed and water tower on the first version were far too big and only when I made them both very much smaller did the effect look right.

I think we have to accept that unlike real railways, where the object is to get by with as few engines as possible, the modeller is frequently likely to have too many. Some can perhaps be found employment in the 'funny train' mode, if you are so inclined, but what of the others? I think we should resist the temptation to have an over-large MPD simply to house them and instead, make an effort to keep some of them out of sight altogether. A good solution is to have a 'working reserve' safely boxed away (or in a display case ready for use) and this can be a very useful ploy for those with exhibition layouts. When we were displaying Garsdale Road, we usually provided at least two engines for every job as an insurance against the sort of failure which could not be rectified during the show; and it always amused the spectators when one of us, usually ex-footplateman Bob Essery (sic!), came out and 'chalked up' the engine rosters for the next display sequence. We even had

a few 'number takers' and repeat visitors when we eventually did this as a regular part of the presentation.

Be that as it may, the locomotives should be operated properly when on the layout. At its simplest, this may be no more than ensuring that vacuum braked stock is operated by a vacuum braked engine, remembering that in the steam era there were many a hundred steam brake only goods engines which were quite incapable of operating an automatically braked train.

The most believable operations will generally be achieved by using as few prime movers as possible: no more than one engine per set of vehicles and less if possible. Thus, unless there is a very good operational reason for doing something different (eg a major city terminal), the same engine as brought a train into a terminus of the kind we would normally model is the most likely candidate for taking it out again, though there may be some slight differences between passenger and freight services in this context.

Dealing with the latter, it was common practice, as I have stated, for the train engine to do its own shunting. The luxury of a 'station pilot' to do the miscellaneous odd jobs was most often confined to busier places and its presence needs to be justified in model terms too if it is to look right. It depends entirely on how much work is to be done and whether the train engine(s) need time for servicing and/or turning on arrival; and even if the latter is necessary, there may still be time for the local freight engine to shunt its own train and be serviced. In this regard, tender-first operating, while disliked, was not ruled out if there was no time to get onto and off the turntable. It was more common on goods trains but not unheard of on passenger services - and, of course, inevitable in one direction if there was no turntable.

With passenger trains, the problems may be a little different. Turn round times may be tighter, barely giving time to run-round, let alone turn or service. In these circumstances, a second engine to take out the incoming train may be a solution and I do this myself with some of the Kendal workings; but it would probably look ridiculous if this happened every time, save for those who are replicating intensive suburban services such as used to operate out of Liverpool Street (the so-called 'Jazz' trains). In any case, these workings simply made use of train engines in rotation. On the whole, therefore, I reckon that pilot engines and dedicated shunting types should be kept to the very minimum on most layouts, unless they happen to be of Toton Yard or some such.

I have used the word 'servicing' several times in the last few paragraphs and a word or two on this subject will not be out of place. The servicing of a steam locomotive could cover almost anything between a quick oil-round by the driver at a station stop to a complete fire drop, coal, turn, water and lighting up again at a more well-equipped location. Moreover, it does not follow, simply because a depot has coal and water facilities that all engines must or would use them, nor even the turntable if present. In fact, especially where tank engines were widely used, it was not uncommon for water cranes to be installed on the platforms as well as at the depots so that tank engines

Main line modelling

I think these two pictures encapsulate, as well as I can, the truly vital main line aspects of the hobby as far as I am concerned. The upper view shows one side of the coin, so to speak, in the shape of the fully matured Gauge 1 railway in my garden with my kit-built Aster LNWR 'Jumbo' 2-4-0 No.5050 Merrie Carlisle and 'bought-in' Midland Compound 4-4-0 No.1000 (both in LMS colours) in charge of my scratch built model of the 10-coach 'Merseyside Express'. Both engines were in steam at the time and putting up a fine performance, but the exhaust was too clean to show up on a warm day.

The other side of the story, the spread and complexity of a fully scenic main line layout, is well shown in this splendid view by Ron Prattley of Neil Corner's Lonsdale station. Though not my own work, and of a size which I could never contemplate building again after my less than happy experiences with the 'Little Long Drag' in 4mm scale, I take much pleasure in seeing the full realisation of one of my designs in a way which I did not at first believe to be possible - see also the notes with Fig.37, Chapter 9. I only fully accepted that it really would happen when Neil and I stood on the bare baseboards and drew out the whole of this station plan full size before the real work started...

A happy compromise

On this last colour page I return to my own Kendal branch and I could not resist re-using the image on the dust jacket - well almost. Barry Lane and I spent some time setting up this scene and took about half a dozen repeats before we got one or two with which we were happy, this being the alternative to that on the cover. It shows Marthwaite station and ex-MR 4-4-0 No.773 setting off with a local to Kendal consisting of ex-LYR stock. I reckon it is just about as good a standard as I am capable of achieving and I am happy with a final compromise which will suffice for me, given that we can't have everything.

And I finish symbolically with the buffer stops at Kendal. It is still a bit squeaky clean, but I already like the view through the archway to the Midland Hotel. This is something which only the camera can see and even that solution will not be possible for much longer - this area is destined to be filled with station canopies in due course.

(which would not normally need the turntable anyway) could take water without going on shed - and I am sure that on many occasions, tender engines would take similar advantage.

As a general rule, the more lengthy servicing (usually in preparation for a spell of duty or the disposal of the locomotive after such a spell) would be carried out at the engine's home base. Visiting engines might have a quick 'fire clean', or top up water tanks and coal supplies, but they would not normally spend too long on shed. It is therefore quite a good idea to determine, at the outset, which of the locomotive fleet is based 'on' the layout and which are simply visiting. Give the 'home' team plenty of time for their many needs but assume that the visitors are well looked after elsewhere. An intelligent use of common sense and an understanding of the basic principles is as good a guideline as any other I can offer.

One area where the modeller can, if so minded, increase the locomotive stock in a realistic fashion is in the realm of out-going trains. Nothing looks more ridiculous on a layout which is being operated to timetable or planned sequence, be it end-to-end or continuous, than to see a locomotive and train, which has supposedly departed for a distant destination, turn up again (sometimes from the wrong direction) a few minutes later. If it is supposed to be on its way to Leeds (or wherever), then give it time to get there before you bring it back in view. The correct working out of a train graph (Chapter 6) will show where this can be done and may even suggest a legitimate need for more rolling stock as well. In particular any strikingly unusual items of rolling stock (passenger or freight) should not reappear a few minutes after being seen to depart, though you may get away with it in the case of humdrum wagons and very ordinary looking carriages.

Finally, it goes without saying that in mechanical terms, the locomotive fleet should be as reliable as your own modelling ability can make it. Nothing destroys illusion more quickly than 'finger prodding' or 'jack-rabbit' starting. Even over-speedy train movements are more acceptable than the poor running characteristics of a badly adjusted locomotive.

Signalling

Apart from the trains themselves, signals are one of the few aspects of the model scene which can also be made to operate properly and I feel it is a great pity that so many fine layouts seem to neglect this fact, sometimes even to the extent of omitting the signals entirely. I speak mainly of the semaphore type of course, because of their obvious visible presence, for who can deny that sense of expectation when watching trains at the lineside and the 'peg comes off'. Colour lights, for all their efficiency, never convey quite the same excitement.

I first appreciated this with my first EM Gauge layout where I had a full array of non-working signals which, on reflection, rather spoiled the show because of their statuesque immobility. I tried to convince myself that it was because I couldn't get them to work anyway, nor did I much like making them; but with Garsdale Road I 'bit the bullet' and installed working signals - and what a difference it made. There were only four of them (a 'home' and 'starter' in each direction), but combined with the correct bell codes, it did serve to create quite a degree of anticipation, something I hope I have made even more apparent in the context of my present system.

I therefore think that a good historical model should have working signals for all running lines. Whether or not this should be extended to working ground signals is perhaps more debatable; they are very small even in 7mm scale and even if they work, this may not be noticed. But I think they should be there if possible, even in static form.

A further advantage of signals is that, at least in pre-BR days (and on the Western Region for many years afterwards), they were so visually distinctive between different railways. In this respect they can play an immense part in creating that sense of 'company' which I covered in some detail in Chapter 2. On my new layout, therefore, knowing that even on the Settle and Carlisle main line the old MR signals did not begin to be replaced until c.1947, and I am modelling a much earlier period than that, there is a full array of working Midland semaphores, some of them still in pre-LMS colours.

Railway signalling is a fascinating subject but, beyond stating that I believe it should be incorporated, I do not propose to elaborate here. For one thing, the basic principles can be gleaned from many standard references and for another, each railway had its own way of doing things.

Model railway control systems

I said at the start of this book that I was not proposing to offer a 'how to make it' account of the hobby, but I think it important that whatever control systems we adopt should be suited to the main purpose of the layout. I therefore thought that I would conclude this section by outlining the principles of my own control system, but using a minimum of technical terms; there are plenty of publshed accounts on this subject for it not to be necessary to go further. The final layout plan is given at Fig.20 in Chapter 6 for any who wish to follow in detail, but to save much page turning, I also append here (Fig.21) a diagrammatic representation of the system.

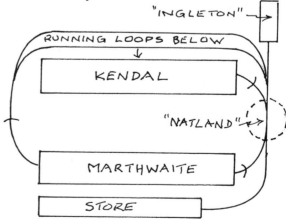

Fig.21: Diagram of the system. *This simplified diagram of the layout, devoid of track detail, is included here simply to clarify the operational aspects mentioned in this chapter.*

145

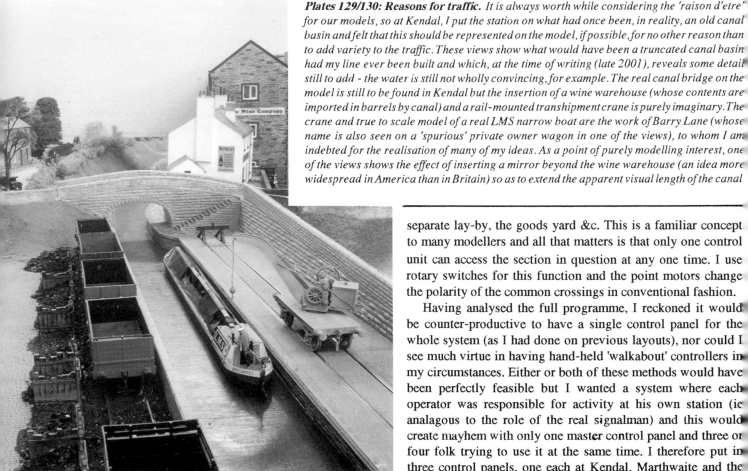

Plates 129/130: Reasons for traffic. *It is always worth while considering the 'raison d'etre' for our models, so at Kendal, I put the station on what had once been, in reality, an old canal basin and felt that this should be represented on the model, if possible, for no other reason than to add variety to the traffic. These views show what would have been a truncated canal basin had my line ever been built and which, at the time of writing (late 2001), reveals some detail still to add - the water is still not wholly convincing, for example. The real canal bridge on the model is still to be found in Kendal but the insertion of a wine warehouse (whose contents are imported in barrels by canal) and a rail-mounted transhipment crane is purely imaginary. The crane and true to scale model of a real LMS narrow boat are the work of Barry Lane (whose name is also seen on a 'spurious' private owner wagon in one of the views), to whom I am indebted for the realisation of many of my ideas. As a point of purely modelling interest, one of the views shows the effect of inserting a mirror beyond the wine warehouse (an idea more widespread in America than in Britain) so as to extend the apparent visual length of the canal*

In essence, I operate a form of cab control whereby the layout is divided into sections, usually defined by the actual track formations and arranged so that each section forms a logical unit such as a fan of sidings from a common throat, a separate lay-by, the goods yard &c. This is a familiar concept to many modellers and all that matters is that only one control unit can access the section in question at any one time. I use rotary switches for this function and the point motors change the polarity of the common crossings in conventional fashion.

Having analysed the full programme, I reckoned it would be counter-productive to have a single control panel for the whole system (as I had done on previous layouts), nor could I see much virtue in having hand-held 'walkabout' controllers in my circumstances. Either or both of these methods would have been perfectly feasible but I wanted a system where each operator was responsible for activity at his own station (ie analagous to the role of the real signalman) and this would create mayhem with only one master control panel and three or four folk trying to use it at the same time. I therefore put in three control panels, one each at Kendal, Marthwaite and the hidden storage area with its two double junctions (referred to as Natland from here onwards). Each location has over-riding control of the track sections at that panel, but every one of them can gain access to a certain number of sections at the other locations on a pre-planned basis.

Plate 131: Station pilot. To justify a separate station pilot, it must have work to do. On the current layout, No.1719 never leaves Kendal and is seen here at one of its most common resting places between turns - the inner end of Platform 4. Purely for the record, the Leyland Titan double decker, yet another means of adding 'period' flavour to the scene, is a kit-based and exact scale model (down to the correct numberplate) of a brand new vehicle delivered to County Motors of Kendal in 1929. It is finished in the correct dark blue and cream livery of County Motors, later absorbed by the more familiar 'Ribble' company, and the model was built for me (along with much other appropriate 'lineside' ephemera) by another of my many friends who have contributed so much to my efforts down the years: Harry (Nelson) Twells.

The basis of my thinking is the prototypical arrangement whereby a particular location is responsible for all movements within its own station limits and for all main line movements *towards* that station. Thus, for example, a train bound from Kendal to Marthwaite will be offered first to Natland and, on acceptance, Kendal will switch the section(s) concerned to Natland, pull off the signals and offer 'train entering section'. At this point, the Natland operator will actually drive the train out of Kendal and does not even need to know from which platform it is coming; he simply drives the train towards his station. The same process is then repeated Natland-Marthwaite and this time, Natland switches the relevant sections to Marthwaite whose operator then takes over the train - and so on, reversing the sequence for in-bound trains to Kendal.

This is all done by bell code and working signals. The latter are not interlocked with the power supply to the track (though they could be), but they will not come 'off' unless a proper route is set, thus giving the operator a visual indication when they do come off that the route is proved, electrically. It does not, of course, prevent operators driving past signals at danger, but that in itself is perfectly in accordance with the pre-track circuit period which I am modelling.

Plate 132: Focus on the signals - 1. All my finished 4mm and 7mm scale layouts have had signals, but not until Garsdale Road did they actually work, largely because I only needed four of them and that was not too onerous a task to contemplate. I include this less than perfect view of that layout because it is the only picture I have which clearly shows the up starter located on the outside of the curve beyond the down main line. This was a common feature of Midland practice wherever the main line was curving to the left (the MR was a right hand drive railway), so as to allow the driver an earlier sighting of the signals - for the prototype inspiration see Plate 67, Chapter 5. The train is a down Saturday 'extra', formed from randomly assembled gangwayed stock, headed by 'Horwich' 2-6-0 No.2803.

Plate 133: Focus on the signals - 2. *Although the 7mm scale Marthwaite (a through station compared with its 4mm scale precursor) has a track layout very much inspired by Garsdale Road, its signalling is more complex because of my wish to terminate certain passenger trains at the station as part of the operating programme. This necessitated the facility to 'start' the railcar in the down direction from the short bay platform and also for some passenger trains to depart 'wrong road' from the up platform. In this view, showing 4-4-0 No.809 approaching from Kendal past the down home on its tall post (for better sighting over the water tower on approaching the station from the river direction), the bracketed 'wrong road starters' from the bay and up platforms can also be seen on their shorter posts. The railcar will depart when the up local has left for Dent Head.*

Plate 134: Focus on the signals - 3. *At Kendal, all main line departures have equal priority, regardless of platform, so all four starter signals are identical and mounted on twin bracketed posts and only one can be pulled 'off' at any one time, depending on the setting of the turnouts ahead of the departing train. In this case the road is set from Platform 2 for the departing sleeping cars, improbably juxtaposed with an Arnside freight in Platform 4, purely for the sake of photography - the trains depart at very different times in reality. Just visible in the background are the miniature signals controlling the exits from the parcels bay and locomotive yard - see also Plates 88 and 89, Chapter 6. Entry to Kendal is controlled by a similar 'one route only' principle, this time by way of a single gantry which features at Plate 86 in Chapter 6.*

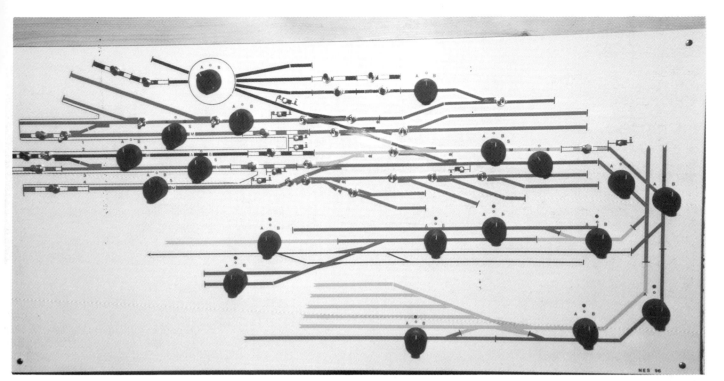

Plates 135-137: Control Panels. Control panels are not the most exciting of visual subjects but these three views give some idea of how I have divided up the layout. On all of them, the actual track sections are colour coded on the panel, each being marked by prominent rotary switches, mounted geographically. The first, more close-up view, shows Kendal, which displays the layouts of the relevant parts of Marthwaite and the storage roads to which it can gain access, this device being adopted so that the railway could be operated by two people if need be. It was made (and photographed) before the slight simplification of the layout in the loco yard - a matter which is now corrected.

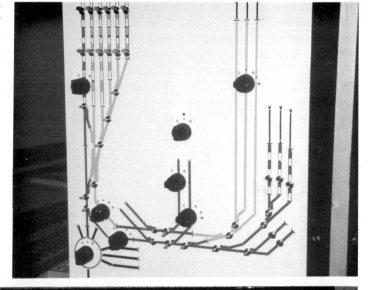

The second picture shows the control panel in the storage area (aka 'Natland'), its orientation being that which operators see when running the system. This, too, has been modified in the light of experience by reducing the complexity of the turntable area and also by adding access to Marthwaite as well as Kendal by way of an additional rotary switch, though not displaying their track layouts in either case - 'Natland' does not need to know precisely from whence the train is coming!

The final picture shows the Marthwaite panel as it was before the addition of the extra siding and slip points - see Fig.20, Chapter 6. It is shown in its operating position - ie hinged out from its vertical 'resting' position. Like the panel at Kendal, it folds down when the layout is not in use so as to make access a little simpler for work purposes. It will be noted that this panel is the only one which has access to the whole circuit. The layout is not normally operated in 'tail chase' mode, but for testing and demonstration purposes, it is useful to have one position from which continuous operation is possible.

Some additional refinements have been added because of the specific nature of the layout. Firstly, it will be seen that a Kendal-Natland-Marthwaite-Dent Head service will return to Natland (via the running loops below Kendal), prior to entering the storage sidings behind Marthwaite. This, in turn, presumes that Natland also functions as Dent Head, so to speak, for trains running in both directions on the main line. In order that the operators at Natland and Marthwaite know from which direction all their trains are coming, we have also adopted a local 'call attention' bell signal: one beat (conventional) for the Natland to Marthwaite trains via the direct route and 'one/pause/one' for the route via the running loops. Natland is also responsible for 'holding' any trains between Kendal and Marthwaite (to ensure that the sequence keeps in synchronisation between these two places) and also for implementing the 'change of train identity' on the Furness line, already explained in Chapter 6. Natland can also change the composition of freight trains from time to time when they are out of sight, so as to simulate activity at the non-modelled intermediate stations.

It will therefore be appreciated that the Natland operator is the key person in the whole sequence, usually being involved in every movement outside the Kendal and Marthwaite station limits. In effect, Natland is a sort of Regional Control Office for the whole layout and acts as 'gaffer' when a full operational session takes place. It works very well for the most part, and it can be very satisfying (and eerily realistic) when, after an hour or two of operating, we realise that apart from bell signals, not a word has been spoken by any of us......

Another refinement is to use the distant signals at the exits from the two stations as route indicators. They were put there mainly for aesthetic effect, but have now been wired so that if they remain 'on', the operator knows that no route is available beyond the station, while if they come 'off', they indicate a clear road and, in the case of the splitting distants at the exit from Kendal and the Kendal end at Marthwaite, also show which of the two routes is set beyond the double junction.

Finally, light emitting diodes are positioned on the control panels to show 'track occupation' on all the hidden running loops and storage sidings, while for 'tail-chasing' and testing, sufficient sections can be switched from Natland to Marthwate to allow the latter panel to run the whole of the continuous circuit in both directions. Under normal operations, the layout is worked entirely in end-to-end mode.

Conclusion

There are no hard and fast rules to model railway operating. In the last analysis, modellers can do as they please and good luck to them. However, I venture to suggest that if you get most of your pleasure by seeing the trains run, as opposed to merely building them, then more permanent satisfaction will be gained by trying to do things properly. We may not all be able to gain access to a rule book, nor be able to draw on our own personal knowledge either, but even if we do not wish to get ourselves totally immersed in all the subtle ramifications of the real railway, it is usually possible to get quite a bit closer to reality than the merely aimless moving of stock.

Even the modern railway - simplified though it may be by comparison with former years - can still repay a bit of careful observation. And if you can still find one, a few hours near to, or ideally inside an old-fashioned manual signal box will teach the modeller a great deal, as will a few hours watching and taking note of activity in a marshalling yard or carriage depot. Much of the action is still recognisably similar in principle; only the characters on stage have changed. It is not as easy as it once was to do this sort of thing, but it is well worth the effort if you can. And remember, even the preserved lines, albeit far more full of stock than they ever were in the old days, still run their trains along traditional methods as far as the operational side of their activity is concerned: they have to, or else they would not be allowed to run trains at all.

CHAPTER 9

General thoughts on layout design

"It's my own invention."
Lewis Carroll, 'Through the Looking Glass'

I CAN THINK of no better way to start my final chapter than by quoting the White Knight, not the first character from one of my favourite literary sources to appear in these pages. For no matter what sort of historical railway model we may prefer to tackle, it must be our own invention or else we are merely copyists of other folk.

I have written this review mainly for those whose preferred choice is the 'total' approach, wherein we resolve to have a go at everything, hopefully to a fairly consistent standard of presentation. I have also stated why 'believable but imaginary' may be easier for most of us than the attempt to model a real place and have also attempted, as far as I am able, to show how this may be tackled in a rational and thought-out manner. It will certainly be less frustrating than tackling a genuine location, if only to keep out of the clutches of 'Johnny Know-all' who will delight in telling us that there never was a trailing single slip to the down main line at Muddlecombe-on-Slush in

1935, much less a ground signal of the type we have modelled. He has never yet made anything for himself, of course, but this, you understand, is only because his researches are not quite complete - a murrain on him and all like him......

But even if we do choose to base our model on a real place at a real time (and I hope my thoughts have helped in this context too), we know, deep down, that it is, essentially, still an imaginary world, however well executed. Therefore, since we can never create a true reality, I began to wonder if there was an alternative expression which would best sum up what I (and I suspect many others) are all trying to achieve; and I found myself homing in on the word 'railwaylike'. Here, what struck me most forcibly was that none of the truly railwaylike models I have ever seen, be they individual items or complete layouts, were in any significant way conditional upon scale, space, standards or any other of the many constraints which we often use to excuse our shortcomings.

Plate 139: The 'total' approach. *This picture, which shows the revised 'exit' at the 4mm scale Marthwaite in its final form (1966-7), also represents the layout in what I like to think was its most railwaylike state in terms of totality. I cringe now at some of the modelling infelicities which it reveals (eg plastic trees - sic!), but at least the main line over the viaduct had a check rail throughout its length - not visible in this view. Ideally, the home signal should be further back from the 'V' of the turnout, whilst the Class 7F 0-8-0 on the empty minerals should certainly have stopped further back from the signal post to let the passenger train take priority; but it was a start. Although there was much improvement still to come on future layouts, there was at least beginning to develop that degree of consistency between the various elements modelled which I place high on the agenda..*

Plate 140: The role of the infrastructure. *The regularly restricted nature of the fixed infrastructure of our railways - see text - can actually work in our favour when faced with limited space and Peter Denny is a past master at this sort of thing. Here we see one his 'trademark' gasworks models tucked into a small corner at Leighton Buzzard - Linslade. In particular note the use of small individual wagon turntables at this most restricted site. Other views of this masterpiece of limited space planning can be seen at Plates 55/56, Chapter 4. (Ron Prattley)*

This, in turn, got me thinking that even if 'railwaylike' was an acceptable and appropriate summation of our activities, it still begged the question to some extent, for such a word can imply many different things and, like so many other aspects of this fascinating hobby, it brings us back yet again to one of my main sub-themes: personal preference. After all, what may be most railwaylike to some (eg the working of a complex signal box in a busy urban environment) would perhaps be anathema to the sort of person for whom the hand-crafting of a superb replica of a favourite item in whatever scale they prefer is sufficient, as long as the end product looks as if the real railway had a hand in its making - two very different sorts of interpretation of 'railwaylike', no doubt about that.

Then there is the tactile pleasure of live steam in its many forms - what could be more railwaylike in the context of the steam era than using the real stuff to make the model work, no matter how many compromises need to be made? And what of those who are happy to accept minimum detail in the models themselves (occasionally with no scenery at all), as long as operation of the system is 100% 'by the book'?

But if we can make the obvious exceptions of the individual 'craftsman' models and/or real life prototype places, where, in both cases, the working parameters we are trying to reproduce are, by definition, 'set' for us already, then I think we can all find common ground if a fully working layout, no matter how simple, is the desired objective. Here, the disposition of tracks and associated matters in accordance with prototype reality is arguably the real common factor, regardless of the scale or standards we may choose. Considerations like this have thus persuaded me that perhaps the best way to sum things up is to look at the matter of layout design by way of addressing those general themes which apply 'across the board', so to speak.

Fundamentally, what I think we all hope to do is produce a track plan which looks as if the real railway might have put it there at the time we have in mind to represent. Here, the main point to bear in mind is that real railways (in the historical British context) usually had a specific way of doing things, often adopting certain cosmetic 'trademark' details along the way which are for the individual to find out as I have already indicated. But I also reckon that most of our principal railways were usually singing from the same 'hymn sheet' in terms of the basics, so this is where I shall concentrate. But before I do so, a bit of historical background may not be out of place.

Historical aspects of layout planning

I start by making the maybe obvious point that track layouts, like rolling hardware, changed with time and although the rate of change was never quite as rapid in the case of track itself (it is, after all, referred to as the 'permanant way'), I think we can identify three main phases in terms of the broader principles, with the usual transition stages between them. The first thing we therefore need to do is decide which is most appropriate to our period of choice, bearing in mind, of course, the implicit dangers of such a simple generalisation.

In the early days of mechanically powered railways, there was little or no appreciation of how the railway idea would grow. In consequence, we built most of our lines to a smaller 'structural envelope' than later experience throughout the world showed was possible. This left Britain with a permanent legacy of tight structure clearances and limited overall dimensions in terms of vehicle width and height. But within this limitation, we singularly failed to make best use of the only dimension which was not quite so critical - vehicle length.

I mention these things at the outset because between them, they set parameters for the fixed infrastructure which began to appear at much the same time. Warehouses, goods sheds, plus not a few passenger stations for that matter, were built so solidly and in such numbers, that they were frequently far too expensive to abandon or rebuild, even after larger vehicles and more track elaboration became technically possible. Even in the passenger arena, such a giant company as the LNWR, until events finally forced an expensive change, chose to keep to its 42ft maximum carriage length for many a long year because of the restricted dimensions of the essential carriage traversers at Euston, or so it is said: no doubt, many other mid-Victorian companies could offer similar examples.

Early track layouts were rather primitive and, in want of knowing anything better at the time, the people who planned the schemes were mostly influenced by the only precedent then available: that of the old horse-drawn wagonways and the like. Such concepts as simple turnouts and diamond crossings were understood at a very early stage but more sophisticated forms of track, not to mention such ideas as transition curves and superelevation took time to evolve. Meantime, such things as short turntables allowing goods wagons, one at a time, to enter warehouses and other places so as to be loaded/unloaded, were common, not to mention stub points, individual (short length) vehicle traversers and other legacies of the pre-steam era. It was simply not appreciated at that time how much in the way of mechanisation and/or sophistication could be achieved.

But perhaps the worst legacy of this 'first phase' as I have chosen to define it, even after the progressive adoption of better track and signalling methods down the years, was to condemn our home railways to a more than century-long love affair with the primitive, inefficient and unbraked four wheel goods wagon, largely because the early building of fixed (and very expensive to replace) elements of the infrastructure in so many places had ensured that they could not handle anything much bigger. This, along with the ever-growing and eventually

Plate 141: Early trackwork. *Finding reasonable views of the early phase of our railways is difficult, but this one drew my attention. I can neither date nor locate the image but the stone sleepers in the sidings suggest an early date, though maybe not as early as it may seem. The wagons in the background could well be turn of the 19th/20th Century in age and the sleepers simply a remnant of older days - an interesting possibility in modelling terms, none the less.*

mechanised road haulage business, was finally to cause a steep decline in British railway freight traffic from the mid-1950s onwards. Mark you, we must also accept that it was not always helped by the singular reluctance of many railways to improve matters where it could be done (eg installing automatic brakes, thus allowing faster speeds), largely because they held a near-total monopoly of the most valuable traffic on offer or, to be rather more accurate, thought they did - until it was too late....

By then, however, we were well into the second phase of track layouts - almost at the end of it, in fact - so when did the essential changes take place? Now I cannot date with precision the move to better track layout design, though some changes took place at a very early stage and most essential elements of what I have called the 'traditional' railway were probably in place by the mid-1870s, no doubt made easier to achieve by the far better signalling and braking standards which were often forced onto the reluctant railway companies during the middle part of the Victorian era. Nor, even were I qualified to do so, do I wish this review to turn into a history of railway safety and signalling; but it does interface with our modelling when we are trying to suggest 'period'. So if you decide to set your model very early in time terms, this is an area where a bit of research will come in handy before you start planning - and it need not be unpleasurable - see Chapter 5.

In general, I regard this second phase as lasting from late or possibly even mid-Victorian days to well into the first 20 years or more of the BR period. During this time, things remained more evolutionary than revolutionary in principle and, again bearing in mind the dangers of broad generalisation, little of fundamental significance changed - a Victorian railwayman of the 1890s would not have found it too difficult to comprehend

Plate 142: Contrasts in track. This official LNER view of Brayton Junction, just south of Selby, was taken in 1945 to illustrate a new facing turnout laid in 110lb heavy duty flat bottom rail - state of the art technology at the time and a piece of pointwork which would not disgrace the modern railway. But note the much older pre-group NER track in the layby to the left, also the difference in ballast texture. There were and are many long term survivors of previous days on our railways and a bit of selective attention to this sort of detail can often help create a good effect. The layout itself is also of interest - a slight variation on the routine double junction arrangement.

the BR system of the 1950s and 1960s, though I doubt that we should be too proud of that fact; but what he may have made of our current railway is a very different story..... More happily from the modeller's standpoint, part of this very long period is almost certainly the most likely choice for most of us and this is where I shall concentrate.

However, before doing so, I think I should tidy up this bit of the analysis by mentioning that we are now, at the start of the

21st Century, firmly in what I see as the third phase of track layout evolution, vast simplification having taken place since the early 1970s. This was usually a response to the need for high speed alignment, together with its concomitant and, very often, computer-controlled, automatic signalling, not forgetting reduced track complexity caused by the diminution in freight infrastructure. Moreover, we should also bear in mind that much of that which does remain in use bears little relationship to the 'norms' of the 'traditional' railway. No doubt it too may well become the inspiration for a later generation of 'historical' models in due course and, indeed, there are signs that this is already starting to happen.

In the meantime, however, and trying to be consistent with my overall themes, I shall now concentrate on that highly interesting c.1885-1965 period (give or take a few years at each end), paying particular emphasis to matters of principle which seem to me to transcend both period of choice and the modelling standards we elect to adopt.

Plates 143/144: Safety Points. *These pictures show mechanically interlocked safety (or trap) points at Blea Moor running loops and Express Dairy sidings at Appleby respectively. The former, protecting the down running loop from the converging lay-by is conventional enough, but that from the dairy was squeezed into a very short space and is sharply curved. Note, in both cases, that the point rodding allows them to be operated as a sort of 'crossover' with the adjoining release turnout to the running lines.*

Some fundamental principles of track design

Before we plan a layout, we need to have a clear understanding of the relationship between track and traffic. Track formations were not random occurrences but were adopted to facilitate the job to be done. And although many traditional prototype track formations, especially at busy locations, can seem incredibly complicated, there was usually an underlying reason for what was provided and no railway would indulge in laying down more complicated pointwork than was needed to do the job on hand. In the first place, pointwork was more expensive to make than plain track, but more importantly, it brought with it

further expenditure by way of the inevitable extra signalling, not to mention additional mechanical complications which considerations of safety demanded.

The first thing to bear in mind is that the nature of the pointwork was driven by the nature of the motive power and rolling stock available at the time. Thus, taking a simple example, if a separate locomotive is required, there will need to be facilities to get it from one end of the train to the other at a terminal location, which, of course, is not synonymous with a terminus - trains could and did terminate at many intermediate places. On the other hand, multiple unit passenger stock with driving cabs at both ends does not need such a facility, only the driver 'runs round' the train, so to speak. And the fact that this type of operation is increasingly widespread in our modern age for main line express formations as well as its long-established suburban role, has much reduced the need for complex point formations of the type once found in many places.

At this point, however, I should mention that if a 'dead-end' terminus, as oppposed to a through station, was sufficiently busy to merit a pilot engine to draw out an incoming train to release the train engine (eg, but not exclusively, the majority of the principal London termini), then the cost of an 'engine release' crossover would not normally be contemplated, even in the days before the more widespread use of multiple unit stock, double-ended HSTs or whatever. There were quite a few exceptions, of course, but these are most unlikely to be relevant to the majority of historical modelmakers.

Mention of safety does, however, raise the matter of the correct way to protect train movements so as to minimise and/or eliminate accident risk. The obvious places where this happens are where the tracks of two or more routes converge or where a siding, lay-by or other lesser track formation makes a connection with the main running lines. In the former case, junctions between routes were protected by signals, but in the latter case, something rather more than a simple turnout from main line to siding was vital to safe operating. At its simplest, this would be a trap point or sand-drag which, operated with the turnout itself, ensured that if anything moved (whether by accident or design) in such a way as to join the main route when it was not safe to do so, then the offending train would simply derail. In many cases, this protection extended to a proper headshunt and at Fig.22 I have offered a few diagrams of the sort of thing which might be found.

Trap points and catch points can be confusing terms and the two are often regarded as synonymous since, in essence, they both did the same thing. They are also referred to as 'safety points' in some sources, but to be strictly correct, a 'trap' point prevented traffic converging onto the main running line if it was not safe to do so and was under the control of the signal box. A catch point, on the other hand, was a spring loaded device placed on the main line itself at the foot of a gradient. Its normally open blades would be 'pushed' into place by a passing train going in the proper direction, but if the train 'broke in two' on an uphill journey (a rare but not unlikely event in the context of freight wagons without any form of automatic and 'fail-safe' brakes), then should the detached portion run away in the wrong direction, the (permanently) open blade(s) of the catch points would derail the miscreant vehicles before they ran back so far as to be a menace to the next following train - again see Fig.22.

Such devices were very common on the traditional railway and can look very good if incorporated in our models.

We next come to the specific track provisions made for the operation of traffic at stations, in which category I also include goods yards, locomotive depots and the like. The most obvious

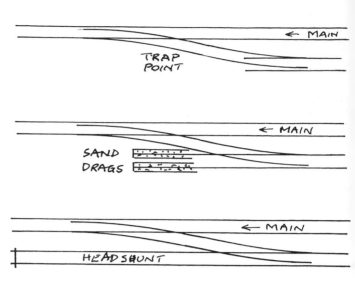

Fig.22: Safety points. *These diagrams show some of the more common methods by which prototype railways protected their main running lines from accidental mishap. In all cases I have drawn both running rails, though to no particular scale or geometry, and their nature should be self-evident.*

of these are the various sidings needed in which to load/unload goods vehicles, store carriages and/or 'park' locomotives when not in use. The vital point to remember here, as I have already mentioned, is to ensure adequate provision for the vast amount of rolling stock which was not actually rolling.... I would even go so far as to say that we usually find ourselves with far too few sidings on most of our models, given the space constraints which the vast majority of us have to face, and that anything we can do to improve this situation is usually worth while.

But it must be done in a rational manner. Thus, there is little point in having lots of sidings if there is no facility to draw vehicles in and out of them for shunting &c. This is commonly an independent 'headshunt', ideally of much the same length as the longest siding, but there were many places where other means were adopted and this can be of help. On my Kendal layout, for example, although Platform 4 (Fig.20, Chapter 6) is signalled for passenger use if need be, this is a rare occurrence and it usually doubles up as a goods arrival road and headshunt facility for the main goods yard.

Having got our sidings, we must then decide how they are to be used. "Obviously," I hear you say, but not if you look at some models I have seen. In most goods yards, although the loading and unloading of vehicles could take place inside the goods shed, if provided, this was usually confined to the most perishable and valuable commodities, the bulk of such activity being carried out in the open air, often using trackside 'goods cranes'. For this, one had to have trackside access (cart roads they were often called) which meant that any sidings intended for loading/unloading were never found at normal track centre spacing in greater numbers than two at a time in order that the road vehicles and crane (if present) had room to manoevre - Fig.23 attempts to show what I mean.

Plate 145: Cart roads. *This picture of the LYR goods yard at North Docks, Liverpool, taken in 1913, clearly shows the wide spaces between sidings to allow road access for the loading and unloading of wagons in the open air. (B.C. Lane collection)*

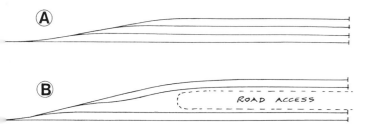

Fig.23: Goods sidings. *These two diagrams attempt to show the essential difference between sidings (eg marshalling yards) where wagons (loaded or unloaded) were stabled temporarily whilst 'in transit' between departure and arrival points (a), and those at which loading or unloading would be expected to take place (b). In this diagram I have followed routine convention by indicating each siding with a single line*

Marshalling yards, where loading/unloading did not take place, were different, of course, as were any sidings used simply for 'parking' purposes, the most likely examples of the latter being sidings designated for already loaded vehicles awaiting despatch and/or goods brake vans awaiting their next turn of duty. Now I am not suggesting that all layouts we may design will be able to incorporate all such refinements, but I am convinced that an understanding of the operational nature of the railway will be of material help when we come to look at the various possibilities on offer.

At this point, as far as sidings are concerned, we next need to consider the difference between passenger and freight stock. Where passenger coaches simply need to be parked out of use until their next job, there is no need for sidings to be any wider spaced than normal, but if carriages need to be serviced prior to their next duty (eg cleaning and/or 'watering'), then some sort of provision is needed for access between sidings, albeit not as much as in the case of a cart road for goods vehicles (above). At its simplest, this may be no more than a raised and

Plate 146: Storage sidings. *By contrast with the previous view, this 1911 picture at Fenchurch Street shows a bank of six goods sidings which are at normal track centres which, in spite of the obvious in-filling between the rails which would allow road vehicles to pass, strongly suggest that they were mostly used for parking wagons before or after loading/unloading in a different part of the yard.*

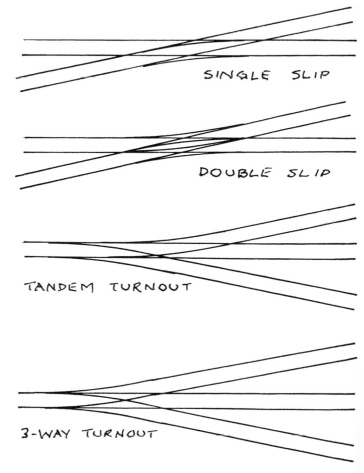

Plate 147: Tandem and Three-way turnouts. *In this view at Cheshunt in 1911, a good example of the common tandem turnout can be seen to the right of the signal box. Such formations, though common enough in themselves, were not often found on the main line; but this one is trailing to the direction of travel and offered no more risk than a normal turnout. However, to the left of the signal box behind the lamp post can be seen a genuine three-way turnout wherein both sets of point blades converged at the same point. These rarer formations were almost always confined to siding areas. Note also a somewhat extended but otherwise conventional trap point to the left of the cattle wagon on the right of the picture.*

SINGLE SLIP

DOUBLE SLIP

TANDEM TURNOUT

3-WAY TURNOUT

narrow platform between sidings so as to allow staff to be able to do their work, possibly allowing space for watering stand pipes; but it does suggest that when we plan our layouts, we need to decide whether we need to offer a 'service facility' for the carriages as well as standing space.

There are two more aspects of carriage working which, if we can model them, help to create atmosphere. Firstly, if gas lit carriages were common at the period we have chosen, then at many major locations there would be found facilities for replenishing the gas cylinders. At really important places these would be part of the permanent infrastructure at the nearest carriage depot, but at many lesser locations, there would often be found a solitary 'gas tank wagon', parked somewhere close to the action, often hard up against the stop blocks at a dead-end platform so as be readily accessible when needed - a fine excuse for an unusual model if nothing else....

Secondly, if you envisage sleeping or dining cars, you may need to offer something appropriate to their needs. In the case of dining cars, food and drink stock replenishment (plus gas in the case of gas cooking) was customary and was often done at the platform itself. But it would not be unheard of, as part of

Fig.24: More complex point formations. This diagram may well be superfluous to many readers but I include it none the less to indicate what I have in mind when discussing such matters in the text. Once again, I have indicated both running rails in the interest of clarity.

158

Plate 148: Slip points. This ladder of single and double slips at Fenchurch Street was photographed in the opposite direction from that shown at Plate 146. The single slip to the bottom left is an interesting variation on the norm, as is the single bladed trap point just beyond it on the left hand running line.

the operating procedure and if timings allowed it, to detach the dining car from a newly arrived train so that servicing took place at a more convenient spot (eg a parcels bay with road access for easier stores transfer), before its next departure.

In the case of sleeping cars, however, we enter the realms of the unmentionable, that familiar exhortation not to use the facilities while the train was standing in the station - sic! This is fine for most normal purposes but what about those trains which allow passengers to remain on board for an hour or two after arrival? In such cases, the usual provision was to have a sort of trough below the arrival platform, through which ran running water and into which the malodorous material could be discharged.... They were often irreverently referred to as 's..t gullies' and their provision on a model can offer an interesting conversation piece if nothing else. More seriously, this is why certain platforms only were allowed to receive arriving sleeping cars at most of our major terminal points.....

As far as locomotive provisioning is concerned, I have gone into this already in Chapter 8, so will not repeat it here, save to emphasise that before planning the facilities, we need to decide just what we shall require and try to avoid the temptation to over-provision just because it looks nice!

I now come to the matter of more complex track formations which were regularly to be found on the traditional railway, by which I am thinking of three way and tandem turnouts, slip points and the like (Fig.24). I have to confess that in this area my feelings are not uninfluenced by the pure aesthetics of such formations if we can find an excuse to use them. They do, of course, rather presume that the track will be hand-built and I know of not a few models where the modeller has fought shy of such features for this reason alone. But perhaps the more important fact to address is why they were used at all (they were expensive formations to make and maintain) and whether or not they are justifiable in the context of a model.

The most usual reason advanced for their presence on the prototype is to save linear space - and this is certainly true in those cases (often terminus stations) where the available space was too limited to allow all desired movements to take place by way of using simple turnouts. All other things being equal, simple turnouts in combination will usually allow the same

Plate 149: Facing and trailing points. *This view of Leman Street (GER) clearly shows the difference betwen facing and trailing points at a double junction. To the left is the facing point for the junction, suitably protected with a facing point lock, while to the right is a turnout without a point lock: it would normally be negotiated in a trailing direction. Note too the use of what might best be described as a 'skewed' double slip to give trap point protection beyond the junction.*

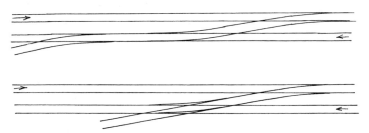

Fig.25: The value of the trailing single slip. *In these two diagrams, I attempt to show how the use of a trailing single slip, in conjunction with a simple turnout to form a trailing crossover, can eliminate the need for facing points on a main line, once again showing both running rails for the sake of clarity. If this is desired in both directions without using a facing point on either of the running lines - eg my revised arrangement at Marthwaite (Fig.20, Chapter 6) - then a pair of adjoining trailing single slips will resolve the problem.*

manoevres to take place, given sufficient length, but slip points and other space saving formations were also found in areas where, apparently, there were no linear space problems so we have to ask ourselves why this was.

One reason was to avoid a facing point on a main line used by passenger trains, where, should simple turnouts be used, a facing point lock would also have to be provided, along with extra mechanical complications and more levers in the signal box, all of which cost money. A trailing single slip, however, will get round this problem in many cases, Fig.25 attempting to show how. It was a commonly adopted solution by many of our railways, not least the Midland, and the cover picture of this book shows how I have used two such single slips on my own layout - see also the plan of Marthwaite at Fig.20.

(Technical note for readers who are uncertain as to the exact difference, begging due forgiveness from those who know these things for stating what might seem obvious: A facing point (aka turnout) is one which presents an approaching train with a choice of routes - ie diverging - whilst a trailing point is encountered when trains approach a single line from converging directions. The facing point is the more dangerous since, if the point blades move when a train is passing, then derailment is a near-certainty, whereas in the case of a trailing point, the weight of the vehicles will normally force the point blades (aka switches) into a 'safe' position. This is why prototype railways avoided facing points on their main running lines wherever they could do so, save in those special cases where the actual routes themselves diverged.

In all cases where a facing point was encountered on a main running line, it had to be further protected by a facing point lock, a mechanical device designed to ensure that point blades could not move when a train was passing and mandatory for all lines used for passenger trains, though 'goods only' running lines (and most sidings, of course) could be, and often were, a little less constrained. This extra protection cost money and many railways (not least the Midland) took this to excess when arranging their track layouts. The Settle-Carlisle, for example, had only one facing point on the main line in the northbound direction when first planned (at Appleby) and none at all southbound, a position which was not changed until WWII when running loops (with facing points) were installed at Blea Moor.)

Plate 150: Main line running loop. This view shows the northbound running loop of the Settle and Carlisle main line at Blea Moor. Taken at the opposite end of the loop to Plate 143 it shows Jubilee Class 4-6-0 No.45732 Sanspareil negotiating the facing point with a Saturday extra train. Note the headshunt on the loop itelf and the miniature signal arm (controlling entry to the loop) bracketed off the running line signal post. Exit at the north end was controlled by a similar miniature arm. The engine smoke hides the up main line signal but the miniature signal arm controlling exit from the similar up loop can be seen on the left.

Double slips were fundamentally different from the single variety, since in whichever direction they are traversed, facing point blades are encountered. Their presence at termini were almost always conditioned by space, but out in the country, many examples of a double slip release to the main line can be found where one might imagine that simple turnouts would suffice (Fig.26). The Midland was very fond of this solution, even when linear space was not restricted, and the Settle-Carlisle was a classic case. In this respect, the only logical explanation I have seen advanced is that although two simple turnouts might be cheaper to provide in theory, the extra cost of grading another hundred feet or so of track bed in order to accept their greater length, compared with that required for a double slip, would be more than the cost of providing a double slip in the first place, the component parts of which would, presumably, be readily available at the nearest permanent way depot. Whatever, it does suggest that if we like the idea of double slips (and I do!), then we do not always need to use 'space considerations' as the excuse....

Multiple turnouts are a different case again. They are rarely found on the main line and if so, almost always 'trailing' to the main direction of travel, suitably protected by trap points and the like. But they do allow the generation of multiple sidings in a relatively short length which, given need for as much siding space as possible (see above) made them very attractive. They would not normally be traversed at high speed and would often be hand-operated in the yards anyway, so the extra cost of maintaining them would not be prohibitive.

Nevertheless, all this said, I must also point out that the modern railway has seen an immense reduction in these more complex formations in favour of the plain turnout (with a facing point lock if needed) and at Fig.27 I have indicated just one way in which a modern junction differs from its traditional forbear - even to the elimination of a diamond crossing.

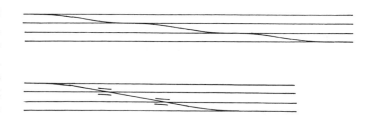

Fig.26: The space-saving property of the double slip. In these two diagrams, using a conventional single line to denote each running road and ignoring the additional complications of facing point locks which would be needed anyway, see text, I have attempted to show (drawn to consistent geometry between the two but not to any precise scale), the linear space saving which double slips offer compared with conventional turnouts.

In the historical model context, as well as having at least some basic understanding of these prototype considerations, we must also take note of the purely modelling parameters of excessively sharp curve radii, crossing angles and many other constricting factors. Adjustments will certainly have to be made in consequence of these factors for most of us and, as I have already indicated, I went one step to far in this respect on Kendal Mk II with both time and cost-wasting consequences. I therefore venture to suggest that even if we cannot resolve all the many conflicting needs, a better appreciation of how and why the real railways went about matters will certainly help us to plan our layouts more coherently and, hopefully, avoid the need for too much 'scrapping and rebuilding'!

There are many more subtle aspects of track planning we might also like to consider, but I hope I have already said enough to point readers in the right direction if they are inclined to take things further. The only additional aspect which I would mention is that no matter what sort of track plan you envisage, it is wise to remember that even the simplest of turnouts, if modelled to reasonable proportions, will take up more linear space then you may imagine. Meantime, I simply offer a handful of layout ideas which I have devised over the years. I do not flatter myself that any or all of them will commend themselves without change, but if they offer even a few useful tips to a handful of readers, I shall be well pleased.

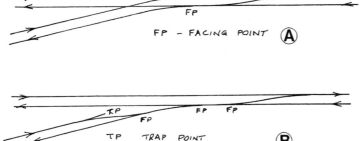

Fig.27: Double Junctions, old and new. Though not intended to exemplify all situations which have taken place during the post-c.1970 period, these diagrams offer just one way by which pointwork at the convergence of two routes has often changed in the more modern era, again using a single line to denote each track. It would seem, these days, that additional facing point locks and bi-directional running through a part of the formation are a more attractive proposition than diamond crossings; but aesthetically, I know which I prefer......

Plate 151: Track complexity at Stockport. I am not sure just how typical of the LNWR was this magnificent array of complex pointwork at an almost deserted Stockport (date unspecified but probably quite early). It repays careful study, if only to note the many and various ways by which the traditional railway ensured that train movements could be as comprehensive as possible. But huge signalboxes were needed to keep everything under control: No.1 is in the left foreground and there is another just as big at the far end. I am tempted to comment that although we can learn much from views like this, it is not too wise to try and model such complexity unless you have a very large space, a very deep pocket and a fair number of willing helpers.....

Some layout schemes analysed

The majority of the plans which follow were prepared in terms of modelling possibilities and problems which I have faced down the years and which, had circumstances been different, I may well have tackled myself - in other words, I rather like most of them! They also include requests by a few folk to help them design a layout and in one case (the most elaborate as it so happens), I have had the very great joy of seeing one of my friends create it, virtually unmodified, in a site space which is well beyond most of us. They all have a 'Midland feel' to them, I suppose, but I hope I may be forgiven for this, given my own specific interests - as I said earlier, I don't think that most principal railways were too different in essence and I reckon that most plans could easily be adapted to meet particular company foibles.

I have rarely suggested much scenic treatment, beyond that which indicates where tunnels, bridges &c might be located, usually to 'vanish' the running lines. My main purpose is to concentrate on the basic geometry of layout planning in terms of what can and cannot be fitted into a given space and though most of the plans could easily be tailored to suit slightly larger site dimensions than I have suggested, I would not recommend

reduction by much more than 10-15% in most cases.

I should also make clear that none of the schemes have been designed to make exclusive use of commercially available and ready-made pointwork, for I do not really think it possible to make a layout look as if a permanent way engineer had a hand in it solely by using left and right hand turnouts of almost never changing geometry. They can be used wherever relevant, of course, and I have often done so - usually in the hidden parts of my layouts - but sooner or later, I reckon that the potential historical modeller will have to face the need to handbuild at least some point formations if the layout is to be totally convincing. By all means use commercial plain track and/or simple turnouts where they make sense, but for better effect, a few properly planned 'tailor-mades' will surely make a world of difference.

Finally, for convenience, although describing the ideas in the usual narrative form and in sequence, I have chosen to refer to them by Figure numbers which follow those of the previous drawings in this book. In most cases, the drawings are offered with a superimposed grid pattern of 12in squares at 4mm scale, other scales in proportion, of course.

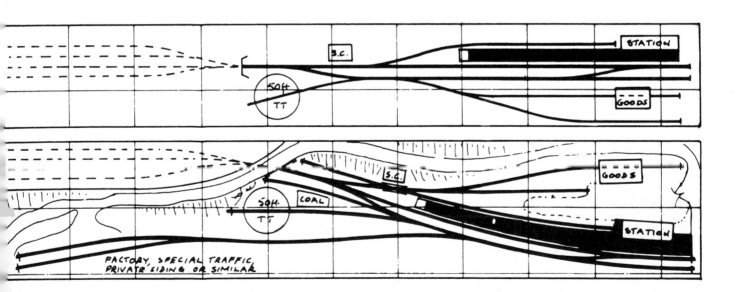

Fig.28: Making the most of limited space

Here, I have tried to show how even a quite short 'straight' site can be persuaded to 'expand' visually. The trick, paradoxically, is to increase the width of the layout and use the diagonal.

The upper plan shows an orthodox 'terminus to storage' system which is typical of many which are are built from conventional and geometrically restrictive proprietary track parts and formations. In my view, it seems pretty dull, may I be forgiven for so-saying; but the lower plan, which only

involves an extra 6-9in width, gives scope for a railwaylike approach. It presupposes a willingness to 'tailor-make' some of the pointwork, and it cannot 'store' any longer trains than the first scheme. But the visual interest is maintained along the whole length of the site by virtue of using the diagonal as the axis of the main line, thus giving enough width to enhance the scenic treatment in front of the 'store'. Note too the beneficial visual effect of using gentle curves in many places rather than rigid straight lines.

163

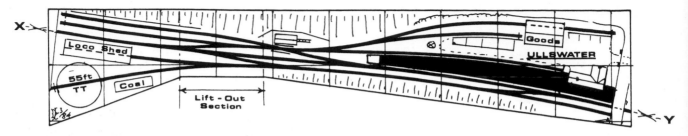

Fig.29: Not quite a terminus!

I have often been accused by my friends of never seriously considering the truly space-starved modeller - and I must admit that I have usually found at least some sort of site for my own efforts wherein dimensions were not too compressed. The plan offered here is derived from Fig.28 and occupies much the same length, being worked out for a keen 7mm scale friend who had but 18ft of space available indoors. He wanted a simple continuous circuit with some main line pretentions and an interesting station as centrepiece. There was prospect of building a portable outside link between X and Y in the form of a simple oval for use in fine weather but it was also wished to have some operational interest in bad weather or if the outside option did not materialise.

The more conventional solution (Fig.28) was not quite what was wanted so we started to consider some 'just supposings' in the context of LNWR c.1905, the desired theme and period. In due course we devised the idea of linking the Windermere branch with the Keswick to Penrith line via Ullswater - single line, of course - as a sort of emergency alternative to the Shap route. The gradients would be fearsome in reality but this would serve to explain big engines on quite small trains.

The result is shown here, wherein all shunting can be conducted between the bridges (ie indoors) but which could function equally well as a passing station if the continuous circuit materialised. The loco shed is for the banking engine which would be needed in context of the main scheme and the carriage sidings are for the Ullswater-Penrith locals. A third possibility is a plug on storage magazine at X (the Penrith end), thus making the layout a branch terminus.

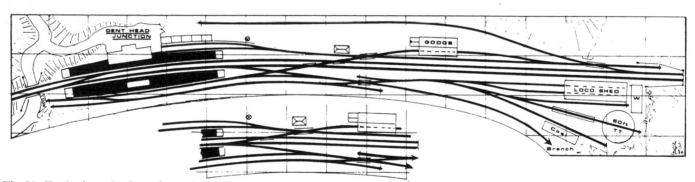

Fig.30: Evolution of a Junction - 1

This is one of my oldest ideas and embodies, in rather more space, the same sort of concepts as offered in Fig.29 - ie a main line 'feel' for someone who does not really have the space for such a notion. It was mostly inspired by the late Norman Wilkinson, a fellow Settle and Carlisle enthusiast who had no real space available for a full presentation, even in his chosen 4mm scale. Instead, he simply built a lovely model of Settle station along the longest wall he could find and had to accept that the main line would simply 'collide' with the wall at each end of his site. He achieved his bit of railway history as a result of these efforts and his model was duly described in the model journals of the 1970s.

For my part, I wondered if Norman's ideas could be adapted to produce the same sort of effects for the main line junction which I had envisaged in context of the original Marthwaite, the idea being to build it in the hope that one day I might have sufficient space available to link the two. As things turned out,

events took a different turn, of course, but it still occurs to me that if modellers feel that one day they might have a bit more space available, then they could do far worse than to build this sort of 'working diorama' as an interim step along the way. The plan, drawn up c.1967-8, would have been built in preference to Garsdale Road had circumstances so decreed - I lived a very peripatetic military life at the time and regular house moves were endemic in the process. Events were to decree otherwise; but I still like it....

The plan is a 'marriage' between Lazonby (Figs.12 and 13, Chapter 4) on the up side and the Hawes branch arrangement at Garsdale. I have offered (inset) an alternative station 'throat' which would cause more shunting problems but might actually look better. It would need about another 25% of length to allow incorporation into a continuous circuit but might be susceptible to a bit of selective shortening. As it stands, it could be shunted properly without any changes.

Plate 152: Company preferences. *Not too many prizes are offered for knowing that this Eric Treacy shot shows Garsdale in early BR days with a rebuilt Royal Scot (probably No.46112* Sherwood Forester*) heading north with the 'Thames-Clyde' express! I have included it mainly to show how many company details remained visible long after both 1923 and 1948 - and some of them are still there in 2001. Typical of the Midland in this view are the double telegraph posts, the diagonal platform fencing, those lower quadrant signals which still remain (quite a few) and the bracket lamp on the fence in the foreground. Note too the characteristic trailing single slips on the crossover which the engine is approaching. These allowed access to the famous stockaded turntable (just visible in the middle left distance) and the Hawes branch bay to the right - the branch itself can be seen to the left of the double-arm signal in the middle distance. These slip points were located to ensure that facing points were absent from the main line. The Midland had something of a fetish about this sort of thing and at Garsdale, even the passenger trains to the branch from the main line had to reverse.*

At this point, and before going any further, I think it might be the appropriate point to introduce the notion of what I call the 'single garage module' when it comes to planning a layout for the most popular choice for most of us - 4mm scale. I have been fortunate in most of my 7mm scale efforts in terms of having a site which would accept the larger scale, but in planning ideas to fit these larger spaces, it has also occurred to me in no uncertain manner that the vast majority of them

would nicely fit into a single garage in 4mm scale - a not unlikely site for many folks.

It does, of course, presuppose that the precious motor car is left outside, but does this matter in any meaningful sense? It will drop in value whatever we do and my engineering friends tell me that if I am not willing to wipe it dry after a wet journey (which I most certainly am not), it is far more likely to develop rust in a dry and heated garage than if left outside to face the elements. My own car (seven years old at the time of writing and without a speck of rust), in spite of having lived all its life outside so that I can use the garage for more creative purposes, seems proof of that, so I commend this approach to any and all who are so inclined......

Whatever, the next few plans are predicated on this sort of site availability, posing the implicit question: 'Why pay good money to house an expensive yet deteriorating asset in a dry and covered area which we could use to far better effect with no loss in terms of intrinsic financial value?' Moreover, in our modern age of smaller houses, this may be the only real space available in which to pursue our hobby, as not a few of my modelling friends have already discovered to their eternal benefit and with no disadvantage to their pockets. Mark you, if what really turns you on is to spend your Sunday mornings by way of careening your four-wheel pride and joy, there is not much more I can say - yes, my prejudices are showing.......

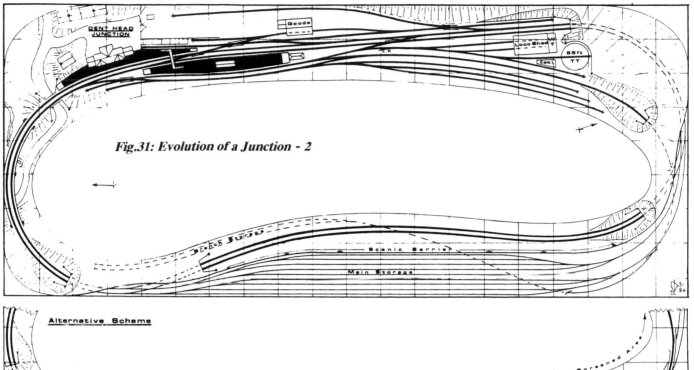

Fig.31: Evolution of a Junction - 2

Alternative Scheme

Fig.31: Evolution of a Junction - 2

This plan is another 'almost but not quite' in my earlier 4mm scale activities - hence the name of the junction. Developed from Fig.30 it is an attempt to produce something similar, including a continuous circuit, in rather less length than would be needed if approach curves were added to Fig.30. Overall, I think the junction layout is better here but the curve over the viaduct is a bit on the sharp side.

Two possible versions are offered. The main drawing hides the storage loops, yet permits trains to be seen for much of the transit of the opposite side of the site by allowing them to by-pass the storage loops in 'tail-chase' mode. The second idea assumes a terminus built above the running loops and this space was calculated to accept the original Marthwaite (Fig.1, Chapter 3) with a slightly revised approach. This plan was resurrected when I changed scale since, in 7mm terms, it would nicely fit the shed. In the end I went for the more complex scheme shown at Fig.6 (Chapter 3)

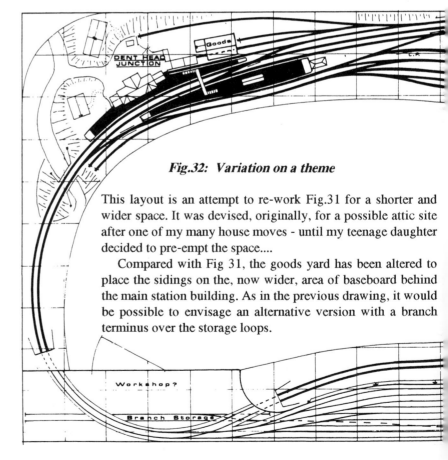

Fig.32: Variation on a theme

This layout is an attempt to re-work Fig.31 for a shorter and wider space. It was devised, originally, for a possible attic site after one of my many house moves - until my teenage daughter decided to pre-empt the space....

Compared with Fig 31, the goods yard has been altered to place the sidings on the, now wider, area of baseboard behind the main station building. As in the previous drawing, it would be possible to envisage an alternative version with a branch terminus over the storage loops.

166

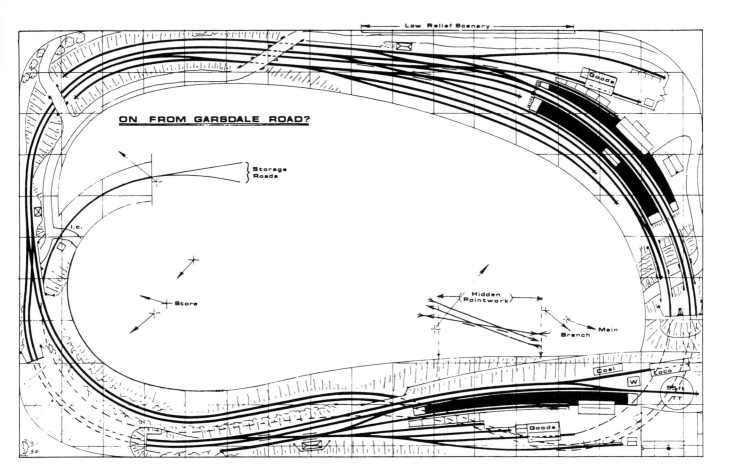

ON FROM GARSDALE ROAD?

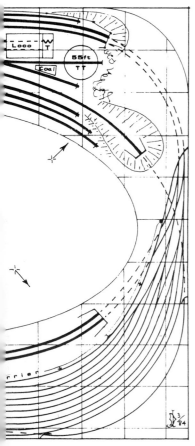

Fig.33: On from Garsdale Road?

Looking back, there is no doubt that Garsdale Road was my favourite 4mm scheme and well before the big shed became a possibility, I played around with many ideas designed to turn Garsdale Road into a junction. None of them came to anything very much, but for this book, I decided to have another try, using the same dimensions as Fig.32 (some 16ft 6in x 10ft at 4mm scale) and then simply let things happen.

The story line is anything within reason and most certainly not tied to the Settle and Carlisle. I see the main station as now being a junction between two companies, one of which operates the main line and the other the single track system which joins it at the junction. The hidden pointwork (it would have have to be made carefully - note the facing single slip...) allows both routes to be fed from the same set of storage roads out of sight of the viewer. Meantime, the modest terminus hides this subterfuge and could be made even more basic than drawn, possibly (maybe better) with a single track approach beyond the double junction. It could be made portable for exhibition work in 'terminus to fiddle yard' mode or form the basis for a solo project. Like the original 4mm scale Marthwaite, the terminus plan is very much based on that which existed at Grassington but this time offered in correct orientation.

The scheme is essentially end to end (storage to terminus via the junction) with the important caveat that much of the traffic from the storage roads would reverse direction at the junction and go back to the store via the 'other company's' line. The capacity of the terminus does not, therefore, have to match that of the storage roads. Had I built it myself, I might have re-written the story to make the main line station a joint Midland/LNWR facility with the terminus belonging to the company which operated the main line, an idea which may hold some attraction for those who fancy having two companies but do not want them equally represented.

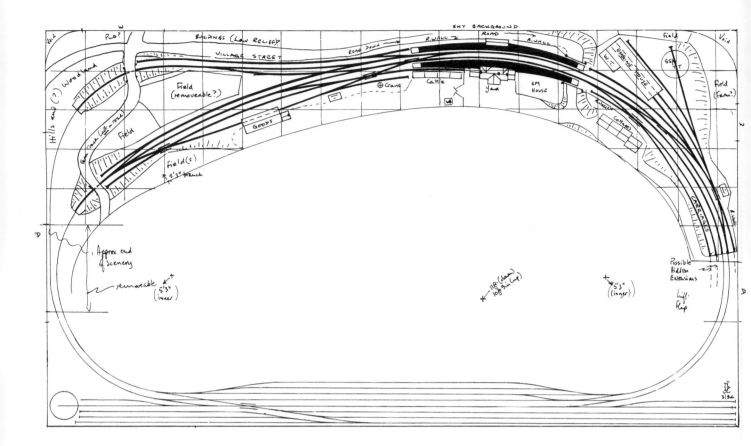

Fig.34: Another secondary junction

When planning Kendal MkIII, I found that any of the three schemes at Figs.31-33 would fit the site, but these were all essentially main line in concept and designed with my original 4mm scale ideas in mind - not quite what was wanted for the new Kendal branch. I thus went back to the drawing board yet again to see what else might be possible. This was the best of the aborted schemes and I had it under active consideration for almost two years while I built the Gauge 1 garden system. In my scenario, the model is now presumed to be a mile or so out of Kendal itself, where the Midland line from Dent Head met the Furness line from Arnside at Natland.

The Midland route (alongside which stands a typical Settle and Carlisle style goods yard) is drawn in such a way that it could be made double track, whilst the carriage sidings and motive power depot are explained by the fact that there is presumed to be insufficient space at the terminus proper. This would offer lots of nice shunting moves of engines and stock between Natland and the now imaginary Kendal.

I think it would have looked well and lends itself to many 'two company' story lines, but although the storage area would be interesting to work, it is hard to see how it could be given any real visual interest - and it occupies almost half the space available too. This, in the event, was the determining factor as far as the final decision was concerned, though I still like the concept itself. I therefore had another try, from which emerged the final version with two stations (Fig.20, Chapter 6).

Plate 153: Coniston station. *This rainy day view of the attractive Furness Railway terminus at Coniston was taken on 10th May 1958 by Tim Shuttleworth and is included here to illustrate the only prototype track layout featured in the plans section of this chapter (part of Fig.35). The engine seen is Ivatt LMS design Class 2 2-6-2T No.41217.*

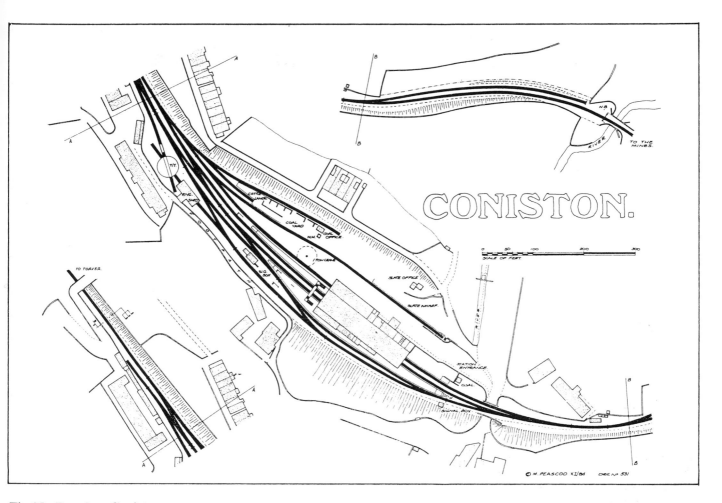

Fig.35: Based on Coniston

I have said elsewhere that I find terminus design rather difficult, and when I designed Kendal MkII (Fig.7, Chapter 3) I made innumerable attempts to get a reasonable arrangement. This was one of them, its track layout being strongly inspired by a plan of Coniston (ex-Furness Railway) drawn by Michael Peascod, who has been kind enough to allow me to use it here in conjunction with my own plan.

The real Coniston was a delightfully different station as

well as being very interesting and I think this adaptation would have been fascinating to build and operate, but in the end I decided that it was not quite comprehensive enough for the pattern of service I had envisaged. I have resurrected it for this book, not because I reckon anyone will have the very peculiar site into which it might have gone, but in the hope that between the two drawings, there might be a few ideas which could be adapted by others.

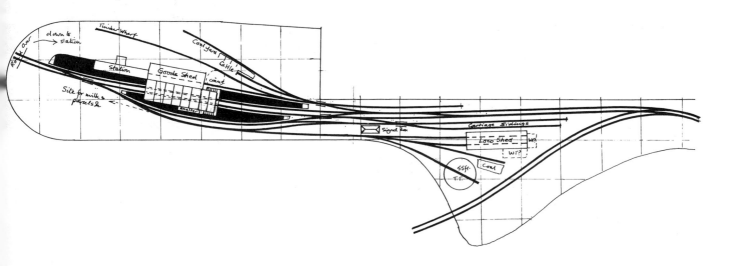

Fig.36: Designs for a small town terminus

As with the previous plan, these schemes were also intended for Kendal MkII, hence the precise site shape. But since they are all only some 14ft long in 4mm scale (ie less than the original Marthwaite), I hope that readers who want a fairly complex facility in a relatively 'tight' area may find a use for some of my solutions.

They could all handle comprehensive freight and passenger services and the longer platforms will take a six coach set -

these being the operational parameters which I set myself for all the many Kendal schemes. I think any of them could form the basis for an attractive 'terminus to fiddle yard' plan and, indeed, I would have built that sort of layout, based on these ideas, had I had no more space than this available to me. In retrospect, it has even occurred to me that if the original 4mm scale Marthwaite had been given this sort of complexity of trackage, it would have been far more interesting to run....

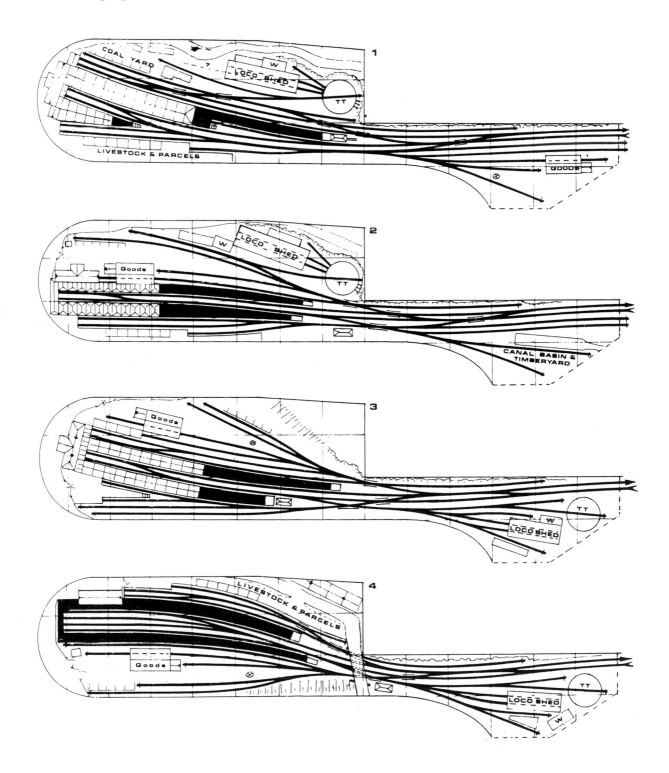

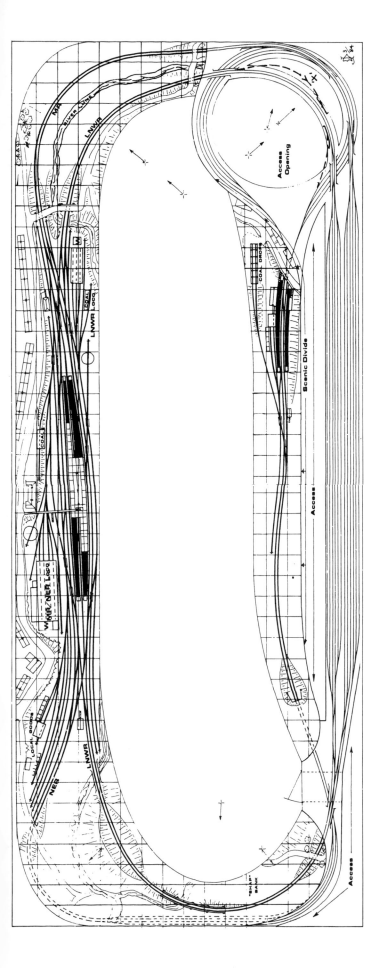

During the late 1970s, I was fortunate enough to meet Neil Corner, a fine mechanical engineer by profession and a keen 7mm scale enthusiast. He told me of his wish to create a large fine scale layout in an empty outbuilding and asked if I would like to design it. His approach was very much influenced by the layout of the late W.S.Norris who had done much the same sort of thing in the 1950s and, indeed, Neil has some of the models which were built for that famous system.

The requirement was for an Edwardian pre-group line on which the LNW, Midland and North Eastern Railways would all feature prominently, but Neil did not fancy the obvious city locations like, say, Carlisle, Leeds or York; he wanted lots of open countryside through which the trains could run. Also, and unlike Norris (whose layout represented no specific area), the layout had to offer an element of prototype feasibility in terms of geography and traffic patterns. In other words, although for much of the time it would function as a display stage (Neil too has his collection of out of period trains) it had to have proper operational potential.

One of the problems of a really big site is that it offers so many possibilities that it is hard to know where to start. But eventually, I recall saying: "Just supposing the Settle and Carlisle had never been built, what would have happened at Tebay?" I chose Tebay because of the NER link at the north end and the net result was to 'rebuild' Tebay in imagination so that it could handle the full weight of the Midland traffic to Scotland as well as that of the LNWR.

We assumed that the real life Low Gill Junction, a few miles to the south, had been discounted as being too cramped for space and that the Midland therefore built a parallel line up the Lune valley on the opposite side to that which the LNWR already occupied. We finally assumed that since it was the Midland which really wanted to get to Scotland, it would have had to foot the bill for the rebuilding of Tebay, which may well, in consequence have grown many Midland characteristics. Neil decided to call it Lonsdale (a nicer and wholly suitable name...) and we reckoned that in spite of our many assumptions, the whole project would have cost the Midland far less than its actual S&C venture....

The junction layout is copied from Hellifield, shorn of its many sidings, and is to scale length, modified only to suit the NER requirement at the north end. The NER station in front of the storage roads is based on typical North Eastern stations and has a set of characteristic coal drops, while all the running loops are long enough to take two full length trains and thus allow end to end running if required (ie, from one end of the loop via the junction to the other end of the loop - or the NER branch to choice). The drawing shows the original plan which has been realised in full with very little modification save for the extra 'one way only' return link (marked 'X') and the later insertion of even more running loops behind the NER station, the latter additions not shown on this plan.

Although a huge layout by conventional British standards, it is essentially both simple in concept and built against a not impossible historical scenario had things turned out a little differently. After all, the Midland genuinely tried to abandon the Settle-Carlisle project in 1869 after reaching agreement with the LNWR. The basic idea could be realised in a smaller space if required and the influence of my own 'Little Long Drag' system (Fig.4, Chapter 3) is not accidental. In fact, when I had gridded this drawing with conventional 4mm scale 12in squares, I found that the overall length of Lonsdale was not dissimilar. Yet I cannot resist the comment that even this layout has to compromise on curvature at the south end, where the approaches would, in the real world, have been straight....

Conclusion

With the description of the origins of Lonsdale, I come to the end of my review in as suitable a form as I can envisage. Like my own latest 7mm scale efforts, it is not quite complete as I write (late 2001), but it is, without doubt, the largest and least compromising layout with which I have ever been involved. I am also delighted that its instigator made very few changes to the plan which I first offered, if only because I like to think that it encapsulates (albeit on on the grand scale) almost all the ideas I have explored in this and previous chapters, not least that of consistency of approach - and that seems to be more or less where I came in............. [HRM]

Plate 154: Departure from Kendal. Though my own final layout is nothing like as spacious as Lonsdale, the departure end at Kendal has a far more 'open' look than I had ever dared to hope, given its restricted length and width. I am also happy that the acute sharpening of the exit curve behind the goods shed, forced on me by site constraints, is almost wholly disguised by the scenery, the distant cottages being modelled in slightly diminishing perspective to aid the illusion of distance. The train is the departing 12.32pm (summer only) 'Lakelander' to Leeds, with its through carriages for Bradford, Liverpool and Manchester, behind ex-LNWR Claughton' 4-6-0 No.6018, Private W. Wood, V.C., *the final addition to the main operating locomotive fleet on the layout. There are obvious signs of work still to tackle (eg cattle pens not yet installed though their base is present) and it still looks a bit 'squeaky clean', I suppose; but even as it stands, it is already beginning to look tolerably railwaylike to my eyes - and what more could I either want or expect to get from this fascinating hobby?*

APPENDICES

ON THESE FINAL pages, I offer a few facsimile extracts from the passenger train marshalling books, issued twice per year for all four divisions of the LMS, together with some selected pages from the LMS 1937 General Appendix, whose instructions, covering 95 pages *in toto*, deal with just about every conceivable aspect of train operation and safety. In the latter case, I have selected the pages of most relevance to modellers while in the former I have simply dipped in at random. They are wholly self-explanatory and give some idea of the detail which went into the planning and operation of the traditional railway. In order to maximise the information, it has been slightly reduced in size compared with the original and, in the case of the General Appendix, arranged sideways on the page. Those who wish to know more are referred to archive sources such as the NRM &c (see Chapter 5), where many of the original documents can be perused in their entirety.

APPENDIX 1: LMS PASSENGER TRAIN MARSHALLING

CENTRAL DIVISION 1935		Marshalling	Balance	Marshalling.	Balance.

CENTRAL DIVISION 1935

Marshalling	Balance
3-40 a.m. LEEDS (Central) to MANCHESTER (Victoria).	
LBL (4B)	8 40 p.m. ex Liverpool **M** — 10 0 p.m. ex Low Moor **MO** — 2032
Brake Van — Attach rear Halifax.	
aBrake Van —ex Normanton	2136
abCompo (corridor) {Newcastle / Liverpool (Ex.)}	6 35 p.m.
abBrake Van **M** {Newcastle / Liverpool (Ex.)}	2137
aFish Truck —ex Normanton	
Attach rear Sowerby Bridge.	
cLoco Stores Van **M** —For Horwich	1530
a Received off 3-9 a.m. ex Normanton.	
b Forward 6-8 a.m. from Manchester.	
c Forward 8-5 a.m. from Manchester.	
Tonnage—130 to Halifax. 190 MO, 210 M Halifax to Sowerby Bridge. 190 MO, 224 M from Sowerby Bridge.	
5-58 a.m. HEYSHAM to LEEDS (Central) M. (Corridor stock) This train is reversed at Morecambe (Promenade) and formation given below is marshalling from engine on leaving Morecambe (Promenade).	
Third Brake / Vestibule Third / First Dining Car / Compo / Third Brake } Leeds (Central)	7 15 p.m.
aThird Brake / aCompo / aThird Brake } Bradford (Ex.)	7 23 p.m.
bBrake Van } Bradford (Ex.) **MS** / Manchester (Vic.) **S O**	2126
cBrake Van —Manchester (Vic.)	2125
dBrake Van —Liverpool (Ex.)	2151
Attach in rear at Manchester (Vic.)	
eBrake Van ThO—Burnley (M.R.)	2125
a Detached at Low Moor and forms 9-41 a.m. to Bradford.	
b Detached at Low Moor and forward 9-41 a.m. **MS**.	
c Detached at Manchester.	
d Detached at Preston and forward 8-8 a.m.	
e Detached at Todmorden and forward 9-40 a.m.	
Tonnage—290 to Preston. 270 Preston to Victoria. 250 ThS, 260 ThO, 230 SO Victoria to Todmorden. 250 MS, 230 S Todmorden to Low Moor. 100 S, 80 SO Low Moor to Bradford. 150 Low Moor to Leeds (Cen.).	

Marshalling	Balance
4-55 p.m. MANCHESTER (Victoria) to BLACKPOOL (North) S. (Vestibule stock)	
Third Brake / Third / 2 Firsts / First Club Saloon (No. 3572) / Third Club Saloon (No. 490) / Third / Third Brake	8 20 a.m.
aFirst } Fleetwood / aThird Brake (corridor)	8 2 a.m.
a Detached at Poulton and attached 6-4 p.m. Poulton to Fleetwood.	
Tonnage—290 to Poulton. 260 from Poulton.	
5-0 p.m. MANCHESTER (Victoria) to SOUTHPORT S. (Vestibule stock) (Class "A" stock)	
Third Brake / Third / Compo / 5 Firsts / Compo / Third / Third Brake	8 5 a.m.
Tonnage—320.	

MIDLAND DIVISION 1939

Marshalling	Balance
12.0 noon ST. PANCRAS—CARLISLE. (Reversed at Leeds.) (Must not convey 4-wheeled vehicles under 15 ft. wheel-base. Class "A" Stock.	
eThird (42) (SO) (L.N.E.)	—
Third Brake (24) (L.N.E.) } Edinburgh (Waverley)	12 10 p.m. 9
Compo. Brake (12-18) (L.N.E.)	
c§Third Brake (24)	
fThird (42) (MO)	1525
bThird (42) (FO)	1672
Third (42)	
Third Vestibule (42) } Glasgow (St. En.)	12 10 p.m. 7
Third Vestibule (42)	
Kitchen Car	
First Vestibule Corr. (18-12)	
cFirst Brake (27)	
Attach front Sheffield:—	
dThird (42) (SX) —Bristol } Leeds	1617
Attach rear Sheffield:—	
dCompo. Brake (9-21) } Do. Glasgow (SX) (St. Enoch)	9 35 a.m. 137
dThird (42) (SX) — Do. do.	1581
Tonnage—277 (307 MO during August, 15th to August 26th) St. Pancras.	

Marshalling.	Balance.
11.45 a.m. (SO) ST. PANCRAS—HELLIFIELD. Class "A" Stock.	
Third (42) —Leeds	1614
Third (42) — Do.	1624
abThird Brake (24) —Carnforth }	195
abCompo. (18-24) — Do.	
abCompo. (18-24) — Do.	201
abThird (42) — Do.	1581
abThird Brake (24) — Do.	201
cRestaurant Car (24) } Sheffield	194
cThird Vestibule (56)	
Tonnage—285 St. Pancras. 210 Sheffield. 150 Leeds.	
a Form 4.8 p.m. Leeds to Hellifield, 5.10 p.m. Hellifield to Carnforth, 7.8 p.m. Carnforth to Leeds.	
c Return 5.35 p.m.	
8.55 a.m. MANCHESTER (Cen.)— ST. PANCRAS. (Must not convey 4-wheeled vehicles between Leicester and London.)	41
AThird Brake (24)	9 25 a.m.
ACompo. (18-24) } St. Pancras	3 30 p.m. (Suns.)
A§Third Brake (24)	
AThird (42) (SO) — Do.	1524
aAFirst R. Car (24) } Do. (MO)	5 32 p.m.
aAThird Vest. (42) } Do. (MO)	64
cThird Brake (24)	
cCompo. (18-32) } Sheffield	562
cThird (64)	
cThird Brake (40)	
Attach front Chinley:—	
A§Third Brake (24) } Liverpool (Cen.)	12 30 p.m.
ACompo. (18-24) } St. Pancras	65
AThird (42) (SO) — Do. do.	1514
Attach rear Miller's Dale:—	
eAThird (42) } Buxton	6 30 p.m.
ACompo. Brake (9-21) } St. Pancras	67
	1549
Attach rear Derby:—	
bFirst R. Car (24) (MX) } St. Pancras	64
bThird Vestibule (42) (MX)	
Tonnage—213 (288 MO, 243 SO) Manchester. 156 (231MO, 216 SO) Chinley. 219 (294 MO, 279 SO) Miller's Dale. 294 (354 SO) Derby. 30 tons less Miller's Dale to St. Pancras (SX) commencing August 28th.	
a Received 3.30 p.m. (Suns.) from St. Pancras.	
b Returns 5.32 p.m. (SX), 3.30 p.m. (Suns.).	

NORTHERN DIVISION 1938

Marshalling.	Balance.

5.0 p.m., Glasgow (Buchanan Street) to Aberdeen.

Marshalling.	Balance.
Third **S O**..................Perth	412 **S O**
Third	400
AInter-corridor Set (3 Vehicles).......... } Aberdeen	40
Dining Car..............	10.35 a.m.
ABInter-corridor Set (3 Vehicles).......... } Dundee	65
BThird **W O**	398
BComposite **W O**........	297
aCompo. Brake.............Comrie	256
Attach rear Perth :—	
DBrake Van ....Carlisle to Aberdeen	—
AECompo. Brake (60ft.)...Edinburgh to Aberdeen.	220

a Transferred Gleneagles to 6.14 p.m. to Comrie.
B Transferred Perth to 6.37 p.m. to Dundee.
D Received Perth off 1.18 p.m. **S X**, 1.28 p.m. **S O** from Carlisle.
E Received Perth off 4.25 p.m. from Edinburgh.

Tonnage—Glasgow 294 **W S X**, 354 **W O**, 324 **S O**; Gleneagles 264 **W S X**, 324 **W O**, 294 **S O**; Perth 220.

5.12 p.m., Glasgow (Buchanan Street) to Oban.

Marshalling.	Balance.
Third Brake .... }	
Third .... } Callander	55
First .... }	
Dining Car.............. }	**C**11.0 a.m.
AInter-corridor Set (3 Vehicles)......... } Oban	50
Attach front Callander :—	
BACompo. Brake **S X** .. }	226
BACompo. Brake (60ft.) } Edinburgh	259
BDThird **F O** .... } to Oban	380a

B Received Callander off 5.3 p.m. from Edinburgh.
C 11.0 a.m. until August 31st; 9.10 a.m. from September 1st.
D Commences September 3rd.

Tonnage—Glasgow 216; Callander 192 **S X**, 162 **S O** (28 extra **F O** commencing September 3rd).

6.8 p.m., Glasgow (Buchanan Street) to Dundee (West).

Marshalling.	Balance.
aThird **W S O** .... }	484a
aThird .... } Aberdeen	396
aAInter-corridor Set (3 Vehicles).......... }	37
CDining Car **S X** ....Perth	12.28 p.m. **D**
Inter-corridor Set (3 Vehicles) .... } Dundee	47(a) **SO**
	44 **S X**
DComposite............... }	
bThird Brake .... } Callander	118
Attach Perth front Dundee portion :—	
ABComposite (18-24)... } Euston to	290
ABComposite (18-24)... } Dundee	277

a Transferred Perth to 3.55 p.m. **S X**, 3.57 p.m. **S O**, Carlisle to Aberdeen.
b Transferred Stirling to 7.2 p.m.
B Received Perth off 3.55 p.m. **S X**, 3.57 p.m. **S O** ex Carlisle.
C Fitted with Adaptors.
D From Aviemore (9.55 a.m. ex Inverness).

Tonnage—Glasgow 318 **W S X**, 346 **W O**, 304 **S O**; Stirling 260 **W S X**, 288 **W O**, 246 **S O**; Perth 158.

4.10 a.m., Glasgow (Central) to Stirling.

Marshalling.	Balance.
CBrake Van (50 ft.) ......Oban	—
HComposite............... }	
HBrake Van (57 ft.) ... } Aberdeen	327
HBrake Van (57 ft.) ......Perth	
HBilsland's Bread Van ...Dundee (West)	
Brake Third **M O** ....Stirling	353
Attach Greenhill rear of Oban Brake Van :—	
JBrake Van ....Edinburgh (Waverley) to Stirling	**B**4.13 p.m.

B To Larbert and forward to Edinburgh (Wav.) at 5.37 p.m.
C Transferred at Stirling to 5.45 a.m. to Oban.
H Transferred Stirling to rear 2.59 a.m. ex Carlisle.
J Received Greenhill off 3.26 a.m. ex Waverley.

Tonnage—Glasgow 158 **M O**, 131 **M S X**.

WESTERN DIVISION 1934

10.0 a.m., MANCHESTER (London Road) TO BOURNEMOUTH.
(Class " A " Stock.)

Marshalling.	Balance.
Inter-Corridor Set (3 vehicles) } Birmingham	C
Two Thirds (MO) }	
Compo. Brake (60 ft.) }	
Compo. Vestibule }	
Third Restaurant Car (68 ft.) } Bournemouth	10 20 a.m.
Third Brake (32) }	
Attach front Crewe :—	
aThird (42) } Liverpool (L.St.) Birmingham	
Attach rear Crewe :—	
aCompo. Brake (60 ft.) } Liverpool (L.St.) Bournemouth	
BaCompo. Brake } Liverpool (L.St.) Southampton	

a Received off 9.40 a.m. from Liverpool (L.St.).
B L M S and G.W. vehicle alternate days.
C 2.50 p.m. (S) from Birmingham, 10.0 p.m. (Sun) from Chelford.

Tonnage—270 (MO), 214 (M) Manchester. 361 (MO), 305 (M) Crewe.

10.10 a.m., MANCHESTER (London Road) TO CREWE.

Marshalling.	Balance.
BaComposite } Bourne-	9 30 a.m.
BaThird Brake } mouth	
BaCompo. Brake } Portsmouth	10 0 a.m.
aBrake Van (Mails) (TO) } Southampton	
Third (NC) (S) }	1744
Composite (NC) (S) } Crewe	
Inter-District Set (SO) }	1155
(3 (NC) vehicles) }	
a Transferred Crewe to 11.1 a.m. to G.W. Line.	

B G.W. and S.R. stock alternate days.

Tonnage—140 (TS), 166 (TSO).

10.40 a.m. (SO), MANCHESTER (London Road) TO WILLESDEN.
(Except April 20th. Also runs (ThO) April 18th.)

Marshalling.	Balance.
AbThird Brake (24) }	10MO55am
AbCompo. Restaurant Car (65 ft.) } Hastings	
AbCompo. Brake }	
Third } Crewe	
Composite (NC) }	1805
Attach front Crewe :—	
AacCompo. Brake —Liverpool Ramsgate	
AabCompo. Brake —Liverpool Hastings	
Attach rear Rugby :—	
AbdCompo. Brake } Birmingham Hastings	

a Received off 10.35 a.m. from Liverpool.
b Transferred Willesden to 3.24 p.m. to Hastings.
c Transferred Willesden to 3.16 p.m. to Ramsgate.
d Received off 12.30 p.m. from Birmingham.

Tonnage—154 Manchester. 156 Crewe. 185 Rugby.

7.0 p.m., EUSTON TO BIRMINGHAM.
(Class " A " Stock.)

Marshalling.	Balance.
Third Brake (24) }	
Composite (18/24) }	
First Restaurant Car (65 ft.) }	B
Third Vestibule(60 ft.) }	
Composite (18/24) } Birmingham	
Third Brake (24) }	
Third (ThO) }	
Third (42) (S) }	C
Third (SO) }	
Brake Van }	12M20 a.m.

B 2.0 p.m. (S), 12.25 p.m. (SO) from Wolverhampton. Works 10.20 p.m., Birmingham to Wolverhampton.
C 8.15 a.m. from Liverpool. Works 8.0 p.m., Birmingham to Euston.

Tonnage—257 (Th), 285 (ThO).

6.15 p.m., EUSTON TO CREWE.
(Runs on April 18th only.)
(Class " A " Stock.)

Marshalling.	Balance.
Brake Van }	
Two Thirds }	
Third Vestibule (56) }	RSD
Compo. Restaurant Car (65 ft.) } Crewe (B)	
Composite }	
Third Brake }	
aThird (42) } Southport	8 50 a.m.
aFirst Brake }	
bScenery Truck } Holyhead	
(with Parcel Containers) }	

a Transferred Crewe to 9.16 p.m. to Edge Hill.
b Transferred Crewe to 8.20 p.m., Birmingham to Chester.
B Crewe to relabel to Heysham and work forward at 9.10 p.m.

Tonnage—290.

6.22 p.m., EUSTON TO STOCKPORT.
(Runs on April 18th only.)
(Class " A " Stock.)

Marshalling.	Balance.
aCompo. Brake (60 ft.) } Colne	7 50 a.m.
aTwo Thirds }	
bThird } Rochdale	—
bCompo. Brake (60 ft.) }	8 45 a.m.
Third Vestibule (56) }	
Compo. Restaurant Car (65 ft.) } Stockport	—
Third }	
Attach front Crewe :—	
cCrewe and Halifax Set } Low Moor	B
(2 vehicles) }	

a Transferred Stockport to 10.2 p.m. to Colne.
b Transferred Stockport to 10.7 p.m. to Rochdale.
c Transferred Stockport to 9.56 p.m. to Low Moor.
B 5.2 p.m. from Stockport.

Tonnage—241 Euston. 296 Crewe.

6.40 p.m. (SO), EUSTON TO HEYSHAM.
(Reverses at Morecambe (Promenade).)
(Class " A " Stock.)

Marshalling.	Balance.
§Brake Van }	
Third (42) }	
Third (42) }	
Third Vestibule (60 ft.) }	
First Restaurant Car (68 ft.) } Heysham	5 48 a.m.
Composite (18/24) }	
Composite (18/24) }	
BFirst Brake Lounge (10) }	
Attach front Crewe :—	
Brake Van —Heysham	

B Replaced by Third Brake on December 22nd and April 20th.

Tonnage—256 Euston. 282 Crewe.

7.20 p.m., EUSTON TO INVERNESS.
(Runs on December 21st and April 18th only.)
(Class " A " Stock.)

Marshalling.	Balance.
§Brake Van }	
Third Sleeping Sal. (60 ft.) } Aberdeen	—
First Sleeping Sal. (65 ft.) }	
Compo. Brake }	
Composite }	
First Sleeping Sal. (65 ft.) } Inverness	—
Third Sleeping Sal. (60 ft.) }	
§Brake Van }	
Compo. Restaurant Car (65 ft.) } Crewe	

Tonnage—296 Euston. 252 Crewe.

B.—MIXED TRAINS.

1.—"Mixed" trains for the conveyance of freight and passengers, in which the freight wagons are not required to have continuous brakes, may be run, subject to the following conditions, namely:—

(a) That the engine, tender and passenger vehicles of such "mixed" trains shall be provided with continuous brakes worked from the engine.

(b) That the freight wagons shall be conveyed behind the passenger vehicles with brake van, or brake vans, in the proportion of one brake van with a tare of 10 tons for every 10 wagons, or one brake van with a tare of 13 or more tons for every 15 wagons, or one brake van with a tare of 16 or more tons for every 20 wagons, or fractional parts of 10, 15 or 20 wagons respectively.

(c) That the total number of vehicles of all descriptions of any such "mixed" train shall not exceed 30, except in the case of a circus train when the number shall not exceed 35.

(d) That all such trains shall stop at stations, so as to avoid a longer run than 10 miles without stopping, but nothing in these regulations shall require a stop to be made between two stations should the distance between them exceed 10 miles.

The distance over which a circus train may run without a stop may be increased to a maximum of 50 miles.

2.—Upon lines where the maximum speed of trains is limited to 25 miles per hour, all trains may be "mixed."

Upon lines where no trains are booked to travel between stations at an average speed of more than 35 miles per hour, half of the total number of passenger trains may be "mixed." Authority to work a larger proportion of "mixed" trains must be obtained from the Minister of Transport.

Upon lines where trains are booked to travel between stations at an average speed exceeding 35 miles per hour, the like authority must be obtained before any "mixed" trains are run.

Circus trains may be run without such authority during the period from March 31st to November 30th in any year whether the maximum average speed of trains run on the section of line concerned is limited or not.

In no case must the speed of a circus train exceed 30 miles per hour.

3.—Trains for the conveyance of horses, cattle or other stock, when vehicles are added for the conveyance of passengers, shall be subject to the same regulations and conditions as apply to "mixed" trains, but drovers, grooms or other persons travelling in charge of such stock shall not be deemed to be passengers

A passenger vehicle provided for the special accommodation of persons travelling in charge of stock must, however, be marshalled next the engine, and be provided with the continuous brake worked from the engine.

4.—When, in addition to one goods brake van at the rear of a "mixed" train, a passenger brake vehicle is included as part of the continuously braked stock, it will not be necessary for a guard to ride in the passenger brake vehicle. If the composition of the train necessitates a second (or third) goods brake van, a second (or third) guard will be necessary, unless communication between the vans is such as to enable the one guard to operate efficiently the hand brakes on the vans.

All trains booked to be run as "mixed" will be so shown in the Working Time Tables, and the foregoing regulations will apply to such trains.

The expression circus train means a "mixed" train in which livestock, traction engines, trailers, caravans, tenting and other equipment and circus employees belonging to a touring circus are exclusively being conveyed.

NOTE.—The above regulations do not apply to troop trains.

TROOP TRAINS.

Troop trains timed at speeds not exceeding THIRTY-FIVE MILES PER HOUR may be made up to a maximum of 30 vehicles over sections of the line where there is no specially restricted load on account of severe gradients, provided the whole of the vehicles are fitted with the continuous brake or through pipe, connected up and working throughout the train. Each vehicle, bogie or otherwise to count as one. Total tonnage not to exceed that laid down for the lines concerned.

WORKING OF CIRCUS TRAINS.

When it is desired to run a circus train 50 miles without stopping and such train starts from a point at which no C. & W. staff is employed, the train must be stopped at the first point at which such staff is available to enable the necessary examination to be carried out.

SHUNTING OF PASSENGER TRAINS FOR OTHER TRAINS TO PASS.

Referring to Rule 146, clause (c), passenger trains must not be shunted from an up to a down running line, or vice versa, for another train to pass.

This instruction does not prohibit a passenger train being shunted on to a branch line at a junction or into a bay line at a station.

EXTRACT FROM THE REGULATION OF RAILWAYS ACT, 1889.

INSTRUCTIONS WITH RESPECT TO CONTINUOUS BRAKES.

A.—PASSENGER TRAINS.

1.—All passenger trains must be worked with the continuous brake in use by the Company.

To facilitate working, however, the following exceptional arrangements are allowed:—

In passenger trains a proportion of unbraked vehicles may be run on the following conditions:—

(a) That all such vehicles shall have continuous pipes of the pattern in use upon the trains with which they are running.

(b) That the proportion of such vehicles shall not exceed one in four in every passenger train running a distance not exceeding 19 miles without a stop.

(c) That the proportion of such vehicles shall not exceed one in six in every passenger train running a distance exceeding 10 miles without a stop.

Provided that for the purpose of conditions (b) and (c) the number of vehicles forming a train be counted as follows:—

Tender engine, 6 or 8 coupled	as 4 vehicles
Tender engine, 4 coupled	as 3 ,,
Tank engine, 4 or 6 wheeled coupled	as 2 ,,
Coaching vehicles, 8 or 12 wheeled	as 2 ,,
Coaching vehicles, 4 or 6 wheeled	as 1 vehicle.
Horse box, carriage truck, fish van or other 4-wheeled vehicle not carrying passengers	as ½

Table showing what proportion of unbraked vehicles (which must be fitted with continuous pipes) may be attached to a passenger train RUNNING NOT MORE THAN 10 MILES WITHOUT A STOP.

To a train (including engine) consisting of braked vehicles equal to—	Unbraked vehicles equal to—
3	may be added 1
3½	,, 1
4	,, 1¼
4½	,, 1½
5	,, 1½
5½	,, 1¾
6	,, 2
6½	,, 2
7	,, 2¼
7½	,, 2½
8	,, 2½
8½	,, 2¾
9	,, 3
9½	,, 3
10	,, 3¼
10½	,, 3½
11	,, 3½
11½	,, 3¾
12	,, 4
12½	,, 4
13	,, 4¼
13½	,, 4½
14	,, 4½
14½	,, 4¾
15	,, 5

Table showing what proportion of unbraked vehicles (which must be fitted with continuous pipes) may be attached to a passenger train RUNNING MORE THAN 10 MILES WITHOUT A STOP.

To a train (including engine) consisting of braked vehicles equal to—	Unbraked vehicles equal to—
3	may be added ¾
3½	,, ¾
4	,, ¾
4½	,, 1
5	,, 1
5½	,, 1
6	,, 1¼
6½	,, 1¼
7	,, 1½
7½	,, 1½
8	,, 1½
8½	,, 1¾
9	,, 1¾
9½	,, 2
10	,, 2
10½	,, 2
11	,, 2¼
11½	,, 2¼
12	,, 2½
12½	,, 2½
13	,, 2½
13½	,, 2¾
14	,, 2¾
14½	,, 3
15	,, 3

2.—Except as hereinafter provided the last vehicle of every passenger train must be fitted with the continuous brake of the pattern in use upon the train.

Where necessary to avoid delay in working, one vehicle only, not being a passenger carrying vehicle, may be placed in the rear of any such train without being fitted with the continuous brake or with the continuous pipe, except on those sections of the line where the practice of running vehicles behind the rear brake van must be provided with the continuous brake or where the vehicles behind the rear brake van is prohibited. (*See respective Sectional Appendices for sections of line affected.*)

NOTE.—Grooms or attendants travelling in horse boxes, etc., are not counted as passengers

SIGNALLING OF TRAINS CONVEYING SPECIAL HORSE OR PIGEON TRAFFIC.

Where instructions are given in the Special Train Notices for trains conveying special horse or pigeon traffic and composed of coaching stock to be signalled by the bell signal of 5 beats (given 3 pause 1 pause 1), such trains must carry No. 3 headlights and take precedence of all other trains except express passenger trains, breakdown van trains going to clear the line, light engines going to assist disabled trains, or fire brigade trains.

TAIL LAMPS AND SIDE LIGHTS ON TRAINS.

Referring to Rule 120; the following instructions apply to trains working over the L.M.S. Railway:—

Mixed trains with a freight train guard's brake van in rear must carry side lamps as laid down for freight trains.

Except where instructions are issued to the contrary, all freight trains or engines with freight train guard's brake van or vans must carry side lights on the rear brake van as follows:—

(A) On main lines where there are only two lines and on single lines...... One red tail light and two red side lights.

(B) On main lines where there are three or four running lines:—
  (i.) On the fast line......... One red tail light and two red side lights.
  (ii.) On the slow, goods, or loop lines.......... One red side light on the side of the van furthest away from the fast line, one white side light on the side of the van nearest the fast line, and one red tail light (see Note).

(C) On goods or loop lines adjoining four main lines.............. One red tail light only. Side lamps must be removed when the train has passed into the loop.

Note.—Certain brake vans are provided with side lamps which cannot be turned, or which, when turned to show a white light to the rear, show a red light to the front. In these cases the instructions in paragraph (B) (ii.) will not apply, and the side lamp instead of being turned must be removed. A signalman will not be required to send the "Tail or side light out, or improper side light exhibited" signal when a train passes his box with side light removed as directed.

Where side lights are shown to be carried the side lamps must, except in the case of local trips, be carried on the rear brake van during daylight as well as during darkness.

The instructions in clause (a) of Rule 120 respecting the carrying, cleaning, trimming, and lighting of tail lamps also apply to light engines.

Tail lamps on passenger trains.—The guard, or rear guard where there is more than one, must see that the tail lamp is properly fixed before signalling the train away. This will not, however, relieve from responsibility any of the platform staff who should affix tail lamps.

Station Masters and inspectors must pay special attention when vehicles are attached or detached, and see that the tail lamp is in its proper position.

A clean trimmed tail lamp must be carried inside the rear van of all trains provided with gas tail lamps, and in each portion where there is more than one van provided with gas tail lamps.

L.N.E. Railway (G.E. Section) coaching stock brake vans with fitted tail lamps.—When one of these brake vans is the rear vehicle on a train, the fixed tail lamp must not be used and an ordinary oil tail lamp must be carried both by day and by night.

Extinguishing lights in side and tail lamps.—At the completion of the train journey and after the train is shunted into a siding clear of the running lines, the guard, before leaving the train, must, unless instructions are issued to the contrary, extinguish the lights in the side and tail lamps.

Freight, etc., trains, assisted in rear—Tail and side lamps.
Referring to Rule 133; when a freight train is assisted in rear by an engine or by an engine propelling one or two brake vans, the guard of the freight train must remove his tail lamp. When the train is assisted by an engine drawing one or two brake vans, the guard of the freight train must, in addition to removing the tail lamp, remove his side lamps, and side lamps must be carried on the rearmost brake van attached to the assisting engine.

ENGINE HEAD LAMPS.

All L.M.S. engines, whether working over the L.M.S. or other Companies' lines, and the engines of other Companies working over the L.M.S. lines, must, unless instructions are issued to the contrary, carry white head lights arranged as under, and trains must be signalled by the bell signals shown:—

Description of train.	Bell Signal.	Head light.
1.—Express passenger train, or break-down van train going to clear the line, or light engine going to assist disabled train, or fire brigade train	4	
2.—Ordinary passenger train, or break-down van train not going to clear the line	3—1	
Branch passenger train (where authorised) ...	1—3	
Rail motor or motor train with engine leading ...	3—1—2	
(When running with driving compartment leading rail motors or motor trains will carry the headlamp on the same bracket as used for the tail lamp.)		
Note.—For arrangements in regard to electric trains see the various electric line instruction books.		
3.—Parcels, newspaper, fish, meat, fruit, milk, horse, or perishable train, composed of coaching stock ...	1—1—3	
4.—Empty coaching stock train	2—2—1	
Fitted freight, fish or cattle train with the continuous brake in use on NOT LESS than one-third the vehicles	5	
5.—Express freight or cattle train with the continuous brake on less than one-third the vehicles, but in use on four or vehicles connected to the engine indicated by ✠ in the Working Time Tables ...	2—2—3	
Express freight or cattle train not	1—3—1	
6.—Through freight train, or ballast train conveying workmen and running not less than 15 miles without stopping	3—2	
7.—Light engine, or light engines coupled together ...	1—4	
Engine with one or two brakes		
8.—Through mineral or empty wagon train	2—3 / 1—3—1	
9.—Freight train stopping at intermediate stations, or ballast train running short distance	4—1	
Branch freight train (where authorised)		
Ballast train, freight train, or officers' special requiring to stop in section or at intermediate siding in section.	3 / 1—2	
10.—Shunting engines working exclusively in station yards and sidings.	1—2—1	Must, whilst in these sidings, carry one red head light and one red tail light.

The lamps must be carried in position day and night.
Note.—Local exceptional arrangements are shown in the respective Sectional Appendices.
When a train running on the L.M.S. Railway is worked by two engines attached in front of the train, the second engine must not carry head light.